A TOUCHSTONE
FOR GREATNESS

Contributions in American Studies
Series Editor: Robert H. Walker

A TOUCHSTONE
FOR GREATNESS

Essays, Addresses,
and Occasional Pieces about

ABRAHAM LINCOLN

ROY P. BASLER

)(

Contributions in American Studies, No. 4

GREENWOOD PRESS, INC.,

Westport, Connecticut • London, England

Library of Congress Cataloging in Publication Data

Basler, Roy Prentice, 1906-
   A touchstone for greatness.

   (Contributions in American studies, no. 4)
   Includes bibliographical references.
   1. Lincoln, Abraham, Pres. U. S., 1809-1865—
Addresses, sermons, etc. I. Title.
E457.8.B353   973.7'092'4 [B]   72-781
ISBN 0-8371-6135-5

Portions of *A Touchstone for Greatness* were previously published and copyrighted:

"Lincoln's Development As a Writer" Reprinted by permission of The World Publishing Company from *Abraham Lincoln: His Speeches and Writings* by Roy P. Basler. Copyright 1946 by The World Publishing Company.

"As One Southerner to Another" Reprinted by permission of Duke University Press from *The South Atlantic Quarterly*, January, 1943. Copyright 1943 by The Duke University Press.

"Lincoln in Politics, 1948" and "Beef! Beef! Beef!" Reprinted by permission of Abraham Lincoln Association from *The Abraham Lincoln Quarterly*, December, 1948 and September, 1951. Copyright 1948 and 1951 by Abraham Lincoln Association.

"Lincoln Country" Reprinted by permission of *The Centennial Review of Arts and Science*, Vol. II. No. 2, Spring, 1958. Copyright 1958 by *The Centennial Review of Arts and Science.*

"Abraham Lincoln: An Immortal Sign" Reprinted by permission of The University of Illinois Press from *The Enduring Lincoln*. Copyright 1959 by The University of Illinois Press.

Library of Congress Catalog Card Number: 72-781
ISBN: 0-8371-6135-5

First published in 1973

Greenwood Press, Inc., Publishing Division
51 Riverside Avenue, Westport, Connecticut 06880
Manufactured in the United States of America
Designed by A. Christopher Simon

To
MY WIFE

CONTENTS

FOREWORD

In presenting this collection of essays on Abraham Lincoln, I am making an assumption, not wholly unwarranted I hope, that the scattered results of forty years' study are perhaps worth collecting. Except for the first piece, most of them have been either published in periodicals or delivered to various audiences, or both. They show a modicum of repetition, particularly of certain quotations which are so memorable that one cannot escape them, but even this repetition exemplifies what Abraham Lincoln has meant to me personally over the years. I offer them now as a cumulation, but I trust not a culmination, of that interest.

Roy P. Basler

A TOUCHSTONE
FOR GREATNESS

AN ACQUAINTANCE WITH
ABRAHAM LINCOLN

"The better part of one's life consists of his friendships..."
—LINCOLN TO JOSEPH GILLESPIE, JULY 13, 1849

Although I was born nearly a century later than Abraham Lincoln, my acquaintance with him began, by curious accident, when we were both about seven years of age. I found him to be a real chum, although he was unaware that I was tagging along, when he and Austin Gollaher went swimming in the creek and Abe nearly drowned, or when his father, Tom Lincoln, took him on a coon hunt. These and other adventures were so nearly identical with some of my own that they blended with mine, their separate identity lost until suddenly dredged up from boyhood memories with startled awareness, as I began to read, many years later, while a graduate student in American literature, the Prologue to Thomas Dixon's novel of Abraham Lincoln, *The Southerner.*

This must have been a story my mother read to me, I thought (later verified), reveling in the reincarnation, as it were, of myself and so many of the experiences of my boyhood which I still remembered, as I suppose Thomas Dixon remembered his own boyhood while transplanting it into his novel of Lincoln. Of all the writings about Lincoln's childhood, I still think none has ever excelled Dixon's Prologue for verisimilitude, however scanty the merits of the rest of *The Southerner* may be as historical fiction.

But where and why I came to be reading Dixon's novel in 1930 marks the beginning of my later acquaintance with the Civil War President, which was to become perhaps the most continuous experience of any kind of friendship throughout my life.

In the summer of 1928 I decided, for personal reasons, to enroll as a graduate student in English at Duke University instead of the University of California. I cannot now imagine a more fortunate or improbable first step toward the study of Abraham Lincoln, which has occupied me consistently, if intermittently, ever since.

The unsuspecting and unsuspected agent of my scholarly fate was an angular Virginian, like myself over six feet in height, whose hair was no longer quite as red as mine, and who had found some twenty years ahead of me that the academic life was about as near as he wanted to come to the respected, if not envied, career of his clergyman father. Jay Broadus Hubbell, professor of American literature, became my mentor and brought me to Lincoln by the most naturally accidental series of inevitabilities that I can imagine.

In the first place, I went to graduate school with a predilection for the English Romantic poets in general and Shelley in particular. I had conceived an amorphous inkblot image of "Shelley's religion" that I thought suitable for a master's thesis. When I went to registration, however, I learned that Duke's Shelley specialist Newman I. White was on sabbatical, and that whatever else I might take in the way of course work, the several courses for which I had particularly opted were out of the question for at least a year. This was a fortunate misfortune, since I elected Hubbell's American literature instead, and at his suggestion wrote my master's thesis on Nathaniel Hawthorne ("The Problem of Sin in the Works of . . ."), which provided a surfeit of literary religion, whatever Hubbell's intention may have been.

I quickly found that this non-professorial, gentle man — who exemplified why the adjective "gentle" and the noun "man" inevitably compounded — could provide just the kind of intellectual guidance and understanding that I was able to profit from at the best. Although his courses were extremely popular, he never seemed to me to be a particularly great teacher in front of his class, or to excel the best of his colleagues in any clearly identifiable manner.

But as a scholarly person he was, and remains in my affectionate memory, the best.

For one thing, our out-of-class intercommunication developed into a friendship which extended the boundaries of the usual student-to-mentor relationship, greatly to my advantage, and I found him to be as much my contemporary as my elder. Out of one of our wide-ranging conversations, while sitting on the steps of the faculty apartment building one hot summer evening (before air-conditioning) came the suggestion which has had more impact on my life than anything else except my marriage to a South Carolina girl the previous summer, a few weeks after her graduation from Duke.

What Hubbell (familiarity between graduate students and faculty was mutually limited to a last name) had been discussing that led up to Lincoln I do not recollect, but I am relatively sure that we had never discussed the Civil War President before. I knew next to nothing about Lincoln beyond the few pages devoted to him in the textbooks, and cared less. I had no Civil War heroes or villains except a few local Missouri bushwhackers whose exploits I had heard of as a boy, luridly tinted by the respective sentiments of the "North" or "South" bias of the narrator. The consensus of my chums, whose families in nearly every case held one or more elders who were still fighting the war with words and such social weapons as every community affords in abundance, was that the whole thing was of no more importance to us than the shotgun weddings, bank robberies, and drunken brawls that ended in shootings, which also were woven into the fabric of Missouri community history. If we played seriously at war to relieve the boredom of Sunday afternoons, it was as Huns and Allies, and our only true mythology was cowboy and Indian.

In addition to mild surprise that my Virginian mentor thought so highly of the Civil War President, I was piqued that he obviously knew so much about the man Lincoln and held him great not only in the political sphere but in the realm of letters, whose citizens as I had understood, along with most conventionally instructed English majors, included Shelley and Scott or Poe and Hawthorne, but hardly Lincoln and Jefferson. Most university English faculties in those days were largely dominated by Harvard-trained Ph.D.s, one of whom superciliously questioned a student who expressed interest in American literature, "And what is that?" Hubbell knew the answer to that type of philological snobbery and helped me learn it.

As dusk settled, our conversation became his monologue, punctuated by my interested questions, and expanded particularly on the subject of Lincoln's appeal to poets who had written one or more of their best poems about the mysterious, enigmatic, symbolic genius of Lincoln. I suppose that my ignorance was at least balanced by my equally obvious interest, for Hubbell finally suggested: "That might be a good dissertation subject, Lincoln in Literature." Neither of us could have guessed the consequence.

I had been for several months searching for a suitable dissertation subject, tentatively adopting and promptly rejecting one after another, for reasons of incompatibility or meretriciousness. As much as I still admired and leaned toward the poets — the land of myth and the language of metaphor — extended excursions, led by the best tour leaders in Shakespeare, Milton, Wordsworth and the Romantics, Tennyson and Browning and the Victorians (not to forget *Beowulf,* and most memorable because truly exploratory in the highest sense, Chaucer), had impressed me that a choice might be far-reaching, if not fatal. Also I had attended one meeting of the Modern Language Association, and had heard typical introductions and descriptions that went "He's a Shelley man" or "I am in Restoration drama, what are you?" Even more depressing were "slave-market" interviews by English department heads, of neophytes in search of an instructorship that might lead at least to an assistant professorship. These interviews sometimes terminated rather abruptly, "Well, we are really looking for somebody in Victorian," or worse, "We want a Milton man." I became concerned, unduly as it turned out, about a friend who would have to admit a year hence to being "a *Piers Plowman* man" and another who was considering the possibility of becoming, with good enough reason, "a Henry James man." As for myself, I had begun to realize that however virgin territory the fiction of James Lane Allen might be to serious literary study, or however venerable William Wordsworth might be (in spite of his then recently discovered illegimate "French daughter"), a commitment might be more difficult to terminate than to consummate. I could not have guessed, however, that some twenty years later I too would have to face the results of my decision. At a leading university in need of "an American literature man," the head of the English department would put it bluntly: "Not in this department! A Lincoln specialist is the last thing we need." The fact that I had published a few pieces about Coleridge, Poe, and other strictly "literary" masters was apparently not enough to offset my original mistake.

In any event, during the weeks following my conversation with Hubbell, in fact for the rest of that summer, I all but buried myself in Lincoln literature — biography, fiction, poetry, drama, some of it extremely turgid. I had received approval by the Duke graduate school of my dissertation subject, "Abraham Lincoln in Literature," under the principal direction of Professor Jay B. Hubbell. That I remained practically buried for a full twelve months was not merely the result of the enormous amount of Lincoln literature, as broadly interpreted for the purpose of my dissertation, but also of the fascination of the man and era and what both had come to mean to so many. For I found that practically every American writer of importance, as well as a host of minor scribblers, had had his say about Lincoln.

That I had married a South Carolinian of the best became evident during the winter 1930—1931, for my wife endured, and could laugh with wry understanding some years later at the pathetic story of the wife of another Lincoln specialist. The poor woman had to be committed to an asylum, in spite of her insistence that she was just as sane as anybody; it was, she said, "just that I have to go to bed every night with Abraham Lincoln!"

A wife who is also an efficient typist, research assistant, and friendly critic frequently contributes more than a writer can acknowledge by whatever amenities in prefaces, dedications, or whatnot. I certainly fared better than most in this respect, and while lovemaking and child-raising continued to be our principal mutual interests over the years, we have also continued the cooperation we began with my first Lincoln study. But I cannot tell her side of this story without ruining my own. The basic assumption is reasonable, however, that whatever I have accomplished, perhaps might have been done as well, or better, otherwise, but not by me!

Barely under the deadline in time for my graduation in June 1931, "Abraham Lincoln in Literature: The Growth of an American Legend" was submitted, I was examined, and the dissertation approved — my final hurdle for the Ph.D. degree. There was the customary additional obligation, if not condition, that I would guarantee publication of the dissertation in an "acceptable manner." Things had been happening to the American economy which affected young Ph.D.s, as well as other people, and my bond to publish would become, perhaps not the greatest, but neither the least of my difficulties during the next few years.

In order to make my study into a publishable book, a thorough revision was mandatory. This was accomplished during the balmy winter of 1931—1932 in Sarasota, Florida, where I had joined the faculty of the John Ringling College of Fine and Liberal Arts. Having seen what the Duke money could do for higher education, I had great hopes for the future of a college founded and to be endowed by the circus king's millions. Others shared in this optimism, but by the end of the first school year the Ringling fortune had been practically wiped out by the depression and the Italian palace in which the great John resided next door to the even more princely and "authentic" palace which he had imported, to reconstruct stone by stone, as the museum to house his multimillion-dollar art collection, was purported on the authority of Ringling's overseer to operate on the twenty-five-cent parking-lot fees paid by tourists who visited the museum. This was the only cash income for many months, so the story went, of an empire rapidly disintegrating, along with the hopes for a major institution of learning dedicated to an ideal blending of the arts. But this, too, is another story.

My revised manuscript, bearing the title "The Lincoln Legend: A Study in Changing Conceptions," I mailed to the most respectable and conservative publisher I could think of among my rather casual title-page acquaintances. There was something impressive, to me at least, about "Houghton Mifflin Company: The Riverside Press, Cambridge" — just the sort of solidly reputable imprint any young scholar might hope for on his first book. If my ego was unduly inflated concerning the merits of my manuscript, it became briefly overblown upon receiving a most complimentary letter from the great Houghton Mifflin editor Ferris Greenslet. That moment was brief indeed, for his letter concluded with the suggestion that Houghton Mifflin would be glad to publish *The Lincoln Legend* if I would subsidize the book to the extent of paying for the typesetting and casting of plates. A toy balloon, blown to its maximum inflation and accidentally released on a skittering trajectory of limp rubberhood — that is my recollection, after more than thirty years, of how reading Greenslet's letter felt.

Such was the state of my innocence in matters concerning publication that I had never dreamed that the likes of Houghton Mifflin published subsidized books. It was customary for scholars to pay part of the cost of publication by a university press, and I had heard of something purportedly less respectable called a "vanity press." For a few days, in my disillusion, I looked askance at every book in my library bearing the Houghton Mifflin imprint, wondering, "How much did that one cost *him*?"

The fall and winter of 1932—1933 was a period of disappointment and disillusion in general. John Ringling's bank failed late in the summer of 1932. We had just the few hundred dollars saved in anticipation of our first baby, expected in December. Monthly salary checks from the college failed to materialize. The friendly CIT Corporation tried to repossess our car in lieu of the final month's installment payment, which we had paid on time by check but CIT had failed to deposit the check before the Ringling bank closed. How did people live for months with no income? That is also another story.

In any event, other circumstances tempered my disappointment as an author, and I replied politely and cagily to Mr. Greenslet, that although my financial status did not permit me to accept his offer at the moment, I nevertheless appreciated his good opinion of the manuscript and might like to reopen the possibility later, if no other publisher could afford to risk publication entirely at his own expense. In the next few months I established the fact that no other publisher was even interested in seeing the manuscript. Under these circumstances, the most currently unsuccessful Lincoln author decided to ask the advice of the most successful.

My first letter to Carl Sandburg described my predicament, outlined my study in some detail, and asked whether he would care to see the manuscript. He replied on December 3, 1933, that, as I described it, he was inclined to say that my manuscript, although largely drawing upon the writings of others, was more an original contribution than a majority of Lincoln items published in recent years. He recognized that a trade publisher might not find such a book profitable, but thought it might be welcomed by some organization devoted to Lincolniana. I might send the manuscript to him or to Paul Angle, secretary of the Illinois State Historical Society.

Since I had already explored, by correspondence with Paul Angle, this very possibility, with negative results, I so replied in my next letter to Sandburg. His friendly reply offered to read my manuscript and see what further suggestions, if any, he might have.

My next letter from Sandburg said some complimentary things about the manuscript but confirmed Ferris Greenslet's judgment that as a book it probably could not appeal or sell widely enough to justify a trade publisher's risking it. Nevertheless, Sandburg thought well enough of it, he wrote, to put it in the hands of a great friend who might see what could be done. I did not learn until a decade later who this was, when Sandburg's great friend became mine also, but with absolutely no recollection on his part of his ever having held my manuscript for over a year, unopened, in one of his Lincoln closets where he kept the most remarkable collection of Lincolniana ever assembled by one man.

Thus matters stood when I migrated in the summer of 1934 from Ringling College, with considerable sand in my shoes, but with few other accumulations except debts, to State Teachers College, Florence, Alabama, where the prospects for collecting at least half of the promised yearly salary exceeded Ringling's best by two hundred percent. The next year, when this prospect had been fulfilled, I retrieved my manuscript and once again laid it in Ferris

Greenslet's lap, together with my check for $600, as first installment on the cost of printing. Annually, at income-tax time, I still get a smug comfort from the fact that the dribbling royalty on the reprint edition of *The Lincoln Legend* is not "income" subject to tax, because I have yet to recover the whole $1,362.58 of this investment.

Whatever the book lacked as a salable commodity, however, when it appeared in the late summer of 1935, reviewers were so good to it, in spite of its eclectic contents, that I have not yet recovered from the effect. They almost convinced me that financial reward was the crassest achievement possible to efforts of intellect. More than this, however, they instigated my shame that the author of so overrated a book had nothing in hand to show how much more he could do. This is the fatality of being printed and favorably reviewed the first time — it confirms one's headiest illusion that this sort of thing is eminently worth doing.

II

Having read practically everything written about, as well as by, Lincoln, I was aware that few among those who wrote about him considered how much his literary instinct or bent had contributed to the development of his character and unique achievement as a public man. Much of the aura of mysterious genius about this man derived from the popular myth, which infused also not a few of the "historical" treatments of his life, that he emerged suddenly from obscurity in 1858 to play the preeminent nineteenth-century role in American history. There was both ignorance and neglect of what and how Lincoln's mind developed, in favor of the touted "facts" concerning what he did and how he lived. The best record of the mind of Lincoln, which directed the actions that led him to his pinnacle in history, was in his words. This is not to say that Lincoln was merely, or even primarily, a literary man, as is true of other great writers, but rather that his literary bent was *sui generis* to his total character and achievement as a historical figure.

It was this view that controlled my continuing study and interest and largely directed my work on Lincoln. In pursuing my work, I became increasingly aware of the need for a definitive text of his speeches and writings, and for the next decade I undertook to find and obtain a photocopy of the original manuscript, or in its absence, the original or best available printed text of his most important letters as well as his major speeches. This intermittent search eventually became a concentrated effort to produce a one-volume selection edited entirely from the best available sources.

Thus in 1942 I had another book manuscript going the rounds in search of a publisher. The obstacles which the depression era had presented to the publication of *The Lincoln Legend* were merely given a new accounting for as World War II developed and the manuscript of *Abraham Lincoln: His Speeches and Writings* kept coming back to rest on my desk. Once again Carl Sandburg tried his best, by now my patron saint as well as my advocate, but without success. Practically everybody in the fraternity of Lincoln scholars knew of the manuscript, had encouraged its compilation, and in many instances had contributed assistance, but their efforts, along with Sandburg's were insufficient, until the proprietor of the Abraham Lincoln Book Shop took the manuscript in hand. Ralph Newman's unique bookstore in Chicago sold more Lincoln and Civil War books, perhaps, than did any other dealer, and thus Ralph was able to convince when he said this large manuscript would make a book he could sell. But it was the fall of 1946, with the war over, before *Abraham Lincoln: His Speeches and Writings* appeared under the imprint of World Publishing Company, much to my satisfaction, bringing, for once, actual remuneration.

The satisfaction of meaningful work for its own sake is always enhanced by a definite product, fruit to which one can point when asked, what have you been doing lately? I recall an alumnae dinner at which one of my sisters had been passing around the table a snapshot. When it came her turn to give an accounting of her several years since school, she responded simply, "Well, you've seen what I've been doing." The snapshot was of her four youngsters. So a book speaks for itself and of the work accomplished in it, but with particular significance to those best able to judge its worth. The reception accorded *Abraham Lincoln: His Speeches and Writings* by the fraternity of Lincoln students was even more gratifying than its relatively wide sale to the general public. But even more important to me personally were the friendships which had grown and would continue to grow from the first acquaintance brought about by my continuing study of Lincoln.

The first and certainly one of the most cherished of these friendships was that with Carl Sandburg. I had met him while in college, although simply for a handshake, as one of an anyonymous crowd of students who went up after one of his inimitable "performances," chanting his poems, intermingled with American folksongs, self-accompanied on the guitar. But our personal paths did not cross again on the same day for more than fifteen years, during which we corresponded intermittently and mostly about our mutual interest. As my bad luck would have it, every time I would be going to Chicago, his activities would be taking him elsewhere. Nevertheless we developed through our correspondence and through several mutual friends a degree of intimacy which led to his writing an Introduction to *Abraham Lincoln: His Speeches and Writings* for which I was wholly unprepared. I had expected the ·customary testimony to the worth of the book and something of the Sandburg view of Lincoln's achievement as a writer. When I received a copy of what he had written, I was so disconcerted by his generous personal tribute that I was moved almost to the point of chagrin. There was, I feared, so little of what would be expected of an Introduction and so much about me personally that it might backfire, particularly when perused by intellectual snobs in the academic realm, to the detriment of the book at the hands of reviewers for the scholarly journals. My state of mind for several days was somewhat like that of a man confronted by a very large suitcase from which the handle has broken completely off. The only solution seemed to be to hug it with both arms and carry it along.

Then I decided to lay out my feelings in a letter to our mutual friend Oliver R. Barrett who had had so much to do with the preparation of my book and, unbeknown to me, with having Sandburg write the Introduction. The upshot was that Carl added several choice paragraphs on Lincoln's greatness as a writer which fitted so well that I suspect few outside of the publisher's office ever guessed that the Introduction as printed could ever have been written without them. In any event, I was to have no doubt, when the book appeared in October 1946, that its brief appearance on the "best-seller" lists was in large measure the result of Sandburg's generous words.

During the academic Christmas holidays that year I resolved to meet my benefactor face to face and introduce my wife and children, for whom his name had become something of a shibboleth. Sandburg had moved his residence some time before from his Chinkaming Goat Farm, in Michigan just outside Chicago environs, to Flat Rock, North Carolina. I had migrated from Alabama to Arkansas and thence to Nashville, Tennessee, during our long epistolary friendship. The return route from my wife's home in Florence County, South Carolina, where we spent the holidays, was through the mountains and passed very near Flat Rock. Thus on New Year's Eve we drove back through one of the worst snow-and-ice storms I have ever encountered, with a call at the Sandburg farm, situated atop one of the rounded foothills of the Smokies.

Sandburg loved children. Ours were not normally shy but "in the presence," as it were, of the silver-haired great man about whom they had heard perhaps enough to put them on strained best behavior, they were somewhat at a loss. Before we left (much too soon for us but with sleet accumulating rapidly outside), they were figuratively if not actually in his lap. The harrowing all-night drive- back to Nashville remains a less vivid memory than the visit by which it was occasioned, and the one-hundred-fifty-dollar damage to our seven-year-old Packard, suffered as we skidded down the narrow farm road from the Sandburg home to the main highway, was a small price to pay.

Carl's love for children was doubtless primarily demonstrated, as it should have been, with his own daughters and with his grandchildren, but the affection with which he recollected his own childhood in *Always the Young Strangers* and the numerous penetrating allusions in his poems and even in his treatment of Lincoln's affection for children in the great biography, showed how deep this ran in Carl's nature. One of his earliest and most poignant poems probes with tender irony deeply into both Lincoln's and Sandburg's humanity and greatness.

In a Back Alley

Remembrance for a great man is this.
The newsies are pitching pennies.
And on the copper disk is the man's face.
Dead lover of boys, what do you ask for now?

Carl's way with children, ours at least, was to meet them on their own terms, as individuals. A wonderful example of this occurred some years later at the dinner table in our home. Our eldest daughter, by this time in high school and inordinately proud of keeping up with contemporary literature, made the most of her opportunity to engage him in literary criticism, and held her own fairly well. The climax came with their discussion of Norman Mailer's recent best-seller *The Naked and the Dead*. Didn't he think it was really the greatest? Carl waited just long enough, looking right across the table eye-to-eye, and exploded, "Why, it's the goddamndest-son-of-a-bitchingest-book I've ever read!"

It was a gem — her gem — but she could not put it in her book report for Miss Graham's English III!

This episode reminds me of another worth telling though somewhat out of the present context. Several years later, after I had been associated for several years with the Library of Congress, Carl was invited to give a lecture at the opening of the Library's Civil War Centennial Exhibit. The afternoon before the lecture he agreed to be available to the press. As usual, some of the reporters who were interviewing him were more interested in something to make headlines than they were in the Library's Civil War exhibit, and for one of them the legal contest over the recent first publication in the United States of Henry Miller's *Tropic of Cancer* seemed the choicest of all opportunities. In answer to the direct question, Carl said he would comment at length on the controversial book if the reporter agreed to report him word for word. His explicit and vivid tribute to Miller's great talent for obscenity was, of course, as unprintable in the newspapers as it was accurate. More significant, to me at least, was the effectiveness with which he exposed the hypocrisy of so much intellectual literary criticism of erotic literature, which discusses the erotic, not in its own best vulgar terms but in the religio-literary frame-of-reference with which D. H. Lawrence liberated literature in the English language — a liberation frequently as false and sentimental in our day as the Victorian conventions were a hundred years ago.

III

Perhaps if I had not committed myself to the study of Lincoln so many years ago, I would never have had the pleasure of Carl's friendship, but I am sure that if some other interest than Lincoln had first brought us together, we would certainly have hit it off eventually just as well because of other mutual interests — our liking for scatological and bawdy humor for instance. We both had a deep and abiding respect and love for the primary source of all humor — the physical reminder to every man that however close to the angels he may ever get, the power that made him used clay, that clay by any other name is still dirt, and that the tenderest emotion or the most metaphysical flight that forgets or neglects this truth for a moment, in that moment becomes false. That this truth was somewhere near the core of Lincoln's great genius we were agreed, and that it accounted in some measure for Lincoln's great love, not only for bawdy and scatological stories, but also for his utter humility at the peak of greatness, as well as his love for a poem beginning "O why should the spirit of mortal be proud."

Related to the subject of Lincoln's earthy humor was the subject of his sexuality — a topic frequently discussed by several of us in the Lincoln fraternity, but interestingly enough scarcely touched upon in print by any one of us. With the exception of Herndon, in private letters but not in his *Lincoln,* the Victorian taboo on sexuality as a topic has been almost completely observed by all Lincoln students, to some extent with good reason. Few of Lincoln's male acquaintances except Herndon, Joshua Speed, John T. Stuart, and a few others, could have known much of anything on the subject at close hand, and only Herndon considered the physical fact important enough (along with Lincoln's chronic constipation and other physiological details) to make anything of it. It would be readily acceded today by almost anyone, I feel sure, that the high degree of sexuality and "powerful attraction to women," which Herndon testified to, was not merely probable but highly significant in Lincoln's personal life. That his conjugal bliss may not have been precisely perfect has been too often noted without any possible relatedness being supposed between his high degree of sexuality and Mary Lincoln's well-known jealousy of nearly every pretty woman to whom Lincoln paid a compliment. I am not suggesting that Lincoln was a Don Juan, but rather that his wife knew better than anybody else what he was capable of, perhaps no less than what some of the flirtatious women were capable of. Likewise, the question is clearly unavoidable today, to any student who would try to understand the aberrant course of Lincoln's courtship and all the self-doubt that went into his breaking off his engagement to Mary Todd on that "fatal first of January," 1841. Lincoln's letters written to his friend Joshua Speed, almost the only intimate letters he ever wrote except to his wife, cannot be read, it seems to me, without recognition of the problem of sexuality that bothered him and Speed not a little, as they mutually, if guardedly, admitted. Speed's testimony to Herndon of Lincoln's visit to a prostitute whom Speed had been accustomed to patronizing, with its humorous denouement when Lincoln failed to have the price needed, places the whole matter in its properly earthy context and "western" milieu, about 1839—1840. Furthermore, if Herndon had the personal knowledge that he claimed to have concerning Lincoln's early venereal infection, that alone could account for much of Lincoln's fits of mental and emotional aberration, his "constitutional" melancholy, and perhaps in quite another direction, no small part of the sympathy and humility with which he invariably looked upon the foibles and shortcomings of his fellow human creatures. It has always been my feeling that Lincoln is in no way diminished by these aspects of his life which have never been given satisfactory treatment by any biographer and would not be in print for the inquisitive reader, were it not for Emanual Hertz's volume *The Hidden Lincoln,* which reproduces many of the documents preserved in the Herndon-Weik Papers in the Library of Congress.

I once discussed this problem along with the problem of sexuality in general with Carl, and the related problem of sex education between generations, parents with children, teachers with pupils, etc. We were more or less agreed that there are no pat solutions, formulas, or ways of even meeting the single problem which is central in the development of every human being. He concluded our discussion with a direct question, to which I found it difficult, and not for the only time in my life, to find a wholly satisfactory answer: "Just what are you going to tell the boy who says, 'I wake up nearly every night, and it's hard, and stays hard, and I can't go back to sleep!' Just what kind of education is there, scientific, moral, or religious, really satisfactory for *that* problem?"

And I think it fair to say Carl and I were in agreement that *that* problem was central to Lincoln's personality and to his genius, no less than it has been to other male human beings of whatever stature or status. Although Carl was by no means reticent or prudish in discussing the problem, he was definitely of the opinion that as a biographer he did not feel he could or should treat it as freely as we could discuss it. Should we not all just assume that Lincoln was powerfully sexed and let it go at that, in writing at least?

Carl was certainly one of the two or three finest raconteurs I have ever known, and naturally enough both of the others were also of the Lincoln fraternity: Benjamin P. Thomas of Springfield, Illinois, and William H. Townsend of Lexington, Kentucky.

Most of Lincoln's best humor of this bawdy variety has been preserved, like the prototypes of Chaucer's fabliaux up to Chaucer's time at any rate, chiefly in oral tradition. A few of Lincoln's stories are referred to in contemporary documents in terms sufficiently explicit that anyone familiar with such folk humor can read between the lines — as for example in the letter written to Lincoln by Moses Hampton, a member of Congress from Pennsylvania:

                                         Pittsburgh
                                      March 30, 1849
Hon Abm Lincoln
Dear Sir
    Do you remember the story of the old Virginian stropping

his razor on a certain *member* of a young negro's body which
you told and connected it with my mission to Brazil — Now
my good fellow, I am "arter" that same Mission, and my object in writing to you just now is to ask the favor that you
will address a letter to Gen Taylor or Mr. Clayton on that
subject — and you may *spice* it just as highly as you please,
I have made up my mind to *stand* it   —   I want that
appointment and *must have it* — Will you have the goodness
to procure a letter from Col Baker, who is well and favorably
known to Gen Taylor — Any influence you may feel disposed
to exert, shall be paid with compound interest if ever in my
power to do so —

I want this application to be like your story of the old
woman's fish — get larger, the more it is handled —
Let me hear from you soon —

Very truly

Your friend &c
M. Hampton

Another example was written down by Lincoln's law partner,
William H. Herndon, for his collaborator Jess Weik, February 27,
1891.

Lincoln was a diffident man — rather shy & not self possessed
in society — especially in a promiscuous crowd of ladies &
gentlemen at a party; he admired audacity — a quick witted
man, one self possessed and not having much cheek — Well
there was a party once, not far from here, which was composed of ladies & gentlemen — a fine table was set & the
people were greatly enjoying themselves. Among the crowd
was one of those men who had audacity — was quick witted
cheeky & self possessed — never off his guard on any
occasion. After the men & women had enjoyed themselves by
dancing — promenading — flirting etc they were told that
the supper was set. The man of audacity — quickwitted —
self possessed & equal to all occasions was put at the head
of the table to carve the turkeys chickens — & pigs. The
men & women surrounded the table & the audacious man be-

ing chosen carver whetted his great carving knife with the steel.
and got down to business & commenced carving the turkey,
but he expended too much force & let a fart — a loud fart
so that all the people heard it distinctly. As a matter of course
it shocked all terribly. A deep silence reigned. However the
audacious man was cool & entirely self possessed; he was
curiously & keenly watched by those who knew him well, they
suspecting that he would recover in the end and acquit himself
with glory. The man with a kind of sublime audacity, pulled
off his coat, rolled up his sleeves — put his coat deliberately
on a chair — spat on his hand — took his position at the
head of the table — picked up the carving knife & whetted
it again, never cracking a smile nor moving a muscle of his
face. It now became a wonder in the minds of all the men
& women how the fellow was to get out of his dilemma; he
squared himself and said loudly & distinctly: "Now by God
I'll see if I can't cut up this turkey without farting." Lincoln
was at the party and said as quick as a bolt of lightning all
the men and women threw off all modesty and broke out, in-
stantly — unanimously — harmoniously, into a universal,
long continued, & boisterous laugh, cheering the fellow for
his complete success — his cunning audacious victory, and became the lion of the evening, swung around the women as
if nothing happened. "I worshipped the fellow" said Lincoln.

     As a matter of course no such thing ever happened and yet
it is a good story to show the power of audacity — self
possession — quick wittedness etc., and as such it pleased
Lincoln admirably. The nib of the thing was what Lincoln was
after. I have heard him tell it often & often.

   Such stories are funny largely as told by a particular raconteur,
whose best art is frequently to convey, ever so slyly, that the joke
is on the teller and/or the listener, or on one aspect of either which
corresponds to the similar aspect of the personnae in the story.
Herndon is trying to make some such point in his sentence intro-
ducing the story of the "Man of Audacity," but I am not sure
he makes the proper identification with Lincoln's diffidence. As
Lincoln told the story, I suspect he may have identified with the
listener who has sat through many a stuffy dinner party and who

will relish the event as well as the audacity of it's perpetrator in flaunting his disrespect for "polite" society by humorous escape from a phony prudery.

Most such stories, however, have never been in print. One of the better ones, typical of Lincoln, I first heard Bill Townsend tell as an example of how Lincoln teased his law partner, in answer to a typical Herndon query.

Herndon perpetually plied Lincoln with questions which grew out of Herndon's omnivorous reading and speculative turn of mind. Frequently Lincoln's humorous answer was an affront to Herndon's seriousness — as when Lincoln replied to Herndon's query concerning what his thoughts were when he visited Niagara Falls. Lincoln said simply, "I thought, where did all that water come from." Herndon in this instance attributed Lincoln's apparently shallow answer to a lack of philosophical profundity, but I have always suspected that Lincoln never divulged to his notoriously quizzical friend the depths of any moment in his life that truly moved him.

On another occasion Herndon, who had been reading a popular scientific work, asked Lincoln if he believed in heredity. As Townsend told the story, Lincoln mused a moment and replied yes, that he had little doubt that not only physical characteristics but also the subtler traits of moral and mental personality were passed on from one generation to another. He had seen too many examples, like-father-like-son, to doubt it, but one instance in particular he was sure Herndon would also recognize — a well-known local character whom Lincoln had first encountered during his New Salem period and who had fathered five sons. Herndon replied that from his knowledge of the sons he failed to see in them any particularly strong evidence of hereditary traits. Lincoln continued, "Well, I know that ——— suffered terribly in the old days from chronic diarrhea, and you know for a fact that every one of the boys has turned out to be a perfect shitass!"

Such stories gain from the occasion as well as the manner of the telling. They derive their "meaning" or their "point" as much from context as from content, and doubtless lose much without Lincoln's voice and timing as well as his apropos subject. His talent for mimicry and dialectical speech also enriched many of the stories

with which he regaled the appreciative audiences that Herndon described in another letter to Weik, November 13, 1885.

> There were three noted story tellers — jokers — jesters in
> the central part of this state especially from 1840 to 1853
> Lincoln of Sangamon County — William Engle of Menard
> and James Murray of Logan: they were all men of mark, each
> in his own way: they were alike in the line of joking — story
> telling — jesting. I knew the men for years. From 1840 to
> 1853 this section was not known for a very high standard of
> taste — the love for the beautiful or the good, We had not many
> newspapers — people in all of these counties would attend
> court at the respective county seats. Lincoln — Engle, &
> Murray would travel around from county to county with the
> courts and those who loved fun & sport — loved jokes —
> tales — stories — jests would go with the courts too from
> county to county. People had not much to do at the time and
> the class of people that then lived here are gone — perished.
> It was a curious state of affairs indeed. As compared with
> the now it was rough — semi barbarous. In the evening after
> the court business of the day was over & book & pen had
> been laid by the lawyers — Judges — Jurymen — Witnesses
> & the people generally would meet at some bar-room —
> "gentlemen's parlor" — and have a good time in story telling
> — joking — jesting etc., etc. The bar room — windows —
> halls & all passage ways would be filled to suffocation by the
> people, eager to see the "Big Ones" and to hear their stories
> told by them. Lincoln would tell his story in his very best
> style. The people — all present — including Lincoln would
> burst out in a loud laugh & a hurrah at the story. The
> listeners, so soon as the laugh and the hurrah had passed and
> silence had come in for its turn, would cry out — "Now Uncle
> Billy (Wm Engle) you must beat that or go home." Engle
> would clear his throat & say — "Boys the story just told by
> Lincoln puts me in mind of a story that I heard when a boy";
> he would tell it and tell it well. The People would clap their
> hands — stamp their feet — hurrah — yell, shout get up —
> hold their aching sides. Things would soon calm down. There
> were politeness and etiquette in it. Each must have his turn,
> by comity, in which to tell his story. The good people would,
> as soon as quiet reigned, would [sic] cry out — "Now is your

time", come Murray do your level best or never come here again to tell your stories." Murray would prepare himself with his best. At first he would be a little nervous, but he would soon gather confidence — rise up — walk about, telling his tale as he moved in harmony with his story: he would tell it well — grandly — and the people would sometimes before the story was ended catch the point and raise such a laugh and a yell that the village rang with the yells — laughs — and hurrahs, etc. Lincoln — and Engle now were nervous and anxious for their turns to come around. Lincoln would tell his story & then followed Engle and then came Murray and thus this story telling — joking — jesting, would be kept up till 1 or 2 o'clock in the night, and thus night after night till the court adjourned for that term. . .

Following one such occasion a bailiff of the court begged Lincoln to write out for him a particularly complicated gem in which Lincoln employed spoonerism to the hilt for bawdy humor. This scrap of paper in Lincoln's hand has been transmitted at enormously inflated prices from collector to collector down to the present, as the only piece, so far as I know, of this variety of Lincolniana in Lincoln's own handwriting.

He said he was riding *bass-ackwards* on a *jass-ack*, through a *patton-cotch*, on a pair of *baddle-sags*, stuffed full of *binger-gred*, when the animal *sterred* at a *scump*, and the *lirrup-steather* broke, and throwed him in the *forner of the kence* and broke his *pishing fole*. He said he would not have minded it much, but he fell right in a great *tow-curd;* in fact, he said it gave him a right smart *sick of fitness* — he had the *molera-corbus* pretty bad. He said, about *bray dake* he come to him-self, ran home, seized up a *stick of wood*, and split the axe to make a light, rushed into the house, and found the *door* sickabed, and his *wife* standing open. But thank goodness she is getting right *hat* and *farty* again.

Typical of the prairie country in which Sandburg grew up and where he as a boy learned many "dirty" stories of the variety that Lincoln purportedly told, either to illustrate a point or merely to regale a courtroom audience when court was not in session, was the bucolic tale of two braggarts proud of their ability to stomach anything, however revolting it might be. I heard Carl tell the story

more than once, with great gusto, as a choice morsel for the true
gourmet of scatology, for all you had to do during the telling was
watch the circle of faces to know who was "in" and who was "out"
at this level. I had heard the story first in my very early boyhood,
as Carl said he had also, and we agreed that it was typical of that
variety of midwestern humor from Lincoln's era to our own.

The two braggarts had been spouting around the neighborhood
for a long time about the strength of their respective stomachs;
so their prowess was brought to a test one Sunday afternoon by
their cronies, who placed substantial bets and finally egged them
on to the trial of strength. First they came to a dead horse. Each
cut in with his knife and carved out a mouthful. The horse had
lain there stinking for months, but each braggart chewed his morsel
and swallowed it down. Then they came to a couple of dead frogs,
which they swallowed with ease. Next on the menu was a dead
rat, which they dispatched between them. Other choice viands in
various stages of decay were devoured promptly. Even a couple
of ancient buffalo chips were swallowed, albeit somewhat
deliberately because of the absence of any water to wash them
down. Next, as if in answer to their drought of throat, they came
upon a fresh cow dropping. There it lay in the green grass like a
custard pie fresh from the oven, with the steam still rising from it.
The first braggart stooped down, took a spoonful, put it in his
mouth, stood up, and swallowed it down. The other one crouched
down in his turn and had his spoonful of the tasty victual lifted to put
in his mouth when he suddenly stood up and hollered out, "I can't
eat it. I can't eat it. There's a hair in it.!"

It requires slight imagination to guess how aptly Lincoln or
Sandburg could use that hair to illustrate a point about what a
man will gag at, having swallowed so much filth by choice.

Even a gargantuan sense of humor, however, is sometimes not
enough, when seeing oneself as seen by others. Like Lincoln,
Sandburg found his sense of humor to be his first and best line
of defense against the ridicule, sarcasm, and disparagement of
critics, but there was a limit to its power to assuage.

When in 1958, shortly after his daughter Helga published her
first novel, *Wheel of Earth,* I found it necessary to write him from
the Library of Congress on official business, I faced a dilemma.

Since I was expected to read the novel, I could scarcely ignore it, and as a great many of the readers I could not avoid the apparent elements of a *roman à clef*. I decided to meet the problem frankly but humorously in only a metaphorical fashion. His reply began all too lugubriously, "It is good to hear from you, either as a person of humor or an official with responsibilities." I was touched, and when some time later he confirmed in person what I had inferred his feelings to be, I thought of his having written, "out of songs and scars and the mystery of personal development, we may get eyes that pick out intentions we had not seen before in people, in art, in books and poetry."

Although Lincoln and Sandburg undoubtedly embellished, I suspect that neither ever created even one of the countless stories for the telling of which both became famous on the prairie. Genuine folk humor is rarely if ever the creation of one teller. Much of it begins in real incident, almost immediately embellished or twisted by someone who has the wit and humor to see its "higher" possibilities, and thenceforth becomes everyone's property. If I have dwelt on some of the most vulgar examples of purported Lincoln stories, as I have found them, it is because they are so seldom available in print. The hundreds of his more polite, though occasionally coarse, anecdotes are well recorded in many books. Sometimes those who retell them do not recognize that the story ever held Lincoln's attention, and sometimes a great tapestry of fiction has been woven over Lincoln's small cloth, as in the case of Mark Twain's "Captain Stormfield's Visit to Heaven." Whether Twain knew it as a Lincoln story or not, he doubtless heard it, as I did when a boy in Missouri, told with locale varying to suit the teller's satiric purpose. It could be told of any town in any state, with the exact effect that Lincoln wanted when he told it about Chicago. As recorded in *Old Abe's Jokes, Fresh from Abraham's Bosom,* 1864, the story goes thus:

> Some years ago, when Chicago was in its infancy a stranger took up his quarters at the principal hotel, and inscribed his name on the register as Mr. J————, of St. Louis. For several days he remained there, engaged in transacting the business which had brought him to the place, and from his exceedingly

plain dress, manners and general appearance, attracted but little attention.

Soon Mr. J——— was suddenly seized with illness, during which he was sadly neglected by his host; and the servants taking their tone from the master of the house, left him to shift for himself as best he could. Thus matters went on, till one morning he was past praying for; his papers were then examined, that the sad intelligence might be communicated to his friends; when to the surprise of all he was found to be one of the wealthiest men in the western country. Arrangements were accordingly made for the funeral; but before the last rites were performed, the subject came to life again, having been the victim of catalepsy, instead of the grim "King of Terror." All were overjoyed at his fortunate escape from so dreadful a fate, and from that time were profuse in their expressions of solicitude, elicited, however, we judge, by "documentary evidence," rather than by any personal regard. At length some one ventured to ask, how things appeared to him while in his trance, to which he thus replied:

"I thought I had come to the river of death, where I met an angel who handed me a jewel to serve as a pass to the other side. On giving this to the ferryman, I received from him another which carried me further another stage in my journey. Going on thus for several stages, receiving at the termination of each, a ticket for the succeeding one, I at last reached the gate of the Heavenly City. There I found St. Peter, who opened the door at my summons, pipe in mouth, seated by a small table, on which stood a goodly mug of steaming whiskey toddy.

" 'Good morning, sir,' said he very politely.

" 'Good morning, St. Peter,' said I.

" ' Who are you, sir?' said he, turning over the leaves of a huge ledger.

" 'My name is J———.'

" 'Very good, sir; where do you live down below?'

" 'I lived at St. Louis, in the State of Missouri.'

" 'Very well, sir; and where did you die?'

" 'I died at Chicago, in Illinois.'

" 'Chicago?' said he, shaking his head, "there's no such place, sir.'

" 'I beg your pardon, St. Peter, but have you a map of the United States here?'

" 'Yes, sir.'

" 'Allow me to look at it.'

" 'Certainly, sir.'

"With that he handed down a splendid atlas, and I pointed out Chicago on the map.

" 'All right, sir,' said he, after a moment's pause; 'its there, sure enough, so walk in, sir; but I'll be blest if you ain't the first man that has ever come here from that place!' "

I have often thought, when quite honest with myself as a student of Lincoln, that if I could choose one occasion out of the past at which I might have been present as an anonymous Lincoln observer, it would not be any of the great historic occasions, some of which have been preserved in eyewitness accounts, but rather, just one of those innumerable sessions in the grubby hotel lobbies and courtrooms, when Lincoln topped the best his confreres had to offer. Neither U. S. Grant, who purportedly would not tolerate, much less participate in, the telling of even mildly "off-color" jokes, nor any other among Lincoln's great or near-great contemporaries, unless it might be the young Mark Twain, could offer any competition for my choice of historic moments. The next best thing to that impossibility has been the not unlike sessions with a few modern masters of the art of storytelling, such as Carl Sandburg, Ben Thomas, and Bill Townsend.

Townsend's repertoire was the most extensive, and included vignettes of the historic characters of the Bluegrass region around Lexington, Kentucky, particularly of Cassius Marcellus Clay, whom Lincoln appointed minister to Russia following Simon Cameron. I have never doubted that this hardy Kentucky abolitionist, nephew of Henry Clay, was one of the truly heroic figures in American history. Although perhaps adequately treated in his historical role by a number of books, he merited the kind of biography which only Townsend could have written but never got around to in his busy life as a lawyer, when his major avocation was Lincoln. The best of Townsend's several books on special aspects of Lincoln, I think, is his *Lincoln and His Wife's Home Town*. But his talent for storytelling is perhaps best suggested by his *Hundred Proof, Salt River Sketches & Memoirs of the Blue Grass,* published in 1964, the year of his death. The biographical sketch of Townsend by his friend Holman Hamilton, which serves as Introduction to the volume, pays high tribute to its subject's artistry as storyteller, but reading it convinces me, as does Herndon's tribute to Lincoln's skill, that printed words cannot do justice to a supreme master of the genre. One has to have been a participant to know how great and how illusory this art can be.

One of Townsend's best stories, "Black Bess," appears as chapter fourteen in *Hundred Proof.* It lacks the rhapsody of rounded periods and not a few colorful words with which its author customarily embellished it in oral delivery. In particular it is bowdlerized at the climax or "punch line," quite in keeping with the old school gentility which blended so naturally with the earthiness of its author when "in the presence of ladies." Townsend was definitely not of the present generation, in which the "fair sex" have achieved the final and complete equality of sharing "off-color" jokes in "mixed company."

I had heard Bill tell the tale of "Black Bess" more than once, but his most historic telling was also perhaps the peak of his entire career as a storyteller, by reason of an unforeseen circumstance that placed Townsend somewhat in the position of Lincoln's "Man of Audacity." The place was the Whittall Pavilion of the Library of Congress; the occasion, a dinner on the night before the Robert Todd Lincoln Collection of the Papers of Abraham Lincoln were opened to the scrutiny of scholars, July 1, 1947. Every Lincoln author and collector, or curator of Lincolniana, of any consequence had been invited to participate in the onslaught on history, scheduled to begin at midnight between July 1 and July 2. To pass the time and put the Lincolnists on their mettle, the Librarian of Congress, Luther H. Evans, had arranged to dine the group, after copious libations. The entertainment was to be furnished by the guests *ad libitum.* It would have been a memorable night in any event, with many a yarn and reminiscence, but the peak was Bill Townsend's narrative "by special request," of the desecration of a most sacred memory of the gray-uniformed Kentucky veterans of the War between the States. For the major portion of the tale

I rely on the version published in *Hundred Proof,* but for the climax I must interpolate from memory.

"I CANNOT REMEMBER the time when I first heard about Black Bess, the mare that John Hunt Morgan rode during the Civil War. The veterans of the Salt River Valley and the old soldiers of the Bluegrass all talked about her with abiding enthusiasm and deep affection.

"Possessed of blazing speed, great beauty, almost unlimited endurance, a strong straight back, exceptional intelligence and a spirited demeanor which reflected her blooded ancestry, Black Bess was remarkably calm and courageous under the heaviest fire. For the general she responded to every wish with prompt and complete obedience. Colonel Dick Morgan, the general's last surviving brother, and other staff officers were fond of relating how their chief — hotly pursued by Yankees — had galloped Black Bess through his mother's house at Second and Mill streets and escaped down a private driveway.

"In 1911 the Bluegrass was full of Morgan's men, most of them hale and hearty despite advancing years. That spring a movement was started to erect an equestrian bronze statue of the general on the courthouse lawn near Upper Street. A fund was quickly raised, and a noted Italian sculptor who specialized in statues of mounted military men — many examples of whose work stood in Washington — was engaged for the undertaking, which everybody hoped would be his masterpiece.

"Promptly he arrived in Lexington and set up his studio in a stone carriage house on Second Street in the rear of what was later the Lexington College of Music. The renowned artist worked alone, and with perhaps a slight touch of arrogance he announced that this statue would be in complete accord with the strictest military traditions.

"At his request he was supplied with several photographs of Morgan, his saddle, and other accouterments. Then inquiry was made about a picture of the "charger" which he had ridden. He was informed that he could be furnished a picture of Black Bess, the mare that had carried the general through so many perilous adventures. However, at the mere mention of a mare, the sculptor's Latin blood boiled over. He shouted, waved his arms, and reiterated that no statue ever showed a military man riding a mare. This would be inexcusably bad art. He would be ridiculed without mercy by competent members of his profession who knew that generals were invariably mounted on stallions.

"However, after it was explained that the veterans and the public generally would never be satisfied with any horse except Black Bess, the sculptor lapsed into sulky silence apparently conceding the point, and it was given no more thought.

"The model was finished sooner than expected and there was considerable disappointment at finding that the sculptor had packed and shipped it to the foundry to be cast in bronze before anybody had seen it. The reason he gave was that other commitments were pressing him so urgently that this work had to be finished at the earliest possible moment.

"When, in due time, the statue came back in permanent form, the sculptor personally supervised the mounting of the canvas-swathed figures on the granite base previously prepared, and then the night before the unveiling he completely draped them with large Confederate flags.

"The ceremonies for next day were eagerly awaited by the old soldiers, their kinsmen, and thousands of others in the Bluegrass. Many dignitaries occupied a temporary platform erected nearby — the national and state commanders of the United Confederate Veterans, high officials of the Sons and Daughters of the Confederacy, the Governor of Kentucky, and both United States Senators. Upper Street from Short to Main, Main Street from Upper to Cheapside, and all available space around the courthouse were packed with a dense throng of enthusiastic spectators.

"Presently the dramatic moment arrived. The band played 'My Old Kentucky Home,' then struck up 'Dixie.' And the beloved 'Stars and Bars,' by ingenious arrangement of the sculptor, slowly and majestically began to roll down from the top toward the base. The crowd broke into thunderous applause, mingled with the Rebel Yell as the head and shoulders of horse and rider were exposed to view — the general, plumed hat in hand as though acknowledging the tumultuous tribute; Black Bess with flowing mane, flaring nostrils, arched neck, shapely head, and those cocked ears which indicated her unceasing alertness the veterans remembered so vividly.

"Then, an instant later as the flag dropped lower, the mood of the vast audience completely changed, and the sultry summer air was filled with cries of dismay and indignation. Incredible as it might seem, the sculptor had transformed Black Bess into a stallion.

"In violence to sex, to history, to honor, and to justice, however properly and artistically hung, there bulged a most supererogatory and majestic pair of balls!"

Bill paused to enjoy the unanimous whoop and prolonged roar of laughter that reward the storyteller's art. But applause could not save him from the utter confusion that descended like a cold, sudden shower of rain, when out of the corner of his eye he saw two young women who, unbeknown to the engrossed all-male audience, had just a moment before slipped unobtrusively into the room to seat themselves against a rear wall. Daughters of two of the venerable guests, they had employed their powers of persuasion, at the late hour, upon the Library of Congress employee stationed at the door to shunt aside members of the press and the public who were waiting in the halls for the arrival of the midnight hour.

Far from a facsimile of Lincoln's "Man of Audacity" at that moment, but nevertheless unable to retreat from the field of honor, Bill continued resolutely, if somewhat stammeringly to the end of his story, finally joining in the ascending hilarity of his audience, a hilarity which was now as much the result of his discomfiture as of his story.

"The veterans almost frothed at the mouth with anger that defied adequate description. Soon, although the dampened ceremonies were not over, small groups began to detach themselves from the audience. They were looking for the sculptor, who had hastily scrambled from the rear of the platform and disappeared.

"But the search for this atrocious desecrator — this perfidious creature — continued. Hearing that he was leaving on the C. & O., which would pull into Lexington shortly, a part of the crowd rushed to the Union Station only to find out later that police officers had taken the bewildered and cringing culprit to Winchester, and he had caught the train there.

"More than fifty years have passed since that eventful and shocking day. The tragic alteration of Morgan's mare has been poignantly related in prose and ballad, to be preserved forever in the folklore of America. But Bess herself still prances proudly on her granite pedestal with unabashed equanimity, heedless of the atrocious anatomical outrage inflicted upon her when Art triumphed over Truth."

IV

With the exception of the Lincoln dinner, the Library of Congress fanfare at the opening of the Lincoln Papers proved to be a rather prosaic affair. As most of us had anticipated, there were no history-shaking discoveries. Hitherto unknown Lincoln manuscripts of great consequence failed to materialize. Old allegations that Robert Todd Lincoln had destroyed documents which would have detracted from his father's image were resurrected by some, but the Moses Hampton letter reproduced earlier in this narrative — certainly a prime target for such destruction — strengthened my belief that Robert Lincoln had not destroyed much if anything.

My personal hope had been to find at most only a few hitherto unknown letters written by Lincoln to his wife. It had always seemed unfortunate to me that the few intimate letters written by Lincoln to his wife derived from the period of Lincoln's term in Congress, 1848—1849, and that they had not been preserved by members of the immediate family. The only domestic letter of any considerable interest during the Presidential years — the famous "Nanny Goat" letter of August 8, 1863 — was preserved in the Lincoln Papers by reason of an almost incredible accident. Lincoln apparently lost it in an unaddressed envelope. It was picked up by a soldier in the Army of the Potomac, but was not returned to Lincoln for many months.

In any event, whether or not Robert Lincoln destroyed any papers before the collection was placed in the keeping of the Library of Congress and sealed for a period of twenty-five years, the opening of the collection afforded little that was startlingly new.

The public ceremonies which followed the midnight opening, at noon on the next day, were therefore an anticlimax for everyone except me. I had been chosen to deliver the "principal address," carried by the national radio networks but cut off in midstream because the allocated air time had been largely monopolized by the master of ceremonies, Senator C. Wayland "Curly" Brooks of Illinois.

My selection for this distinction, I attributed to several circumstances besides the favorable reception of *Abraham Lincoln: His Speeches and Writings* the preceding year and my recent appointment by The Abraham Lincoln Association to edit a definitive edition of Lincoln's work. For one thing I was not a competitor among the several eminent historians and biographers of Lincoln, the choice of one of whom might have been viewed askance by the proponents of others. More important, however, as I learned later, was my recommendation by the dean of the Lincoln fraternity, Oliver R. Barrett, who had become my good friend to whom I already owed more for kindness and good opinion than I could ever repay. His unique story has been told so amply and well by Sandburg in the remarkable book, *Lincoln Collector, the Story of the Oliver R. Barrett Lincoln Collection* that all I hope to do here is illustrate the generous contribution of time and trouble with which he made possible my work as well as that of so many others. Sandburg's monumental *Lincoln,* Albert J. Beveridge's fine biography, James G. Randall's several important books, and practically every other significant Lincoln work of this century could not have been written without Barrett's assistance.

Barrett was the "friend" with whom Sandburg had deposited my manuscript of *The Lincoln Legend* in 1934, and from whose vault he had reclaimed it unread to return it to me in 1935, when I decided to accept Houghton Mifflin's offer to publish. What had happened will presently become, if not clear, at least understandable, but I must double back on my trail somewhat.

During the Christmas holidays in 1940, I had spent a few days in Chicago, ostensibly to attend the annual meeting of the Modern Language Association, but in reality for the purpose of learning whether I might obtain access to the Barrett Collection, without which my job of editing a volume of Lincoln's writings would be impossible. When his secretary put my telephone call through, I said, "I am Roy Basler from Florence, Alabama, and I would like very much to have an appointment." He asked, "What do you want to see me about?" I replied, "Abraham Lincoln." "Very well," he said, "come at two o'clock."

He received me very cordially, if at first rather aloofly. It was obvious that whatever Sandburg had told him about me several years before had left absolutely no record in his memory and that he was only indifferently curious about an Alabaman professing an interest in Lincoln. I was self-conscious about interrupting an obviously busy and big-time lawyer, whose (to me) very opulently furnished office bore testimony chiefly to the fact that I should state my case succinctly and impose no longer than necessary.

Somewhat hatchet-faced in appearance, with eyes that darted their sharp, quizzical appraisal across his huge desk, he lolled in a high-backed, leather swivel-chair and gave me the works. What brought me to Chicago? Just where was Florence, Alabama? Where was I born? (I didn't sound like an Alabaman.) How did I become interested in Lincoln? And so it went for more than an hour, during which I seemed never to get an opening to mention *The Lincoln Legend* or to broach the subject of my proposal to edit a volume of Lincoln's writings. But we did talk about Lincoln, and I expounded my views, particularly of Lincoln's literary style, with which Barrett took exception. Lincoln had no style; he just wrote carefully. So I defended my view and demonstrated my points.

I remember almost entirely the gist, and a great deal verbatim, of our discussion of Lincoln's style and the question of just what style is. He contended Lincoln had no style, that he wrote "naturally" as he spoke, that clarity was his only concern. "Even in the Gettysburg Address?" I interjected. "Yes, especially there." "Do you think the poetic effects there are accidental then?" "Not accidental, but natural, inspired." "Out of what? You don't think Lincoln's reading of the Bible had anything to do with how he wrote then?" "Not consciously." "Perhaps not when he was writing the Addresses but surely when he was reading the Bible, especially aloud, he was conscious of the rhythms, imagery, especially the metaphor of its poetry and made it a part of his literary paraphernalia of understanding, which he might or might not use sometime, don't you think?" "Maybe, but that's not style."

At this, I became genuinely puzzled. Perhaps I didn't know what

Barrett meant by style or he what I meant. "Well, if it isn't, what is style? What would you cite me as an author's style?" "Maugham's *Cakes and Ale,* that's style." "How right you are! I agree, but don't both derive, each from the different literary experience of the man writing, as well as from the rest of the life experience of the man who is creating something in words?"

He thought about it a moment and said, "Yes and no."

Then we left the question of Lincoln's style, with my promise that I would do something to demonstrate Lincoln's style, or styles, for he had more than one. Some of my subsequent efforts to do so have appeared in print.

I became aware that the day was darkening outside his windows and wondered what to do, but he would not let me come to the point until it was well after four o'clock. "All right, tell me why you want to go to the trouble of editing another book of Lincoln's writings. The Nicolay and Hay edition seems good enough to me."

I listed specific instances where Nicolay and Hay did not seem to me to have met modern scholarly standards of editing, and in the process noted that Barrett seemed unaware in most instances that this was the case. Finally he stood up, signifying that our session was at an end, and smiled for the first time. I knew that I was "home free." "When do you want to work on the things I have?" I replied that, at his convenience, I should like to obtain photostats but if he preferred I could come up sometime during my summer vacation. "Very well," he said, "write to me."

As he walked me down the corridor, I became aware that we were about the same size and that something had happened during the afternoon. It was the feeling that Oliver Barrett and I would thenceforth get along together, but I did not guess how rich a friendship was ahead.

Like most collectors, Barrett was reluctant to furnish photocopies of his treasures, even at the researcher's expense. It was not so much the trouble of photostating dozens of documents, for the inconvenience of providing the originals and an office to work in surely offset that. It was rather the feeling that once photocopied the document lost something of its uniqueness. This chariness was the occasion of one of the most memorable weeks

I have ever spent, the last week in August 1941. All day long, with my wife's assistance, I copied and/or corrected the text of Lincoln letters and other documents. During the evening we visited the Barrett home and explored his unbelievable collection of other historical and literary treasures — from Columbus to Lincoln, you named the person and Oliver Barrett produced the manuscripts: Napoleon, Wellington, Washington, Sherman, Grant, Molière, Dryden, Shelley, Poe, Whitman, Tennyson, Byron — there was scarcely a major literary or historical figure from the seventeenth century to the twentieth not represented by several manuscripts, obviously chosen for some particularly interesting human revelation. Barrett had collected for half a century with a catholicity and discrimination that made him a veritable Croesus among manuscript collectors. In the process, he had explored bypaths of history and literature that no organized, formal study could have opened up, for it had been his custom to acquaint himself with the surrounding circumstances of every piece he owned. Although somewhat of a patchwork, his learning was certainly as brilliantly colorful and idiosyncratic a quilt of knowledge as is imaginable. From cellar to attic the modest two-story frame house in which the Barretts lived was literally crammed — closets, bureaus, trunks, and boxes — with those things he most frequently liked to handle and study; the less attractive, but by no means less valuable, were relegated to a very large bank vault.

What sort of wife could put up with a hobby that preempted every nook and cranny and practically crowded her out of house and home? Pauline Barrett had married the hobby along with the man and could joke about her problems in good humor which nevertheless needled, covertly and harmlessly, her spouse's idiosyncrasies. She was small, plump, and wifely, keeping her house a most intimate home in spite of her husband's every tendency to turn it into a museum and archive. The personality of the house was hers more than his — lived-in and lived-with in every modestly handsome piece of furniture, fine china, and old silver. So well tucked out of sight were his treasures that no casual visitor could possibly have guessed at the wealth hidden away. Even the numerous museum pieces of furniture and knickknacks "belonged" so to the atmosphere that one would not recognize them as historic relics until a second look brought forth a fascinating story.

She and my wife became friends immediately, with family gossip about children and all of the distaff side of things, and it was to her that our mutual friendship as two couples owed even more eventually than to Oliver, and continued through other visits and correspondence for many years after Oliver's sudden death from a heart attack in March 1950. We helped her select the plot in Oak Ridge Cemetery, Springfield, Illinois, where Oliver's ashes would be interred, a stone's throw from Lincoln's tomb, simply appropriate for the resting place of one whose admiration never wavered for all that Lincoln was and represented.

During our visit that memorable August, I mentioned *The Lincoln Legend*'s absence among Oliver's books and told him I would rectify the omission upon returning home. I did not mention the fact that he had once held the manuscript for several months. When he received the book, he wrote: "I am greatly obliged to you for the book, and the flattering inscription. I have read it from cover to cover, and am astounded with the contemplation of the fact that I had no knowledge of the existence of a book so important to any Lincoln student, or to any collector of Lincolniana. I cannot explain how I could possibly have missed the reviews or some mention of a book of such interest and importance. . . . . When I spoke to Carl about your book, he told me that I had seen the manuscript and read it when he had it, before the book was printed, which leaves me more mystified than ever, because I have not the slightest recollection of it." Carl was wrong, I knew, about Oliver's having read it, for when it came back to me in December 1934, it was sealed in the same wrapping in which I had mailed it to Carl, with a new address label, prepared, as I guessed, by Oliver's secretary, who probably dug it out of a pile in the not-too-tidy closet in his office.

Although it is tempting to dwell on other pleasant occasions when I enjoyed Oliver's hospitality and friendship, I will recount only one — an occasion when I unintentionally displeased him. On February 9, 1946, I was Oliver's guest speaker before the Caxton Club. This prestigious if informal organization of bookmen was surely the most awesome group I had ever faced, up to that time, and I prepared accordingly. When we were assembled at table I saw before me, as before every man present, a full bottle of bourbon — a time-honored custom and a challenge, come what would! Even a bad speech might pass, I suspected, as I watched with mounting awe each capacity seated at the table, the contents so rapidly diminishing in every bottle, my own like all the rest.

There was one part of my speech in which I contrasted with particular pains the deterministic philosophy of Karl Marx with Lincoln's own determinism. The talk seemed to hold my audience, and I flattered myself that the applause was not wholly the product of alcoholic euphoria, either mine or theirs. When the meeting adjourned, Oliver and I returned to his office and he paid me several fine compliments on the way. Not until we were saying goodbye did I learn that I had wounded him in a tender spot. "It was one of the best talks we've ever had and I am happy to have credit for inviting you," he said, "But I have a suggestion for improving it if you ever give it again. Leave out the part about Marx. It is wrong even to mention Marx in relation to Lincoln, in any way whatsoever." I was astonished and replied, "But wasn't my very point to show to Lincoln's advantage his humanism versus the cold mechanism of Marx, which lies at the roots of the most incredibly inhuman excesses of Stalin's regime?" Oliver shook his head. "You can't even name them together without lending, even unintentionally, respect to the most despicable of all views of human nature."

I have reflected on this many times and have recognized some truth in Oliver's admonition, but I have continued to try, on occasion, to show that the difference between the philosophy of those two men is still the crucial issue before humanity at large, in the conviction that Lincoln's must endure — recognition of freedom as the true necessity versus recognition of necessity as the true freedom.

V

In September 1947 I moved my family to Springfield, Illinois, and took over, as executive secretary of the Abraham Lincoln

Association, the task of collecting and editing Lincoln's works. The association had a unique history, dating back to 1909 when the centennial of Lincoln's birth had been observed with great eclat in Springfield under the auspices of the newly formed Lincoln Centennial Association. Organized as a patriotic effort, in some parts perhaps with a guilty civic conscience, to redeem Lincoln's home town from the memories of its race riot the preceding year, one of the most inexcusable blots on our national history. For several years thereafter, the Centennial Association had attempted annually on February 12 to emulate the grandeur of the first occasion, with a gargantuan banquet and addresses by leading statesmen and political figures of the era. Fine wine and exotic viands as well as speakers imported from the four corners of the earth gradually began to pall, however, and the association fell into desuetude, until 1922 when it was reorganized under the leadership of Logan Hay, distinguished attorney and citizen of Springfield who was also a nephew of Lincoln's secretary, John Hay. Logan Hay assembled a membership and a modest reserve fund to further a continuing program of research and publication, as well as the annual observance of Lincoln's birthday, in order "to contribute something solid and lasting to the appreciation of Lincoln's life." The need to sift particularly the local Illinois sources of Lincoln's early career, and replace encrustations of fiction and legend with recovered facts was the laudable object to which Hay and his associates dedicated the reorganized association.

To do the spade work as well as the more dignified chores, Hay brought in as executive secretary, Paul M. Angle, a twenty-four-year-old graduate of Miami (Ohio) University who had just received his master's degree from the University of Illinois. Under the guidance and stimulation of Hay, Paul Angle began publishing in the association's *Bulletin* a series of thoroughly researched and well-written papers that quickly commanded the respect of the professional historian who had for too long largely neglected the Lincoln story. In addition, the annual meeting was devoted to speakers willing to produce "something solid" rather than the fusty political oratory of yore, and the resulting annual volume of *Papers* challenged equal respect. It was not entirely coincidental, I think, that the labors of Carl Sandburg and Albert J. Beveridge on the Lincoln story began about the same time, for there was indeed much to be done.

The membership of the Abraham Lincoln Association extended into all parts of the United States, and even abroad. In cities such as Chicago, Los Angeles, and Washington, D.C., among others, there were (and some still *are*!) Lincoln groups, Lincoln fellowships, etc., whose memberships often numbered up to a hundred or more. Their practice was to gather at least annually on Lincoln's birthday, and frequently also on other commemorative dates, such as that of the assassination, the Emancipation Proclamation, the Gettysburg Address, etc. Like the Civil War Round Tables, groups which developed somewhat later and enlisted more members from below the Mason-Dixon line, these Lincoln organizations were comprised of the most varied assortment of lawyers, teachers, preachers, railroad men, or whatnot (even an occasional historically oriented bricklayer!) that can well be imagined.

The one thing these persons had in common was their passionate devotion to the study of Lincoln in particular and the Civil War period in general. Some were inclined to idolatry, but not all by any account. Otto Eisenschiml's *(Why Was Lincoln Murdered?)* fascination with Lincoln sometimes seemed to me to be motivated by a hardly concealed contempt (comparable to that held by Edgar Lee Masters) on the other hand, and Edgar DeWitt Jones *(Lincoln and the Preachers)* and others of his persuasion, seemed to me almost to approach a secular kind of idolatry, in which Lincoln replaced Jesus as an image of worship. And in all of the Lincoln groups one found every shade of variety between these extremes.

Over the years, I kept finding myself engaged in an unintentional epistolary controversy with some of these Lincolnites. To the pietists among them, perhaps my most unforgivable single sin was publication in the *Abraham Lincoln Quarterly* (September 1948) of a monumentally researched article by Roy Hays, proving once and for all that the Lincoln cabin enshrined in the marble temple at Hodgenville, Kentucky, and maintained as a national monument, is a fraud, albeit originally, perhaps, an unintentional fraud. I well remember a blistering letter received from one old-fashioned GOP newspaper editor who believed devoutly in preserving all Lincoln's halos, in which I was denounced along with other reprehensibles who purportedly want to prove Lincoln a bastard and to destroy the shrine in which the place of his hallowed birth is preserved.

The most curious of many such controversies, however, was the one I got into with Otto Eisenschiml as a result of my article written for *The South Atlantic Quarterly* during World War II ("As One Southerner to Another: Concerning Lincoln and the Declaration of Independence," *SAQ,* January 1943). Reprinted as a brochure by the Abraham Lincoln Book Shop, this venture into historical polemics received a wide and timely distribution and brought some acclaim for the view expressed therein — namely, that in a period when the United States was engaged in a war against fascist powers dedicated to the myth of the Aryan superman, it seemed singularly inappropos for "Southern" historians to continue to belabor the self-evident truths of the Declaration of Independence as "self-evident lies."

To my considerable surprise, I received among my "fan mail" only one expression of disapprobation and that one was cast in polemic terms so bitter that I, at first, thought it could only be a joke. How could it be possible, in the era when Hitler was exterminating Jews by the millions, that an Austrian Jewish immigrant, who had "made it" in America, would bitterly defend, with antebellum vigor, the right of Southern gentlemen in the midst of World War II to denounce as of old the "self-evident" truths of American democracy, as "self-evident lies"? Although I came to know Eisenschiml personally, and to recognize his essential quixoticism, I never found a completely satisfactory answer to this question.

It was his intention, he wrote me, to submit for publication in *The South Atlantic Quarterly* his piece "As One Gentleman to Another," a copy of which he enclosed — as a gentleman — so that I might know the chastisement I had coming. "If you think that I am factually in error, or that I am hitting you below the belt, please tell me so frankly. I have an idea you were pretty hot under the collar when you wrote your article. I often feel that way myself, but I usually allow myself a cooling-off period. I shall do so also in this case."

In answer, I sent him a copy of my reply to his reply, which I proposed to send the editor if he should follow his expressed intention. Sometime later he wrote me again, "The more I read your letters the more convinced I become that I should drop my original intention of airing my impressions in public." There the matter rested. Some years later I had the opportunity of becoming better acquainted with this truly quixotic, difficult, and brilliant man, but I never felt really comfortable in our quasi-friendship, because I never really knew where he stood.

Although not every member of a Lincoln group or fellowship was as colorful as Otto Eisenschiml, the fact is that an interest in Lincoln has proved to be, over the years, as good an intellectual index as I have found to those qualities of human nature which prove to be interesting in others. It beats even an interest in poetry or poker, which I have found, much as I enjoy them, to be somewhat unreliable as an index to character.

Among the "professionals" whose personal acquaintance grew into personal friendship during these years, in addition to Paul M. Angle, were Benjamin P. Thomas, Harry E. Pratt, and W.E. Barringer, all of whom preceded me in the office of executive secretary of the Abraham Lincoln Association. Ben Thomas in particular, and his lovely wife Sally, whose Christian name we heard only when Ben expressed affectionate astonishment (My God, Salome!) at some unanticipated revelation of her many social talents, were the best of friends. They both provided me and my wife with about our only entry to that singularly closed "open society" which characterized Springfield no less than other middlewestern, more or less static communities, which lack the distinction of being Lincoln's home town. Following a brief stint as college teacher of history, Ben had succeeded Paul Angle as executive secretary of the association for four years (1932-1936), enticed to Springfield in part by the fact that it was his wife's home. As executive secretary he produced his quota of association publications, most notable of which was the especially well-written little volume *Lincoln's New*

Salem. Neither the salary nor the position of executive secretary was, however, quite commensurate with the social circles in which the Thomases moved, and Ben decided to go into business. When he had sufficiently proved to himself and others his business acumen, he sold out for a tidy sum and returned to writing about Lincoln as a serious hobby. His biography of Lincoln published in 1952 brought him not only well-deserved fame but financial rewards that so overshadowed his earlier business successes, and so impressed certain of his somewhat patronizing fellow citizens, that he enjoyed an all-too-brief prestige, cut short by his suicide, instigated by cancer, in 1956.

Ben's friendship was in many ways one of the finest of my life and provided a confidential rapport and understanding which I sorely needed on occasion during the five years I labored for the association. I like to think that perhaps I brought something to him, as well, something which he did not find elsewhere in Springfield except in his most affectionate family. At any rate, I treasure the sentiment which Sally wrote me following his death — that he might not have committed suicide had I remained in Springfield, available for one of our talks.

Perhaps less professional, and to some extent less intimate, was my friendship with the president of the association George V. ("Gib") Bunn, Jr., who nevertheless was the source of my absolute support and the guarantee that, when the till began to run dry, *The Collected Works* would not fail of completion. Of Gib Bunn I can testify that I never found a single contradiction of what Paul Angle had said by way of persuasion in recruiting me for the job. "You'll never find a finer man to work with than Gib Bunn." Paul could be exceedingly noncommittal, as well as categorical, in his opinions of people, but he was never more reliable than in this one.

In addition to Ben Thomas and Gib Bunn, my editorial advisers numbered two outstanding professionals, both of whom had taken Lincoln for their specialty long before my time; Paul Angle, the director of the Chicago Historical Society, and the University of Illinois' distinguished Professor James G. Randall. Although as a group the advisers were convened only once, to discuss, revise, and approve the set of editorial rules I had drawn up, they gave individual advice and encouragement upon request, at frequent intervals.

In addition to his no-nonsense, practical advice on approaching any and every problem of historical research, Paul was most congenial company, as was his good wife Vesta, and together with the Thomases, although less often because of the distance between Chicago and Springfield, they provided some of the best social hours the Baslers ever enjoyed. But it was Jim Randall and his wife Ruth who seemed most familial, not fatherly or motherly, but like one's best uncle and aunt, in their regard for us and our labors in what was, after all, a kind of family project of the whole membership of the Abraham Lincoln Association. Sometimes family solidarity was needed, as matters would develop.

By the time I assumed my duties as executive secretary of the Abraham Lincoln Association, more than twenty years of solid research and distinguished publication had not only mined all the veins of early Lincoln ore in Illinois, but had brought the association to a position of eminence as a historical society with limited objectives. There remained the one big job — a new edition of Lincoln's works — which had been for years anticipated as the culmination of the association's program, but which could not be brought to fulfillment until the Lincoln Papers in the Library of Congress were released for study. Beginning with Paul Angle and continuing with each of his successors, photocopies of Lincoln's writings and speeches had been collected sporadically in connection with particular research projects. It was obvious, however, that a major, organized effort of collecting would be necessary as the first step in the project which I optimistically hoped I could finish in three years, but which would prove to require a little more than five. The dispersal of Lincoln manuscripts, as a result of the demand for Lincoln autographs among collectors, was not confined to the United States, and in spite of sizable holdings in historical libraries and in the magnificent Barrett collection, a very large portion of the letters and other minor pieces were held by individuals, for the most part unknown to any one source of information — in other words, several thousand needles in hundreds of unidentified haystacks. Lincoln seldom kept copies of his letters or speeches, and the letters he received prior to 1860 for the most part were not preserved. Although the Lincoln Papers in the Library of

Congress proved a treasure trove of the correspondence he received after 1860, drafts or copies of letters he wrote as President were less often to be found in the Lincoln Papers than were the originals in the departmental archives, taken over by the National Archives after its establishment in 1934.

Prior to this time, however, a great many of the Lincoln manuscripts in departmental files had been "lifted" by persons who had access to them, to be given to friends and autograph collectors, or sold to autograph dealers. Likewise, county courthouses in central Illinois were rifled for the documents Lincoln penned as a lawyer. Although autograph collectors unquestionably were responsible for preserving many items that might otherwise have been lost, some aspects of the autograph business neither the collector nor the historian can be proud of. Here is the typical story told by an autograph dealer in 1948, of how sixty-eight Lincoln autographs came to be offered for sale by another dealer.

> Mr. Meegan was offering the lot to my father for the price of $300. Neither of us could quite believe our eyes, yet Meegan was a reliable dealer and perfectly trustworthy. The speed with which our check went off need not be described. . .
>
> "Whether these slips of paper on which Lincoln's writing appeared — most of them were one inch by two inches in size or slightly larger — came to Mr. Meegan in this form, we do not know. All were endorsements written by Lincoln and cut from letters of appeal to him. These begging letters to the President have been referred to by many historians. To Lincoln, the kind and the merciful, the reading of these often heartrending appeals was a terrible chore, and yet one which he could not and did not choose to delegate. It was his custom to write on the back of each letter his note, referring the matter to the Secretary of War; or ordering a young boy under age, to be returned to his parents and discharged from the army upon refunding his bounty; or issuing a pardon to a prisoner; or recommending the appointment of an officer, and so on endlessly. A complete letter of appeal, with Lincoln's endorsement, generally fetches from $35 to $75 today, and the price was higher in 1936. Only the cut endorsements, however, were offered to us. Some vandal, who believed that Lincoln's writing alone would be of value, and not the mes-

sage of the petitioner, had, the story goes, cut out these endorsements of Lincoln from some hundreds of letters of appeal. The actual figure was never verified. Whatever the number, Mr. Meegan, sure, would never have perpetrated such an act of vandalism. The fact remains, however, that he acquired the group, from what source is not known, and disposed of them rapidly to the trade. Needless to say, this flood of Lincoln A.D.S.'s drastically reduced their price for a number of years. Now they have been mostly absorbed, and values are gradually on the increase again. *

The only comment I wish to make on this narrative is that these Lincoln endorsements were all taken by someone from the records of the War Department and that no "reputable" dealer could pretend ignorance of this fact. This is only one instance among many of the dealer's, and ultimately the collector's, indifference to the moral implications of acquiring stolen property. I can speak with knowledge of the extreme difficulty with which public repositories of documents undertake to safeguard their collections from theft. Without the cooperation of dealers and collectors, which I am happy to say is greater than it was some years ago, the vast collections of public records, national, state, and local, cannot be adequately preserved intact.

Our first problem was to cast a large net with small meshes which would catch as many items as possible. We sent out several thousands of letters to libraries, museums, autograph dealers, and private collectors, asking their cooperation and enclosing a form for reply. If no reply was forthcoming, a second letter was sent, and often a third or fourth.

We sought in every case to obtain a photocopy of each Lincoln manuscript, at our expense, and in most cases we succeeded. Without the modern techniques of photocopying — photostatic or photographic prints, microfilms, etc. — our task would have been all but impossible even in so far as the mere collecting was concerned, and of course when the editing process began we could not have achieved anything like the degree of accuracy which was possible, if we had had to rely on transcriptions such as earlier editors were forced to use to so large a degree. When one considers that nearly

*The Collector, December 1948, LXI, no. 12, 265-66.

seven thousand separate titles, varying from one page to over one hundred pages, were thus collected, the benefit of photo techniques can be appreciated.

Correspondence was by no means an adequate method of finding or obtaining copies of Lincoln manuscripts. Many miles of personal travel and all too many hours of personal interviews on the part of one or another member of our staff were necessary before the reticent collector delivered the needed photocopy, and in a few cases where photocopies were taboo we had to make our own transcripts. Also there were some major jobs of searching the tremendous bulk of records in the National Archives, or the papers of many a Lincoln contemporary which reside uncalendared and uncatalogued in historical societies and libraries throughout the country. Of course, it was only the uninitiated who believed that archivists would know whether their hoard of documents contained one or more Lincoln manuscripts, but I have found it a matter of surprise to most people that we had to do our own searching in such matters. The general idea seems to be that manuscripts in libraries and state archives are individually catalogued in the same manner as books. One can only wish that it were true!

Then there was the job of searching the catalogs of autograph dealers and auction houses accumulated over a period of fifty years, not merely for leads to present location of manuscripts but also for a text, sometimes the only extant text of a manuscript that had temporarily disappeared or had been permanently lost or destroyed. We also combed newspapers of the period, published reminiscences, biographies, and autobiographies of Lincoln's contemporaries, and printed compilations such as the *Official Records of the Union and Confederate Armies,* for texts of speeches, telegrams, orders, and letters of which no manuscript could be found.

Thus when we finally went to press, it was not a stroke of imagination which prompted the late Jim Randall to suggest that the best title for the job would be *The Collected Works of Abraham Lincoln.*

Since I have lapsed from the singular *I* to the plural *we* in this narrative, it is about time to pay tribute to my assistants. When I accepted the job of editing Lincoln's works, I found that Miss

Marion Dolores Bonzi, a student of Jim Randall's at the University of Illinois, had already been employed by the association as assistant editor. Zealous to the point of obsession with ensuring accuracy of Lincoln's text, she was also indefatigable and practically lived at her desk until her marriage in 1950. As my second assistant, I recruited Lloyd A. Dunlap, one of my own graduate students whose phenomenal talent for finding the necessary facts to fill in a definitive footnote I had discovered the preceding year. With his talent he combined an indefatigability equal to that of Marion Bonzi, and the two of them complemented with great success whatever I brought to the task myself. Perhaps a brief description of our teamwork may be in order.

As photostats and typed copies (as well as mere references) accumulated, they were processed according to the steps we devised. A card index was developed to catalog every source or mere reference that came to our notice. Cards were made for each item — one for the chronological card file, and one or more for the alphabetical card file, depending on the number of names or topics involved. As the photostats or other copies were acquired, they were filed chronologically. At first an extremely large number were relegated to an undated and unclassified section but in the process of editing we were eventually able to assign dates to all but a few of the many undated items.

Although it was impossible to adhere completely to a division of labor in any stage of our work, a division of a sort was evolved for the process of editing. A manuscript was typed (first copy and two carbons) either from the photostat or other copy, or from the best printed source. The second carbon was filed as a reserve in case of loss or damage to the other copies. The first carbon became our working copy, and the first copy, as corrected and supplied with notes, was eventually sent to the press. Lloyd Dunlap performed the bulk of the research which went into the annotation, and Marion Bonzi performed the bulk of checking the manuscript from photostats and other sources. I prepared the annotation and coordinated and reviewed the work at the two extremes of research and final checking. Each of us, however, had at all times a large concern with the work of his associates, and there is probably no page in the

Collected Works which does not bear some testimony to the effort of each, not merely in his own but also in his colleagues' sphere, to produce as nearly as possible a definitive annotated text.

But, to return to the earlier chapter of the story, the job got done, the page proofs of volume seven of *The Collected Works of Abraham Lincoln* were completed, and I took my departure from Lincoln's home town late in August 1952.

When I reflect on the five years spent on this project, I have no regrets, in spite of the fact that it was the only job I ever had in which I failed to receive a single raise in salary. Although I understood the reasons for this, at the time, I never understood why the officers of the Abraham Lincoln Association, all my friends, later on turned back all the royalties (a good many thousands of dollars) on *The Collected Works* to Rutgers University Press, at a time when I could have used a portion to help send my children to college.

During the interval between September 1947 and September 1952, practically everybody I knew in the academic world or elsewhere had enjoyed some increase in salary, and many were substantially better paid. But this was the least of my worries during the spring of 1952, when I had to face up to the fact that as a result of having been for five years out-of-the-line of regular candidates for academic advancement, no university seemed to have the slightest interest in hiring an ex-editor of Lincoln back into the role of professor of literature. The abrasion to my pride was lessened not at all when the only academic offer forthcoming proved to be a conditional one-year appointment at the university where I had first embarked on Lincoln scholarship. The reason for the one-year conditional trial period, so I was told, was that the then president of Duke University was concerned because so much of my teaching career had been spent in teachers' colleges. This was not the first time I had encountered the cultural snobbery of the anti-pedagogical academic world, which was displayed at its most ridiculous by alumni of second-or-third-rate liberal arts schools. I suppose no one other than my wife ever knew how nearly an answer to prayer was the offer of a position in the Library of Congress, where I would remain until I retired.

One further chapter in the story of *The Collected Works* may be briefly told, as it centers on one of the most remarkable men I have ever had the privilege of calling "friend." Earl Schenk Miers, director of the Rutgers University Press 1944—49, had negotiated with the association prior to my coming on the scene an agreement whereby Rutgers would be the publisher of all association books. I found this a very agreeable arrangement, since it enabled me to work directly from the beginning with the publisher whose imprint *The Collected Works* would bear. Within my first year, however, it became apparent that the genius of Earl Miers for developing a hitherto rather minor press into a major publishing house brought about certain traumatic convulsions in an organization not yet equipped to handle major enterprises.

Earl was above all a man of ideas, particularly for new books. Since he had more ideas than he could execute himself, he generously handed them out to his friends. One such notion was for a book of readings about Lincoln, excerpts selected from the enormous accumulation of Lincoln books. The brilliant idea could scarcely have been better executed than by Paul Angle as *The Lincoln Reader,* with a success that brought Book-of-the-Month adoption, as well as a series of less successful imitations by other publishers.

Hitting the bigtime competition, although it brought Rutgers what was, for a minor university press, an unprecedented status, did not suffice to bridge the difficulties which accumulated from Earl's entrepreneurial drive, and he left Rutgers to pursue his career as writer-editor-publisher, with continuing success elsewhere.

That Earl had been a victim of cerebral palsy from birth was the first thing one recognized on meeting him. It was also the first thing one forgot thereafter, since it became merely the camouflage, as it were, of a brilliant personality and an ebullient disposition that created intelligent social intercourse as good as I have ever had the privilege of sharing.

With his departure, it became evident at Rutgers that the prospect of publishing *The Collected Works* was producing a mild case of jitters, to say the least. While Earl's successor, Harold N. Munger, did not precisely indicate an intention of abrogating the agreement with the association, he nevertheless did not conceal his perturbation, and upon my initiative, agreed that the association might seek another publisher if we chose to do so. I felt so confident of obtaining a contract with a major trade publishing house that I struck out at once, working at the top level. "Struck out," in fact, is the precise idiom for describing the result of my efforts. Not one of the major publishers was interested, although one of them went so far as to conduct a field survey of probable sales. When I received the letter announcing that the survey indicated a top expectancy of less than 500 sets of a multivolume collection of the works of Abraham Lincoln, I knew the survey was worthless. The only way to prove it was to conduct a survey of my own, limited to the membership of the association and the principal research libraries in the United States. Tabulation of the results of my survey indicated a firm expectation that sale of more than 1,000 sets could be reliably counted on prior to publication. With this evidence in hand, I reopened the question with Harold Munger, and the upshot was that Rutgers University Press decided to proceed on the assumption that the basic costs could be recovered on publication, if *The Collected Works* were priced for a minimum sale of 1,000 copies.

One of the great satisfactions of my life was the communication received early in February 1953 from Harold Munger, notifying me that well over one thousand copies had been subscribed for prior to publication.

As this is being written, some thirteen years later, I am reliably informed by William Sloane, director, Rutgers University Press, that, "It's rather pleasant to think that there are some 40,000 sets around and about in the world." Rather pleasant to me, indeed.

Of the approximately $100,000 expended in preparation of *The Collected Works*, Rockefeller Foundation grants had provided $54,000, and the rest had come from the association's reserve fund and gifts from members. The association had gone for broke, but I doubt that any comparable major historical project has ever been, or ever will be, accomplished with less money — or more headaches.

Thus *The Collected Works of Abraham Lincoln,* published on February 12, 1953, was not only the culmination of the distinguished purpose for which the Abraham Lincoln Association had been founded and nourished for thirty years by citizens of Springfield, Illinois; it was likewise the occasion of the association's desuetude. *The Abraham Lincoln Quarterly's* final issue for December 1952 carried a notice of the closing of the association office and the transfer of all its files to the Illinois State Historical Library. The financial statement published in the preceding September issue of the *Quarterly* had told why.

Money available for the project had been $96,464.99; total expenditures had been $96,455.70. Balance $9.29.

My acquaintance with Abraham Lincoln did not come to an end with publication of *The Collected Works,* of course, but with my entrance into a new career as a library administrator it is true that I found less and less opportunity to pursue research and writing. It is a further truth, however, that the change was welcome although I secretly nourished for several years the notion that I would one day return to write THE biography of Lincoln, which I felt, and still feel, is yet to be written. When I finally and reluctantly acknowledged to myself that it would never be written by me, I thought of this personal narrative, within its limited scope, as perhaps the best further contribution I could make to the study of Lincoln. The better part of one's life consists, as Lincoln said, of his friendships, thinking only of the living. But how frequently those whose personality, mind, and spirit survive in some measure long after their bones are dust, have participated in our friendships among the living! And of all those, Lincoln remains in his greatness the most companionable.

LINCOLN'S DEVELOPMENT
AS A WRITER*

I

Concerning Lincoln's early life, the facts which he considered significant enough to relate in his autobiographical sketches written
in 1859 and 1860 are still those which most concern a student of
his writings, and there seems to be little need to do more than refer
the reader to them.

A word of caution should be sufficient to prevent one's falling into
the common error of supposing—as Lincoln did—that this period
is notable only for its barrenness. A certain type of biographer has
made much of the hardships, poverty of educational opportunity,
and undistinguished culture of the frontier settlements in which
Lincoln grew up; and in reaction, another type has attempted to
glorify the same environment as the paradise of opportunity for
virile American genius. In any event, Lincoln's early life sufficed
to provide him with a great store of practical knowledge and a
deep understanding of and sympathy with the people among whom
he would live most of his life. This knowledge and understanding

*Written as an introductory piece for the book *Abraham Lincoln: His Speeches
and Writings* (World, 1946), and reproduced here with the publisher's permission,
this essay combines and extends the results of the author's earlier studies—in particular his "Abraham Lincoln—Artist" *(North American Review,* Spring 1938) and
"Abraham Lincoln's Rhetoric" *(American Literature,* May 1939).

provided a firm footing which served him more dependably than an elaborate schooling served many of his contemporaries.

Anyone inclined toward the various types of "progressive" education which are sponsored today by the pedagogically elite—with their emphasis on "social living," "cooperative endeavor," "discussion-action," and "learning by doing," might, in fact, conclude that Lincoln's early educational advantages were nonpareil. He learned the fundamentals of farming, surveying, business, and politics by doing them, and his need directed the acquisition of manual and mental skills in what "progressive" educators today might call "meaningful situations." In short, he received an abundance of the practical kind of well-rounded education which it is becoming customary in the twentieth century for financially favored urban parents to send their children hundreds of miles, with hundreds of dollars, to get.

What is perhaps more important is the personal philosophy of education which Lincoln developed during these years, and which he did not materially alter during his mature life. It is summarized in the succinct and homely adage, "a man is never too old to learn." Of his several expressions which state this attitude, one of the best is the following piece of advice on studying law, written in 1858:

> When a man has reached the age that Mr. Widmer has, and has already been doing for himself, my judgment is, that he reads the books for himself without an instructor. That is precisely the way I came to the law. Let Mr. Widmer read Blackstone's Commentaries, Chitty's Pleadings, Greenleaf's Evidence, Story's Equity, and Story's Equity Pleadings, get a license, and go to the practice, and still keep reading. That is my judgment of the cheapest, quickest, and best way for Mr. Widmer to make a lawyer of himself.

And also, Lincoln might have agreed, it is the best way for one to grow in general intellect.

In keeping with this philosophy is the constant development in Lincoln's whole personality throughout his entire life. If there is one incontrovertible theme that runs throughout the biographical sequence of facts, opinions, and legends concerning Lincoln, it is that as a personality he never ceased to grow in a unique pattern, which was both organically logical and objectively adaptable. There is only a half-truth in the famous statement of Charles Francis Adams, Jr., that "during the years intervening between 1861 and 1865 the man developed immensely; he became in fact another being. History, indeed, hardly presents an analogous case of education through trial." Lincoln did grow between 1861 and 1865, but in no essential did he become a *different* being. The failure of numerous biographers to bridge the gap between his early life and his presidency might have been avoided had they given as much attention to his writings as to the minutiae of his daily living.

Something should be said of his schooling and study during his boyhood years. His own testimony that he went to school "by littles" which in "the aggregate did not amount to one year" has been accepted by some as a statement indicating relatively slight acquisition of knowledge or skill. Actually, this means that Lincoln attended school for several years, short terms of two or three months being the general rule, and many school terms averaging less. Need one be reminded that even yet in the United States in certain areas it would require three years of schooling to accumulate an "aggregate" of twelve months? Or, that if concentrated attention on the skills of learning—all the frontier school concerned itself with—be considered, then four or five grades, and perhaps more, of a modern curriculum would be required to furnish the equivalent of Lincoln's twelve months? One year, by littles, of learning to read, write, and cipher enabled Lincoln to acquire the basic tools which he used and kept sharp until he could at twenty-three study Kirkham's *Grammar,* a difficult textbook, and within a few months write with a clarity that few college graduates ever achieve today. This fact need not startle us when we consider that although undeniable advancement has been made in the manner of education, the essentials of logic and rhetoric and the basic skills are still matters which one *learns* rather than is *taught.* The intellectual avidity of the child is more important than methods of instruction, and good books, with the opportunity and desire to master them, need little from a teacher when in the hands of an exceptional student.

The textbooks which Lincoln studied probably provided as good an opportunity for learning the essentials and the graces of expression then, as the best modern textbooks do now. Dilworth's *A New Guide to the English Tongue*—the leading elementary textbook of the day, with lessons in spelling, grammar, and reading; tables of homonyms; exemplary fables and recommended prayers—is in spite of its stilted precepts, pedagogically sound. *The Kentucky Preceptor* and Scott's *Lessons in Elocution,* with well-chosen selections of prose and poetry, might be criticized as too mature and difficult for the slow-to-average child, but are excellent collections for a child intellectually alert. A careful examination of these and other textbooks which Lincoln studied both in and out of school will not impress anyone with Lincoln's poverty of opportunity for the study of grammar and rhetoric. It is safe to say that few children today learn as much through twelve years of formal schooling in these two subjects as one finds in the several textbooks which Lincoln is supposed to have studied.

Thus, one may conclude that Lincoln came to his study of Kirkham's *Grammar* in 1831—1832 as an advanced student, ready to form a permanent habit in writing. This was his own testimony, allowing for modesty, in 1860, when he wrote in his "Autobiography": "After he was twenty-three and had separated from his father, he studied English grammar—imperfectly, of course, but so as to speak and write as well as he now does." That this was no idle claim, the student may determine by analysis of his early writings from 1832 to 1840. Noting the possible but unlikely truth of the tradition that his friend Mentor Graham assisted him in composing the announcement, "To the People of Sangamo County" (1832), the student will, nevertheless, recognize predominantly the certainty and deliberateness in style which marked Lincoln's mature writing.

By his twenty-eighth year Lincoln had acquired the facility in fundamentals of rhetoric which marks all his later work. "The Perpetuation of Our Political Institutions" (1838) contains many passages comparing favorably with more famous paragraphs often admired in his later speeches. Other speeches of this early period show similar facility, and if they err, it is in the excessive use of rhythm and trope. Lincoln's taste improves much thereafter, as his literary stature increases; but the very sins of his early public style, subdued, become the virtues of his mature public style. His private style as revealed in his early letters is constant throughout his later letters in its idiomatic, loosely deliberate, and colloquial effectiveness.

But even his worst rhetorical blandishments in his early speeches exemplify his deliberate seeking for effect. There is, for example, the concluding paragraph of "The Sub-Treasury" (1839), a campaign speech in which Lincoln attacked the Sub-Treasury and defended the National Bank. The fact that his audience loved such rhetoric perhaps made the performance expedient, for certainly the speech as a whole, though a tight bit of reasoning, could hardly have been inspirational and needed some political fireworks as a tailpiece.

Aside from textbooks, the efforts of biographers have uncovered a good many books that Lincoln indubitably read before 1831, but the list is undeniably spare, perhaps largely because the records of his life prior to this date are poor at best, and because books were without doubt scarce in his younger life. Among other works, Lincoln read *Arabian Nights,* Ramsey's *Life of Washington* (the book damaged by rain and paid for with two days' labor topping corn, as first narrated by John L. Scripps in his campaign biography), Grimshaw's *History of the United States,* Aesop's *Fables,* Bunyan's *The Pilgrim's Progress,* Defoe's *Robinson Crusoe,* Weems's *Life of Washington,* and the King James Bible. In so far as his early reading may have influenced his later style as a speaker and as a writer, the two most significant of these are the *Fables* and the Bible. His technique in telling stories to enforce a truth and his fondness for rhythmic parallelism and balanced structure may have derived chiefly, though not entirely, from these two sources.

II

Lincoln went to New Salem, Illinois, in July 1831, and during the next six years his intellectual horizon extended rapidly. Apparently it was during the first year that he began his study of grammar, possibly as tradition has it, under the tutelage of his appropriately named friend, Mentor Graham; for he composed and published on March 9, 1832, his political announcement, "To the People of Sangamo County," his first writing of importance, so far as is known. Just how much Mentor Graham had to do with this composition is not certain, but what is certain is that the announcement was ably written, and that the few letters written by Mentor Graham which are preserved in the Herndon-Weik papers do not even suggest a competence in grammar or rhetoric sufficient to account for any material assistance that Lincoln may have had in writing this piece. With whatever assistance, Lincoln continued his study and reading and in the fall of 1833 mastered the rudiments of surveying in order to work for the county surveyor, John Calhoun.

In addition to the schoolmaster, Graham, Lincoln had for friends a number of well-educated people whose libraries and conversation were educational gold mines. Among these was Jack Kelso, whose love for and knowledge of Shakespeare and Burns became a legend to a later generation. If Lincoln's fondness for these poets had not developed before this time as a result of his early reading, possibly his reading and discussion of them with Kelso may have served to fix a literary preference that remained strong until his death.

Without attempting to give an inclusive list of books that Lincoln read during his residence at New Salem, one may note that accounts of this period agree in portraying him as ransacking the private libraries of his friends, though they do not always agree as to the specific books read. William H. Herndon's biography has Lincoln running a gamut from newspapers and the sentimental novels of Caroline Lee Hentz through Thomas Paine, Voltaire, Volney, and Rollin, to Burns and Shakespeare. It is unlikely that Lincoln acquired a fondness for the novels of Mrs. Hentz during this period, since the earliest was not in print until 1846, and most of them were published in the fifties; but that Thomas Paine in particular may have been one of Lincoln's favorite authors seems not improbable. In philosophy, no other writer of the eighteenth century, with the exception of Jefferson, parallels more closely the temper or gist of Lincoln's later thought. In style, Paine above all others affords the variety of eloquence which, chastened and adapted to Lincoln's own mood, is revealed in Lincoln's formal writings. From reading such as this, rather than from the instruction of a frontier schoolmaster, Lincoln derived his most important literary education. Aside from general reading during this period Lincoln studied law, borrowing books from his friend, John T. Stuart, and purchasing a copy of Blackstone's *Commentaries* at an auction in Springfield.

Lincoln's writing was apparently not confined at this time to letters, legislative bills, and political speeches. Herndon refers to a predilection for scribbling verses which began when Lincoln was a youth in Indiana, and expresses the opinion that it is just as well none are extant. Perhaps during this period also Lincoln began a practice of writing pseudonymous political letters to the *Sangamo Journal*, ° which he continued until 1842, when one of them resulted in a challenge to a duel. The problem of assigning pseudonymous or anonymous letters and editorials to Lincoln is, however, a dangerous one, and requires more careful study than has sometimes been given to it. Of these writings one may say that Lincoln's authorship has not been finally established for any except those included in *The Collected Works of Abraham Lincoln* (1953). Several political letters which appeared in the *Journal* in 1837-1838, signed variously "Sampson's Ghost," "Old Settler," and "A Conservative," seem certainly to have been written by Lincoln, but in no instance do they add to his literary accomplishment. In racy idiom, satire, and humor they are distinctly inferior to the second "Rebecca" letter, which will be discussed later.†

Lincoln's move from New Salem to Springfield in April 1837, brought a further extension of his social and intellectual horizon. Springfield became the state capital in 1839, Lincoln having largely directed the legislative maneuvering that deprived Vandalia of this

°The name of this newspaper was originally *Sangamon Journal* (1831-1832), but was shortened to the colloquial *Sangamo Journal* (1832-1847), and became *Illinois Journal* (1847-1855), and finally *Illinois State Journal* (1855 to date).

†For a discussion of these pseudonymous letters see Glen H. Seymour, " 'Conservative'—Another Lincoln Pseudonym?" *Journal Illinois State Historical Society*, July 1936; *Bulletin*, The Abraham Lincoln Association, No. 50, December 1937; Roy P. Basler, "The Authorship of the 'Rebecca' Letters," *The Abraham Lincoln Quarterly*, June 1942.

distinction. But before this event Springfield was a thriving town in its own right, containing among other advantages "a State Bank, land office, two newspapers . . . the Thespian Society, the Young Men's Lyceum, a Colonization Society and a Temperance Society."‡To the Young Men's Lyceum on January 27, 1838, he delivered the address previously mentioned, which was his first considerable literary effort, though he had a year earlier delivered before the legislature a speech defending the National Bank, which is significant for its logical analysis and close argument.

"The Perpetuation of Our Political Institutions" is resoundingly conservative in its treatment of the theme of law and order, swelling deeply with moral and patriotic fervor but completely ignoring the greatest moral issue of the day—the abolition of slavery. In the set of "objections," which Lincoln together with Dan Stone drew up in March 1837, opposing resolutions passed by the legislature in support of slavery, Lincoln stated carefully "that the institution of slavery is founded on both injustice and bad policy, but that the promulgation of abolition doctrines tends rather to increase than abate its evils." The position taken in these conservative "objections," Lincoln maintained until he was elected President. On the whole the "Lyceum" address probably represents Lincoln's personal ideas during this period fairly accurately, and as such it must be judged, though inferior when compared with his later expressions, of great interest for its ideas as well as for its rhetoric. Herndon certainly underestimates it as "highly sophomoric," but comments that it created for "the young orator a reputation which soon extended beyond the limits of the locality in which he lived."

In his early speeches Lincoln reveals himself clearly as the intellectual and spiritual child of the romantic era no less than Emerson, Thoreau, Whitman, Whittier, and Lowell, as well as William Ellery Channing, Theodore Parker, William Lloyd Garrison, and many lesser lights. The philosophical ideas that animated American thought from the time of the American Revolution to the Civil War were perhaps no less potent in Springfield than in Boston. Among the ideas which run through both

‡Harry E. Pratt, *Lincoln,* 1809-1839, p. lviii.

"The Perpetuation of Our Political Institutions" (1838) and the "Temperance Address Delivered before the Washington Temperance Society" (1842) are the concepts of human perfectibility and the progressive improvement of human society through education; the exaltation of reason, of "all conquering mind," as the human attribute through which progress may be achieved; and the ideal of liberty, equality, and brotherhood. These concepts composed the essential humanitarianism of Thomas Jefferson, which consistently held men above things. Likewise they were the essentials of Lincoln's philosophy, though subdued by the innate conservatism that held him aloof from the radical reformers of his day.

It is clear in "The Perpetuation of Our Political Institutions" that the fundamental theme of the "Gettysburg Address," which was later to be woven out of these very concepts, was essentially in 1838 what it was in 1863, the central concept of Lincoln's political philosophy. Lincoln thought of American democracy as an experiment in achieving human liberty, relatively successful though far from completed, and threatened most by the mobocratic spirit and the failure of the citizens to observe and preserve the duly constituted authority of government. One sentence from this early speech contains the essential germ of the "Gettysburg Address." Speaking of the founders of American political institutions, Lincoln said, "Theirs was the task (and nobly they performed it) to possess themselves, and through themselves us, of this goodly land, and to uprear upon its hills and its valleys a political edifice of liberty and equal rights; 'tis ours only to transmit these—the former unprofaned by the foot of the invader, the latter undecayed by the lapse of time and untorn by usurpation—to the latest generation that fate shall permit the world to know." In 1863 he was to say, "It is rather for us to be here dedicated to the great task remaining before us. . .that government of the people, by the people, for the people, shall not perish from the earth."

Curiously woven into the texture of these essential concepts is Lincoln's belief in the "doctrine of necessity," which he defined as the "belief that the human mind is impelled to action, or held in rest by some power, over which the mind itself has no control." Like several of the early nineteenth century romantics, Lincoln made a correlation of his belief in "necessity" and his belief in human progress and perfectibility. William Godwin's "doctrine of necessity," which so deeply influenced Coleridge, Wordsworth, Shelley, and others among the English romantics, was such a correlation of necessitarianism and perfectionism. Godwin himself began as a Calvinist, came under the influence of Condorcet, Rousseau, and others of the French school, and eclectically concocted his own philosophy from the concepts of his masters by correlating the "doctrine of necessity" with the romantic doctrine of human perfectibility rather than with Calvin's doctrine of human depravity.

Although Lincoln probably had not read Godwin's *Political Justice,* Godwin's theories along with those of Rousseau may have come to him as to many, in the never ending succession of ripples in popular thought created by the original intellectual splash produced by the writings of those worthies. It is just as possible that Lincoln made somewhat the same correlation in his own thinking without benefit, either at first or second hand, of Godwin's philosophy. In any event, necessitarianism and perfectionism were inextricably woven into Lincoln's personal philosophy during these early years and remained strong with him until his death.

Though Lincoln's writings are few between 1838 and 1842, these were otherwise busy years during which his legal practice was growing, his political leadership of the Illinois Whigs was becoming firmly established, and his social position was gradually elevated. He courted the Kentucky belle Mary Todd, jilted her, suffered terrific hypochondria, recovered, and re-established his position as favored suitor to marry her November 4, 1842.

III

The year 1842 is one of considerable literary significance. Lincoln's remarkable friendship with Joshua Speed, apparently the only intimate personal friendship of Lincoln's life, is recorded in an interesting series of letters. The "Address before the Washington Temperance Society" was delivered on Washington's birthday. A "Eulogy on the Death of Benjamin Ferguson," delivered before the same society on February 8, displays a solemn rhythm and elegiac diction not matched in literary effect by anything he had written prior to this time. But most interesting is Lincoln's participation in a series of pseudonymous political satires published in the *Sangamo Journal* during August and September. The second "Rebecca" letter, the only one of the series which Lincoln wrote, reveals a bent indicative of a wider scope in his literary possibilities than he had shown before. The fact that he afterwards eschewed such literary activity, perhaps largely because of the unpleasantness which followed, does not diminish the letter's significance to the student of Lincoln's growth as a writer. It displays an ability to portray character, a skill in handling dialogue, a realistic humor, and a biting satire, which mark him at this time the potential equal of his Southern contemporaries, Augustus Baldwin Longstreet and Johnson Jones Hooper, if not of the later Mark Twain.

Lincoln's literary activity during the next four years is relatively slight in significance except for his writing a series of poems. During the political activity of the campaign of 1844, he revisited his boyhood home in Indiana, and in typically romantic fashion was prompted, as he said, to "feelings. . .which were certainly poetry; though whether my expression of those feelings is poetry is quite another question." These powerful feelings, apparently "recollected in tranquillity," resulted in a group of poems beginning with the nostalgic "My Childhood Home I See Again," and including "The Bear Hunt" and perhaps others that have been lost. A literary friendship which he formed with Andrew Johnston, a lawyer of Quincy, Illinois, occasioned Lincoln's enclosing parts of the first, and perhaps all of the second of these poems in letters written to this friend. The manuscript of a third section of the first poem seems to have been lost.

Another piece of writing doubtless the result of his friendship with Johnston is the narrative of a "Remarkable Case," a murder trial with an unusual denouement, which appeared in the *Quincy Whig,* April 15, 1846. Lincoln had told the story earlier, shortly after defending the accused, in his "Letter to Joshua Speed," June 19, 1841. As he wrote it for publication in the *Quincy Whig,* it is a well-told mystery story, worthy of careful study as one of his few ventures in narrative.

Without danger of exaggerating their importance, it is safe to say that Lincoln's poems are superior to the average run of verse published in America before 1850, and that the first and best of them reveals a quality which wears better than Lincoln's biographers have supposed. One cannot read "My Childhood Home I See Again" without sensing faintly the manner and mood of minor English poetry in the late eighteenth century, a typical example of which, William Knox's "Mortality," was Lincoln's favorite poem at this time. Although these verses suffer much when placed beside the "Farewell Address" or the "Second Inaugural Address," they are by no means the pure doggerel that many of Lincoln's biographers have termed them. As literary critics, Lincoln's biographers have displayed, with few exceptions, a lack of literary perspective exceeded only by their preoccupation with political facts. Again, however, the student must find these poems interesting as an art form which Lincoln abandoned along with the realistic satire of the "Rebecca" letter. They are most significant as literary experimentation, which showed promise of growth but was frustrated by the environment and the events of the milieu in which it occurred. In Lincoln we have a literary artist, constrained by social and economic circumstances and a dominant political tradition to deal with facts as facts, yet always motivated by his love of words and symbols and his eternal craving to entertain people and to create beauty. It is this love of words, never completely subservient, which finally flowers in the unique art of his "Gettysburg Address," "Farewell Address," "Second Inaugural Address," and even earlier in his "Concluding Speech" in the campaign of 1858. Lincoln spoke as an artist because he was first of all an artist at heart. Had he otherwise developed these talents, it is not difficult to imagine for him an important place among American poets or writers of fiction.

Of special interest to the student of Lincoln's literary growth is the partnership in law practice which he formed in December 1844, with William H. Herndon, who earlier had clerked in the store of Lincoln's friend, Speed, and had been a student in the law office of Logan & Lincoln. The partnership continued until 1861, and up to the time of Lincoln's departure for Washington perhaps no other person contributed more to his intellectual development, directly or indirectly, than Herndon did through his perpetual reading and discussion of books. The general impression abetted by Herndon's testimony that Lincoln came to books chiefly through his partner's library is, however, not compatible with the fact that Lincoln's own library was of considerable extent and that he had convenient access to the state library. The student must gauge carefully Herndon's statement that Lincoln "comparatively speaking had no knowledge of literature. . . . He never in his life sat down and read a book through," as the statement of an omnivorous reader who was more impressed by Lincoln's intellect than by the breadth of his literary culture.

Lincoln's growing prestige in local Whig politics culminated in his election to Congress from the Seventh Congressional District of Illinois in 1846. During the campaign he met strong opposition in the candidacy of Peter Cartwright, the famous Methodist circuit-rider, not on the national issues of the day so much as on personal, moral, and religious issues. Cartwright and his supporters resorted to the "grape-vine telegraph" in spreading reports of Lincoln's infidelity, and the charges thus made clung to Lincoln's name, in spite. of his forthright denial, until long after his death. The most significant piece of writing which resulted was the "Letter to the Editor of the *Illinois Gazette,*" August 11, 1846, and a political handbill in which Lincoln expressed his religious views. Both of these items were rediscovered in 1941 by Mr. Harry E. Pratt. They contain perhaps the most complete statement of personal religious philosophy which Lincoln wrote during his early career. The nub of his statement, a part of which has already been cited, is as follows:

> That I am not a member of any Christian Church, is true; but I have never denied the truth of the Scriptures; and I have never spoken with intentional disrespect of religion in general, or of any denomination of Christians in particular. It is true that in early life I was inclined to believe in what I understand is called the "Doctrine of Necessity"—that is, that the human mind is impelled to action, or held in rest by some power, over which the mind itself has no control; and I have sometimes (with one, two or three, but never publicly) tried to

> maintain this opinion in argument—The habit of arguing thus
> however, I have entirely left off for more than five
> years—And I add here, I have always understood this same
> opinion to be held by several of the Christian denominations.
> The foregoing, is the whole truth, briefly stated, in relation
> to myself, upon this subject.

Lincoln was elected by an unprecedented majority of 1511 votes, and went to Congress with prospects as bright as any first-term congressman could have wished. His experiences in Washington were doubtless important to his growth in many ways. Although politically adept in the Illinois legislature, he was new to the larger activities of Congress and proceeded to work diligently, attending to routine duties and "learning the ropes." Contacts with congressmen from other parts of the nation gave him an understanding of political currents outside Illinois. Particularly, he was acquainted with the rising importance of slavery as a national issue, not only through the sometimes heated arguments of fellow congressmen who stayed at Mrs. Spriggs' boarding house and through the serious discussions in Congress of various bills and resolutions for abolishing slavery in the District of Columbia and limiting its spread into new territories, but also through his speech-making tour of New England states during the presidential campaign in the summer of 1848. Most of the political animus engendered in Congress by the issues of the Mexican war was concerned directly or indirectly with the question of the extension of slavery, and conservative though he was on the question of abolition, Lincoln took his stand with his party against a war denounced by Henry Clay as being "for the purpose of propagating slavery." In the "Spot Resolutions," which Lincoln introduced on December 22, 1847, shortly after the session opened, and in the speech which he delivered on January 12, 1848, he was sticking close to the tactics of Henry Clay, whom he had heard declare only a few weeks earlier in Lexington, Kentucky: "This is no war of defence, but one of unnecessary and offensive aggression."

This important Mexican war speech was essentially an apologia for himself and for all those Whig members of Congress who had voted what amounted to a general censure of President Polk for starting an unnecessary war. As exposition it is one of the ablest speeches Lincoln ever delivered and deserves to rank with the best of his later expository writing, though the unpopularity of its theme may make it as difficult of appreciation for some students of his works as it was for his contemporaries. In spite of the vigorous diction and strong figures in which he condemned Polk's action and defended the Whig position, many of his constituents saw in the speech only a betrayal of the national destiny, and as a consequence, his political future became overcast. His letters to Herndon and Linder, written a few weeks later, in spite of their merit as further statements of his case, apparently did little to change the rapidly forming opinion among even his closest friends that his political career was finished.

Of the other speeches delivered before the House, one in particular deserves notice as perhaps the best example of his popular, rough-and-tumble style as a stump speaker. It was delivered on July 27, 1848, shortly after the Whig Convention in Philadelphia had nominated General Taylor, "Old Rough and Ready." The purpose of the speech was entertainment at the political expense of the Democrats, who had nominated General Lewis Cass, and in ridiculing Cass, Lincoln gave satire, sarcasm, and rough humor a free rein. Although it scarcely adds to his stature as a statesman, it has real significance in his development as an artist. His inclination to entertain his audience had been both a strength and a weakness throughout his political career up to this time, getting votes from the people on the one hand and arousing suspicion of demagoguery on the other. The *Illinois Register,* in commenting on one of his political debates in 1839, had noted: "Lincoln's argument was truly ingenious. He has, however, a sort of *assumed clownishness* in his manner which does not become him. . . . Mr. Lincoln will sometimes make his language correspond with this clownish manner, and he can thus frequently raise a loud laugh among his Whig hearers. . . .We seriously advise Mr. Lincoln to correct this clownish fault before it grows upon him." Like the "Rebecca" letter, however, this speech is interesting as a good example of a variety of expression that Lincoln gradually abandoned in his later speeches, except for an occasional recrudescence during the great debates with Douglas in 1858.

At this point perhaps it may be well to comment briefly on Lincoln's use of humor and satire, and in particular on his use of anecdotes, since this speech is one of the few in which Lincoln displays his forte as a humorist and a storyteller. In the first place, the stories for which he was famed were generally confined to his impromptu speeches and personal conversations, and became as a result largely a matter of oral tradition. Secondly, by all accounts they depended as much on grimace and mimicry as they did on inherent humor or point in producing their effect, and hence many of them have become but poor reading as told second- or third-hand. Evidently, however, Lincoln was a master of the art of telling the incident and at the same time withholding the point until it served with an immediate snap at the conclusion to clarify and give meaning to the whole story. This is the fundamental pattern of all good anecdotes, but added to this is Lincoln's practice of withholding not only the point of the story, but also his particular application of it, until the end.

Although in many of the stories credited to Lincoln with a fair degree of authenticity he seems to have been working with didactic purpose, certain apologists have erred in the assumption that he told them only for serious purposes. His love for the writings of Artemus Ward, Petroleum V. Nasby, and other humorists indicates a respect for humor in its own right, and his indulgence in stories as well as his general clowning on the platform was doubtless an expression of a genuine and deep-seated comic urge, not necessarily incompatible with high sincerity when blended in the genius of an artist. Today one can lament only that so few of Lincoln's stories have been preserved in the actual manner of telling which he gave them. Even the most authentic often show less of Lincoln than they do of the person who is authority for the tale.

Flashes of humor repeatedly occur in his letters. In these flashes the humor is less satirical than in his political speeches, and it grows mellower through the years. Nothing in his later writings equals the biting satire of the second "Rebecca" letter, but even in the letters written during his presidency his humor is sharp. He once wrote Secretary Stanton that he wanted Jacob R. Freese appointed colonel of a colored regiment "regardless of whether he can tell the exact shade of Julius Caesar's hair," and another time asked Cuthbert Bullitt, who had written a letter criticizing Army policy at New Orleans, if he would carry on war "with elder-stalk squirts charged with rose-water." But he was as ready to see humor at his own expense and to satirize his own situation. In the "Letter to R. P. Morgan," he returned an expired railroad pass and requested a new one thus: "Says Tom to John 'Here's your old rotten wheelbarrow. I've broke it, usin' on it. I wish you would mend it,case I shall want to borrow it this arternoon.'" In these instances, as in nearly all of Lincoln's humor, the general allusions and the association of ideas for humorous effect are drawn from common experiences of everyday life. In substance it is the common humor of his time, but in the skill with which it is used it is Lincoln's.

In the study of Lincoln's writings it would seem unnecessary to emphasize the necessity of a sense of humor and an appreciation of irony, but, as H. B. Van Hoesen has pointed out in a brochure entitled *The Humor of Lincoln and the Seriousness of His Biographers,* Lincoln's humor has not always been perceived by his readers, though the audiences to which he spoke could scarcely miss the point. This circumstance is the result, in part at least, of the fact that Lincoln's humor is so often ironical, and that the point emphasized by vocal inflection is not always so obvious on the printed page. Even his most serious speeches, such as the "Address at Cooper Institute," contain humor which a reader may miss unless he reads with awareness, but which Lincoln's audience fully appreciated, if one may judge from contemporary newspaper accounts of the occasion. An interesting example of humor missed by Lincoln's editors occurs in the "Speech at Peoria." After a lengthy analysis of Douglas' arguments extolling the virtues of the Nebraska Bill, Lincoln sarcastically continued, "If Nebraska Bill is the real author of these benevolent works, it is rather deplorable, that he has, for so long a time, ceased working altogether." In three separate instances in the same paragraph Lincoln made use of the personification for humorous effect, and in each his editors humorlessly revised the phraseology to read "the Nebraska Bill," and in the sentence quoted emended the pronoun *he* to *it*.

The political eclipse which followed Lincoln's term in Congress was paralleled by an eclipse in his writing and speaking. Until 1854 he devoted himself almost entirely to his law practice, and in consequence achieved a considerable legal reputation and a comfortable income. Aside from the personal letters written during these years, his only work of much literary significance is the "Eulogy on Henry Clay Delivered in the State House at Springfield," July 6, 1852. This was a labor of love and genuine admiration to which Lincoln carried a sympathetic understanding of Clay's personality and a fine assessment of his political worth. It shows what was perhaps unconsciously running through Lincoln's mind, the indebtedness of Lincoln to Clay both politically and intellectually, and the remarkable degree to which their personalities and genius held similar and contrasting qualities. One can hardly read any paragraph in it without feeling that Lincoln was, unconsciously or consciously, inviting comparison and contrast of himself with his "beau ideal of a statesman."

The presidential campaign of 1852 in which Pierce and Scott were opponents produced another speech, worthy of mention only because of its perfunctory mediocrity and because Nicolay and Hay either ignored or conveniently overlooked it when compiling the *Complete Works*. It is entitled "Address before the Springfield Scott Club, in Reply to Judge Douglas's Richmond Speech." Its very mediocrity and the futile sarcasm are indicative of the senility of Whig politics at the time. Apparently Lincoln could not, even by choice, find anything worth saying in support of a party which was dying because it strove only to avoid the great issues of the day and could do no better than lift the slavery plank of an opposition platform. Even the satire and humor of the speech are far below Lincoln's average.

IV

Lincoln's political inactivity ended in 1854 with the passage of the Kansas—Nebraska Bill. The next five years saw his steady rise from comparative political oblivion to a position of national importance as the leading opponent of Douglas' doctrine of Popular Sovereignty, and as one of the leading national figures in the new

Republican party. The contrast between Lincoln in 1852 and 1854 is remarkable. From a sarcastic politician with a party allegiance but no issue, he emerged a serious statesman with a great issue but as yet no party to lead. From the futile mediocrity of his "Address before the Springfield Scott Club" he rose to the impassioned seriousness of the "Speech at Peoria." The contrast is immense but not mysterious. Lincoln had simply found a theme worthy of his best, and the high level of literary merit in his speeches and other writings is a record of his emotional conviction. Although he did not reach his peak as a literary artist until an even greater theme—preservation of the Union—began to dominate his thinking, during the next six years he composed a body of speeches and letters which in power and distinction of style is second to none other in American political literature.

Careful study of Lincoln's works of this middle period (1854-1861) emphasizes the fact that his later beauty of expression was not an accident of inspiration, as thought by many of his biographers, which simply happened to a man who had no particular care for finely wrought sentences. Indeed, the "Speech at Peoria" (1854), "A House Divided: Speech Delivered at Springfield, Illinois" (1858), and the "Address at Cooper Institute" (1860), to mention only three of the many, have in a large measure the technical distinction of style that is generally credited only to his later masterpieces. It is not so much in technical command of style as it is in power of feeling and imagination that his later works surpass those of his middle period.

A critical examination of Lincoln's more important works of this period reveals the supremacy that has always existed in the works of an indisputable master of language. With vital imagination he infused into the political matter of the pre-Civil War epoch great poetic significance: "If we could first know *where* we are, and *whither* we are tending, we could better judge *what* to do, and *how* to do it. . . . 'A house divided against itself cannot stand.' I believe this government cannot endure, permanently half *slave* and half *free*. I do not expect the Union to be *dissolved*— I do not expect the house to *fall*— but I *do* expect it will cease to be divided. It will become *all* one thing or *all* the other." In language seemingly effortless and yet grandly beautiful he phrased the emotional convictions upon which he believed human political progress to be founded: "Repeat the Missouri Compromise—repeal all compromises—repeal the Declaration of Independence—repeal all past history, you still cannot repeal human nature. It will be the abundance of man's heart, that slavery extension is wrong; and out of the abundance of his heart, his mouth will continue to speak." He took, and made his own, the thought and spirit of those phases of the epoch which he has since come to symbolize, in such a manner that, though others spoke before him and others have spoken since, today one can scarcely think of the common matter of his argument except as matter that is particularly and peculiarly his. From the "Speech at Peoria" to the "Address at Cooper Institute" Lincoln displayed again and again his power to synthesize without recourse to illusive transcendental generalities, and to stamp with unity without narrowing to personal bias, political matter covering nearly a century.

The "Speech at Peoria" was one of many that Lincoln made during the campaign of 1854, most of the others probably expressing the same anti-Nebraska Bill sentiments, and in fact one of them delivered at Springfield on October 4 being the same speech later delivered at Peoria. On one occasion at Bloomington when Stephen A. Douglas was the principal Democratic speaker and Lincoln's friend Jesse W. Fell attempted to arrange a debate, Douglas declined. The "Speech at Peoria" was Lincoln's fourfold answer to Douglas' sponsorship of the Kansas-Nebraska Bill: first, the bill was a reversal of all historical precedents established for limiting the extension of slavery; second, there was no necessity or public demand for repealing the Missouri Compromise; third, the repeal was morally wrong in that it violated a compact agreed upon by two parties and denied that the Negro had any human rights; last, only the restoration of the Missouri Compromise could prevent ultimate political disintegration.

When the election was over, it was clear that anti-Nebraska sentiment had prevailed. In the Illinois legislature anti-Nebraska men held a majority of five. Since Lincoln had led the fight, it was only natural that he be the choice for United States Senator, although there is no indication in his writings that he entertained any such ambition before the election. What happened afterward is told by Lincoln in his "Letter to E. B. Washburne," February 9, 1855. In short, to ensure an anti-Nebraska senator, Lincoln threw his support to Lyman Trumbull, an anti-Nebraska Democrat.

Although the year 1855 was one of political inactivity for Lincoln and apparently no speeches were written, his letters show constant evolution of ideas. The "Letter to George Robertson," August 15, 1855, concludes with a paragraph adumbrating the famous opening of the "House Divided Speech," still three years away: "Our political problem now is, 'Can we as a nation continue together permanently—forever—half slave and half free? The problem is too mighty for me—may God, in his mercy, superintend the solution." The "Letter to Joshua F. Speed," August 24, 1855, shows his resolution to continue the fight for restoration of the Missouri Compromise, and likewise his insistence that he was still a Whig and certainly not a member of the American party:

> I am not a Know-Nothing. That is certain. How could I be? How can any one who abhors the oppression of negroes, be in favor of degrading classes of white people? Our progress in degeneracy appears to me to be pretty rapid. As a nation, we began by declaring that *"all men are created equal."* We now practically read it "all men are created equal, except negroes." When the Know-Nothings get control, it will read "all men are created equal, except negroes, *and foreigners, and Catholics."* When it comes to this I shall prefer emigrating to some country where they make no pretence of loving liberty—to Russia, for instance, where despotism can be taken pure, and without the base alloy of hypocrisy.

In the next year, 1856, Lincoln definitely lined up with the new Republican party and took active lead in organizing the state convention at Bloomington in May. It was here that he delivered the famous so-called "Lost Speech," which according to the local tradition was the supreme effort that fused discordant elements into a unified party. The tradition has it that even hard-boiled newspapermen were so overpowered by his eloquence that they forgot pencil and pad to sit enraptured. A report of the speech, reconstructed by Henry C. Whitney from notes taken at the time, and published in 1896, probably follows the general argument very well, but it hardly reproduces the rhetorical effect claimed for the utterance. In any event, however, the speech did inspire the convention with unity of purpose. Within a month Lincoln's national importance was recognized by delegates to the Republican National Convention, when 110 of them cast their votes for him on a nomination for Vice President.

Although Lincoln made many speeches in the campaign that followed, none has been preserved in entirety except the "Speech Delivered at Kalamazoo, Michigan," August 27, 1856. In it Lincoln insisted that the issue of the campaign was, "Shall the Government of the United States prohibit slavery in the United States?" and that it was "very nearly the sole question." He pointed out the political power and position of white men in slave states whose representation in Congress was enhanced by the slave population to the point that a white man's vote in the South was worth two in the North. He stressed the importance of free labor as an essential to the future development of democracy. He claimed that Buchanan, the Democratic candidate, was committed to the extension of slavery into the territories. Finally, he scouted the idea that the election of the Republican candidate, Fremont, would bring disunion. In all it was perhaps his frankest anti-slavery utterance up to this time.

Of two fragments of other speeches made during this campaign, one is preserved in a manuscript entitled "Sectionalism," apparently a portion of a speech which he delivered a number of times. It holds the distinction of being the only considerable speech manuscript known to be in existence from this period. In it Lincoln tried to show that Republicanism was not inherently sectional, and that if it appeared so, such appearance was not its own making but that of the Southerners who refused to take anything but a sectional attitude toward it. This argument he would recur to in later years, but with particular effect in the "Address at Cooper Institute."

In 1857, an off-year in politics, came the Dred Scott decision, handed down by the Supreme Court on March 11. In his one important speech of the year, delivered in Springfield, June 26, after paying his respects to the dilemma of popular sovereignty in Utah and to the election in Kansas, Lincoln attacked the Dred Scott decision and Douglas' speech of two weeks earlier upholding it, and indicated the line of future Republican action: "We know the court that made it has often overruled its own decisions, and we shall do what we can to have it overrule this." Ignoring—as Douglas had done—the merits of the decision, Lincoln nevertheless cut deeply into the ground that Douglas had taken in maintaining that the decision was acceptable and should be respected and upheld. He cited the action of Andrew Jackson in ignoring a court decision—and incidentally Douglas' approval of Jackson—as precedent for Republican endeavor to have the decision reversed. The Republican attitude was particularly justified in that the decision was not unanimous, was not "in accordance with steady practice of [government] departments," and was "based on assumed historical facts which are not really true." Although the speech contains some of the most memorable passages in his writings, it lacks the unity of effect which marks his best. The truth is that Lincoln had no solution to the problem of slavery except the colonization idea which he had inherited from Henry Clay, and when he spoke beyond his points of limiting the extension of slavery, of preserving the essential central idea of human equality, and of respecting the Negro as a human being, his words lacked effectiveness.

V

From June to November 1858, Lincoln delivered more than sixty speeches which, though they failed in their immediate purpose of defeating Douglas in the campaign for the United States senatorship, made Lincoln's national reputation and eventually led to the Presidency. He began on June 16 with his famous "House Divided Speech" in Springfield, accepting the unanimous nomination of the Republican State Convention as its "first and only choice" for the Senate. A greater speech had never before been delivered to an American political party gathering, and yet, although Lincoln said in it the essential things that he would repeat over and over during the next months, he found so many new ways, some of them memorable, of modifying and clarifying and emphasizing these essentials, that it is exceedingly difficult to eliminate any single speech of the campaign from analysis and comment. He closed his campaign on October 30 in Springfield with a speech which marked yet another peak in political oratory. The striking contrast between the "House Divided Speech" and the "Last Speech in the Campaign of 1858" is in mood rather than in power of expression. The former is an electrifying challenge to conflict; the latter, an avowal of faith and resignation, phrased with lyric calm and cadenced beauty of expression which Lincoln had never before equaled, and would afterward excel only in the three or four passages that are graven in the mind of humanity more permanently than in the granite of all the monuments to his greatness. The summer of 1858 was the literary, as well as the political, climax of his middle period.

His theme in the "House Divided Speech" was that political acts and events had for years been building a trap which would, unless avoided, catch and forever imprison the essential ideal of human liberty. Under the guise of allaying controversy and establishing national unity, the Democratic party had constantly pushed slavery into new territory and had thwarted all efforts aimed at control and ultimate extinction of the evil. The crisis was at hand and the issue clear: either national politics would have to control slavery, or slavery would control national politics. The speech concluded with a plea for party harmony and support of Republican principles.

In a fine though homely figure of speech Lincoln pictured the political "machinery" built for the extension of slavery by the Nebraska Bill and the Dred Scott decision, which would work with the "don't care" policy of Douglas' popular sovereignty not to permit local determination of the issue in the territories, but to guarantee extension of slavery in spite of local opposition. The figure of the "house or mill," constructed by the Democrats for the perpetuation of slavery, constantly reappeared in his other speeches of the campaign and was the spearhead of his attack upon Douglas, implying as it did that Douglas had been consciously or unconsciously working for the extension of slavery. The idea was not new with Lincoln: Republican leaders everywhere had attacked the Supreme Court for complicity in a scheme to spread slavery. It remained for Lincoln to make the charge vivid and persuasive in a figure of speech and to so involve Douglas by implication that the entire effect would weigh heavily not only in the immediate contest, but in any future contest as well.

> We can not absolutely *know* that all these exact adaptations are the result of preconcert. But when we see a lot of framed timbers, different portions of which we know have been gotten out at different times and places and by different workmen—Stephen, Franklin, Roger and James, for instance—and when we see these timbers joined together, and see they exactly make the frame of a house or a mill, all the tenons and mortices exactly fitting, and all the lengths and proportions of the different pieces exactly adapted to their respective places, and not a piece too many or too few—not omitting even scaffolding—or, if a single piece be lacking, we can see the place in the frame exactly fitted and prepared to yet bring such piece in—in *such* a case, we find it impossible to not *believe* that Stephen and Franklin and Roger and James all understood one another from the beginning, and all worked upon a common *plan* or *draft* drawn up before the first lick was struck.

There has prevailed among students of American letters a notion that Lincoln was as a writer and speaker "plain homespun;" and that his usual style was unadorned with figures of speech and other rhetorical devices. It would be difficult to find a plainer misstatement of Lincoln's style than the comment of V. L. Parrington in *Main Currents in American Thought:* "His usual style was plain homespun, clear and convincing, but bare of imagery and lacking distinction of phrase. . . . Few men who have risen to enduring eloquence have been so little indebted to rhetoric." Study of Lincoln's works must find otherwise.

Lincoln's use of figures of speech is one of his most distinctive stylistic traits. He is consistently and naturally figurative. His pithy quips, his almost legendary stories, and his most serious analyses as well as his poetic passages constantly reveal this trait. In many

instances his figure provides the texture of his thought so
unobtrusively that a casual reader may not even be aware of
metaphor. Although Lincoln tends to use figures more rather than
less than most orators of the time, in his later works he employs
them, if not less often, at least less obviously than in his early
works, and during his middle period they become more effective
and dramatic, though they remain consistently natural, even
homely, in quality. Even his finest figures in his later writings are
couched in terms that will appeal to the common man. Metaphor
in the grand manner of Webster's famous peroration to the "Reply
to Hayne" Lincoln seldom uses, and in early speeches where he
does employ something of the sort, he seems merely to be
experimenting with a technique not compatible with his own style.

Yet one can scarcely agree with Daniel Kilham Dodge's summary opinion expressed in his monograph, *Abraham Lincoln: The
Evolution of His Literary Style,* that "Lincoln's figures almost always serve a useful purpose in making an obscure thought clear
and a clear thought clearer." The implication of a purely utilitarian
motive hardly does justice to Lincoln's imaginative quality of mind.
Herndon insisted, and others have agreed, that Lincoln had "no
sense of the beautiful except in a moral world." Such a limitation
means nothing in an experimental or scientific sense, but even if
we grant it we need not presume that Lincoln was oblivious to all
but the utilitarian advantage in analogy and metaphor. All of
Lincoln's contemporaries did not agree with Herndon. Stephen A.
Douglas, as we shall see, thought Lincoln loved figurative language
for its own sake.

Lincoln's figures are of two kinds: those which he uses as a method of explanation or a basis for drawing inference, and those which
he uses as rhetorical assertions for purposes of persuasion. Only
the first type are primarily utilitarian, and then seldom in the sense
that Dodge supposes. If Lincoln had been writing scientific
treatises, such an employment of analogy might have been very useful, though its usefulness would have diminished as the inferences
drawn tended to escape from the realm of unquestioned fact. But,
since Lincoln was making political speeches, this type of figure often became more effective in discomfiting his opponent, as the

inferences drawn from it tended farther from the unquestioned facts. In Lincoln's speeches the inferential values of such figures nearly always seem to outweigh their explanatory values, and as this is more or less evident in any particular figure, Dodge's comment seems less or more true.

If we examine Lincoln's figure in the "House Divided Speech" as he carries it through the various stages of inference, we shall very likely understand why Douglas sarcastically charged in the "Ottawa Debate": "He studied that out—prepared that one sentence with the greatest care, committed it to memory. . .to show how pretty it is. His vanity is wounded because I will not go into that beautiful figure of his about the building of a house. . . . " Douglas replied in the only way one could reply—with sarcasm—to an effective figure of speech which carried in careful phrases an unforgettable image with implications of something more than rational analysis could maintain. If this figure works toward "making a clear thought clearer," that clearness is like the glass near the edge of a lens, capable of distorting vision rather than improving it. Lincoln's analogy, we may admit, was effective in explaining to his hearers how the Dred Scott decision and the Nebraska Bill were working together for the extension of slavery, but its further and more important immediate implication that Douglas was deliberately working for the extension of slavery seemed to Douglas a distortion of truth. Yet it was true, as Lincoln saw it, that Douglas' political activity did in fact facilitate the extension of slavery, and as Lincoln had observed of another figure of speech with political consequences, "the point—the power to hurt—of all figures, consists in the *truthfulness* of their application."*

Lincoln's repeated use of the figure in later speeches leaves no doubt as to his reason for making it. The pressure which this figure brought upon Douglas, through constant repetition, set the scene for the "Freeport Heresy." Douglas had no rhetorical technique other than sarcasm with which to combat the implication, and sarcasm was insufficient. Then came Lincoln's question: "Can the people of a

*See "The Presidential Question: Speech in the United States House of Representatives," July 27, 1848.

United States Territory . . . exclude slavery from its limits . . . ?"
Asked and answered earlier without the preparation, it could never
have produced the impact that it did at Freeport. Lincoln knew
Douglas' answer before he asked the question. Douglas had said over
and over that slavery could not exist without favorable local
legislation. So did nearly everyone else know it. The only purpose
Lincoln could have had in asking it was to destroy forever any
possibility of Douglas' effecting a *rapprochement* with Southern
Democrats. Under the implications of Lincoln's figure, constantly
pressed, Douglas was constrained to make a statement of opinion
that, although it immediately cleared his way in the senatorial
contest, eventually cost him the Presidency.

It would be difficult to find in all history a precise instance in
which rhetoric played a more important role in human destiny than
it did in Lincoln's speeches of 1858.

In Chicago on July 10, after listening to Douglas' speech on the
night before, Lincoln delivered his second important speech of the
campaign. And again in Springfield on July 17, he covered much
the same ground. In these two speeches he explained his declaration
of belief that the country would become either all slave or all free.
It was not, as Douglas had charged, a statement of wish for or
purpose toward disunion, but rather an unpleasant prediction that
arose from his interpretation of the direction of political events.
He argued again that Douglas' "popular sovereignty" had been
emasculated by the Dred Scott decision. He continued his attack
on the moral indifference of Douglas' "don't care" attitude toward
the extension of slavery. He admitted that, of course, the
Declaration of Independence was not meant as a statement of fact
that all men were "equal in all respects." The statement was rather
an ideal principle to be worked toward: "I say in relation to the
principle that all men are created equal, let it be as nearly reached
as we can." In his discussion of this principle in the latter part
of the "Chicago Speech" he reached high points of persuasion and
beauty of language. He concluded the second "Springfield Speech"
by renewing his charges of conspiracy, which Douglas had up to
this time ignored. Then came the challenge to debate and Douglas'
acceptance.

The debates are on the whole inferior to Lincoln's preceding speeches, but for the purpose of comparing and contrasting the rhetorical effectiveness of the two men they offer the student perhaps a better opportunity than the earlier speeches. The first debate at Ottawa was in a sense the climax of the campaign viewed from Lincoln's side. In it, as we have already noted, he finally forced Douglas to take notice of the charge of conspiracy and particularly of the "beautiful figure." In the next debate at Freeport came the denouement in the form of a list of questions, and among them the one that Douglas answered to his eventual undoing.

After the seventh and last debate at Alton on October 15, Lincoln continued making speeches up to the end, and on October 30 concluded in Springfield before "a giant Republican rally." This speech, in style and emotional context, is a foretaste of the later lyric mood of the "Farewell Address," "Gettysburg Address," and the conclusions of the two "Inaugural" addresses. The sentences flow easily with a subtle cadence, unobtrusive but poetic. The diction is simple, but the words play a rich pattern of assonance and alliteration.

> My friends, to-day closes the discussions of this canvass. The planting and the culture are over; and there remains but the preparation, and the harvest.
>
> I stand here surrounded by friends—some *political, all personal* friends, I trust. May I be indulged, in this closing scene, to say a few words of myself. I have borne a laborious, and, in some respects to myself, a painful part in the contest. Through all, I have neither assailed, nor wrestled with any part of the Constitution. The legal right of the Southern people to reclaim their fugitives I have constantly admitted. The legal right of Congress to interfere with their institution in the states, I have constantly denied. In resisting the spread of slavery to new territory, and with that, what appears to me to be a tendency to subvert the first principle of free government itself my whole effort has consisted. To the best of my judgment I have labored *for,* and not *against* the Union. As I have not felt, so I have not expressed any harsh sentiment towards our Southern brethren. I have constantly declared, as I really believed, the only difference between them and us, is the difference of circumstances.

I have meant to assail the motives of no party, or individual; and if I have, in any instance (of which I am not conscious) departed from my purpose, I regret it.

I have said that in some respects the contest has been painful to me. Myself, and those with whom I act have been constantly accused of a purpose to destroy the Union; and bespattered with every imaginable odious epithet; and some who were friends, as it were but yesterday have made themselves most active in this. I have cultivated patience, and made no attempt at a retort.

Ambition has been ascribed to me. God knows how sincerely I prayed from the first that this field of ambition might not be opened. I claim no insensibility to political honors; but today could the Missouri restriction be restored, and the whole slavery question replaced on the old ground of "toleration" by *necessity* where it exists, with unyielding hostility to the spread of it, on principle, I would, in consideration, gladly agree, that Judge Douglas should never be *out,* and I never *in,* an office, so long as we both or either, live.

VI

Although Lincoln lost the ensuing election, the national publicity given the debates and his other speeches placed him among the few top leaders of the Republican party. As shown by his letters during the next few months, he was not immediately aware that he had become important among the various prospective Republican candidates for the next presidential election, but he worked consistently for party harmony and neglected few opportunities to keep himself before the public, filling political speaking engagements during 1859 in Ohio, Indiana, Wisconsin, Iowa, Missouri, and Kansas. These speeches repeated most of the arguments he had used in the campaign of 1858.

He was also in demand for popular lectures and even prepared a somewhat colorless disquisition on the growth of American civilization under the title, "Discoveries, Inventions and Improvements." Although he delivered it a number of times, he never thought much of it, and in truth it did not measure up to his other nonpolitical address delivered before the Wisconsin State Agricultural Fair on September 30, 1859. Lincoln was not at his best in making speeches for their own sake, but on this occasion he had in the general theme of agricultural improvement and the dignity of labor something about which he knew well from his own experience and felt deeply from his own nature. The passages on labor are perhaps the most significant utterances made on that subject by any important political figure of the era:

> The world is agreed that *labor* is the source from which human wants are mainly supplied. There is no dispute upon this point. From this point, however, men immediately diverge. Much disputation is maintained as to the best way of applying and controlling the labor element. By some it is assumed that labor is available only in connection with capital — that nobody labors, unless somebody else, owning capital, somehow, by use of that capital induces him to do it . . . But another class of reasoners hold the opinion that there is no *such* relation between capital and labor as assumed; and that there is no such thing as a freeman being fatally fixed for life in the condition of a hired laborer; that both these assumptions are false, and all inferences from them groundless. They hold that labor is prior to, and independent of, capital; that in fact, capital is the fruit of labor, and could never have existed if labor had not *first* existed; that labor can exist without capital, but that capital could never have existence without labor. Hence, they hold that labor is the superior — greatly the superior — of capital.

> They do not deny that there is, and probably always will be, *a* relation between labor and capital. The error, as they hold, is in assuming that the *whole* labor of the world exists within that relation . . . .
> . . . As each man has one mouth to be fed, and one pair of hands to furnish food, it was probably intended that that particular pair of hands should feed that particular mouth — that each head is the natural guardian, director and protector of the hands and mouth inseparably connected with it; and that being so, every head should be cultivated and improved, by whatever will add to its capacity for performing its charge. In one word. free labor insists on universal education.

His growing popularity as a speaker brought him an invitation to speak in New York before the Young Men's Central Republican Union. The place was Cooper Institute. Evidently Lincoln prepared the address for this occasion with more care than he had given to any speech prior to this except the "House Divided Speech" of two years earlier. In architecture it is if anything the more carefully balanced of the two, and in dignity and precision of expression it is fully the equal of the other, but it lacks perhaps something of the dramatic fire with which the earlier speech burns. The earlier speech is superior as a whole in imagination and feeling, and the later is more consistently polished and perfect in all its paragraphs and sentences. In no prior address, speech, or letter are Lincoln's stylistic effects more carefully calculated. His handling of the sentence taken as a text from Douglas' "Speech at Columbus, Ohio" is for repetitive effect one of his most skillful and adroit rhetorical successes. His straight exposition of the attitude taken toward slavery-extension by the founding fathers is excellent historical analysis based on painstaking factual research. His tempered statement of Republican principles, although a repetition of what he had said often in 1858, is in succinctness and force perhaps his best statement up to this time. His employment of balanced structure in the paragraph which clinches the political point of this analysis and concludes the first part of the address is rhetorically the highwater mark of the piece:

> If any man at this day sincerely believes that a proper division of local from federal authority, or any part of the Constitution, forbids the Federal Government to control as to slavery in the federal territories, he is right to say so, and to enforce his position by all truthful evidence and fair argument which he can. But he has no right to mislead others, who have less access to history, and less leisure to study it, into the false belief that "our fathers who framed the Government under which we live" were of the same opinion—thus substituting falsehood and deception for truthful evidence and fair argument. If any man at this day sincerely believes "our fathers who framed the Government under which we live," used and applied principles, in other cases, which ought to have led them to

understand that a proper division of local from federal authority or some part of the Constitution, forbids the Federal Government to control as to slavery in the federal territories, he is right
to say so. But he should, at the same time, brave the responsibility of declaring that, in his opinion, he understands their
principles better than they did themselves; and especially should
he not shirk that responsibility by asserting that they "understood the question just as well, and even better, than we do
now."

The dramatic analogy of the highwayman, with which he exposed the
irrationality of the more intemperate secessionists, is one of his most
successful figures:

Under all these circumstances, do you really feel yourselves
justified to break up this Government unless such a court decision as yours is, shall be at once submitted to as a conclusive
and final rule of political action? But you will not abide the
election of a Republican president! In that supposed event,
you say, you will destroy the Union; and then, you say, the
great crime of having destroyed it will be upon us! That is
cool. A highwayman holds a pistol to my ear, and mutters
through his teeth, "Stand and deliver, or I shall kill you, and
then you will be a murderer!"

His peroration is one of his most effective and memorable conclusions:

Neither let us be slandered from our duty by false accusations
against us, nor frightened from it by menaces of destruction
to the Government nor of dungeons to ourselves. Let us have
faith that right makes might, and in that faith, let us, to the
end, dare to do our duty as we understand it.

VII

To survey the body of Lincoln's writings during the years of his
Presidency, commenting on each significant letter, message,
proclamation, or address in chronological order, is perhaps less desirable at this point than a discussion of Lincoln's style in these

respective types, with some observations on significant examples of each; for, in fact, one could otherwise hardly decide which pieces to omit from consideration on principle of merit or interest. Among students with a newly acquired interest in Lincoln's writings as well as among inveterate admirers, there is so much diversity of taste and individual preference for one piece over another that one with a catholic taste may well be amazed at the bias with which students of Lincoln privately claim top honor for their favorite passages. The wide range of choice afforded by the writings of the years 1861-1865 has not tended to discourage this diversity of preference.

Particularly difficult is the problem of selecting the best of Lincoln's letters. The most famous of all his letters of condolence, the "Letter to Mrs. Bixby," although it is undoubtedly a gem, can nearly be matched in artistic effect with the "Letter to Colonel Ellsworth's Parents," May 25, 1861, or the "Letter to Fanny McCullough," December 23, 1862.

The differences between these three masterpieces are not differences in literary success and felicity of phrasing so much as differences in purpose and effect. The "Letter to Mrs. Bixby" is a public letter, written, as were many of Lincoln's letters, with the probability of publication in mind, to a woman whom Lincoln knew only through War Department records as a bereaved mother, and about whose sons he knew only the supposed facts stated in the letter. His phraseology, though felicitous in place, might have seemed pompously insincere in the "Letter to Fanny McCullough." Likewise, the personal fatherly tone and the pleading simplicity of phrase in the "Letter to Fanny McCullough" would have been intolerable in the "Letter to Mrs. Bixby." The eulogy of Colonel Ellsworth to his parents is as fine in its way as either of the other two, and in purpose and effect holds a middle ground between them. Lincoln had known Colonel Ellsworth well as a student in his own law office, had admired and loved him, and in this letter wrote his noblest tribute to a friend.

But when all is said, the "Letter to Mrs. Bixby" is not likely to give way to either of the others in popular appeal, for like the "Gettysburg Address" it so links the private theme of sorrow with the public theme of preservation of freedom, that the letter is in itself an emblem of a national ideal. As Carl Sandburg has poetically phrased it, "Here was a piece of the American Bible. 'The cherished memory of the loved and lost' — these were the blood-colored syllables of a sacred music."

The distinction between Lincoln's public and private style must be kept in mind likewise in reading his letters and telegrams to government officials, army officers, and various public figures. On the one hand Lincoln could write a public masterpiece like the "Letter to Horace Greeley," August 22, 1862, and on the other hand a private masterpiece like the "Letter to General Joseph Hooker," January 23, 1863. The one he expected to be published, the other he expected only Hooker to read. Lincoln found an inimitable manner of writing for each specific occasion that arose.

The degree to which his letters are informal and personal varies considerably with the occasion. The sequence of letters and telegrams to General McClellan runs from strictly formal to informal and personal, and the variations in tone from one occasion to the next make the sequence the most interesting group of letters written by Lincoln to one man. Lincoln used every manner and device he knew in his attempt to handle McClellan, and all failed. His letters are a fascinating literary triumph in the midst of executive failure. Certain of his letters, such as the "Letter to James C. Conkling," August 26, 1863, are in effect public addresses and as such display qualities of argument and style which are typical of Lincoln's addresses of this period rather than of his letters either formal or informal. In logic and in rhetorical effectiveness they are in no way inferior to the best of the addresses.

It may be said that during his Presidency, although he often wrote hurriedly and without revising, Lincoln never wrote a bad letter. A study of every letter, its purpose, and its adaptation of language to that purpose, will reveal, even in the less known pieces, as high a degree of felicity in phrasing, and as remarkable an adaptation of tone to theme, as can be found in the more famous letters. Two days before he wrote the famous "Letter to Mrs. Bixby," he composed a short "Letter to General Rosecrans," November 19, 1864, which in its limited sphere is as succinct, as delicately

worded, and as definitive an achievement of language as Lincoln
ever composed. Similarly, two days after the excellent public "Letter to Erastus Corning and Others," June 12, 1863, he penned a
short "Telegram to General Hooker" which in its small way is
no less an artistic triumph: "If the head of Lee's army is   at
Martinsburg, and the tail of it on the Plank road between
Fredericksburg & Chancellorsville, the animal must be very slim
somewhere — Could you not break him?" In short, even Lincoln's
most casual pieces bear the inimitable marks of literary excellence.

VIII

In his official proclamations and executive orders Lincoln presents
a peculiar problem to the biographer and critic. Many of them are
of little or no literary significance, being legal documents in precise
legal phrase properly utilitarian and without stylistic individuality.
Even the "Emancipation Proclamation" has in it little that is
distinctly Lincolnian. There is, however, in the proclamations of
thanksgiving and fast days, a style of expression which has become
the subject of some discussion because it is peculiar to these pieces
and is not generally found in any of Lincoln's other writings. Since
these proclamations are jointly signed by Seward as Secretary of
State and by Lincoln as President, and since the facts concerning
their composition are not fully known, the conjecture has been
made that Seward wrote them. Joseph H. Barrett, an early
biographer of Lincoln, first made the conjecture, but Nicolay and
Hay took no notice of it and included the proclamations without
question in the *Complete Works*. Daniel Kilham Dodge in his
admirable little book, *Abraham Lincoln: Master of Words,*
comments on the conjecture but arrives at no definite conclusion,
though he seems to assume Lincoln's authorship, while recognizing
the possible influence of *The Book of Common Prayer* on the style
of the proclamations, and the fact that Seward was an
Episcopalian. The chief stylistic trait which sets these pieces apart
from Lincoln's other writings is the use of words and phrases in
pairs, as for example in the following passage from the
"Proclamation of a National Fast Day," August 12, 1861:

> And whereas it is fit and becoming in all people, at all times,
> to acknowledge and revere the Supreme Government of God;
> to bow in humble submission to his chastisements; to confess
> and deplore their sins and transgressions in the full conviction
> that the fear of the Lord is the beginning of wisdom; and to
> pray, with all fervency and contrition, for the pardon of their
> past offences, and for a blessing upon their present and pros-
> pective action . . .

This is a general characteristic of phraseology in legal documents as well as in *The Book of Common Prayer,* but in legal documents the effect is, according to legal tradition at least, to make every statement incontestably clear, whereas in *The Book of Common Prayer* the effect is primarily one of incantation. Obviously, the effect in Lincoln's proclamations is nearer to that of *The Book of Common Prayer,* but it does not therefore necessarily follow that *The Book of Common Prayer* is the source of the device. The fact that the proclamations as official pronouncements are in their na- ture legal documents may well account for Lincoln's use of a device with which he was thoroughly familiar as a lawyer, and his use of it for rhetorical ends is only natural, in view of the solemnity of the theme and the occasion.

The fact that few of the manuscripts of proclamations are entire- ly in Lincoln's hand neither adds nor subtracts evidence, since it was customary for the official copy to which signatures and seal were to be affixed to be engrossed by an official scribe, and unless preserved by reason of unusual historic significance (e.g., the Pre- liminary Emancipation Proclamation), first drafts, either in Lincoln's hand or that of another, most often have not survived.

In these proclamations, then, it may be supposed that we have examples of a formal style which Lincoln adopted for the specific purpose, and which for sonorous effect and solemn rhythm is not less interesting than, though different from, the style of his addresses. In his early writings, as we have seen, Lincoln experimented with various forms of writing and several styles, and it is only logical to assume that in this later period, when con- fronted with the necessity of composing an expression which re- quired something distinct from his usual style of public address,

Lincoln adroitly made use of a device long familiar to him. Of course, the majority of routine proclamations, executive orders, etc., which bear Lincoln's signature, were drafted by someone else.

IX

Presidential messages to Congress have rarely ever been noted for literary significance. Their very purpose and nature limit their content to summary of national progress and recommendations for congressional action. And of all Lincoln's writings aside from legal papers and executive orders, his messages are the most strictly utilitarian and necessarily prosaic. In spite of these considerations, several of Lincoln's messages so transcend the limitations of the occasion as to be worthy of inclusion among his best writings. With one exception they suffer generally in comparison with his great addresses, but in certain passages, such as the conclusion to the "Annual Message" of December 1, 1862, they reach peaks of eloquence unsurpassed in the annals of history.

Above all, the messages to Congress demonstrate again the rhetorical care and precision with which Lincoln composed even his most factual statements, and his feeling for exact coloring of phrase and choice of word. The well-known incident concerning his use of the term "sugar-coated" in the "Message to Congress in Special Session," July 4, 1861, exemplifies the care with which he chose his words. The public printer John D. Defrees objected to the lack of dignity in the term as used in the sentence, "With rebellion thus sugar-coated they have been drugging the public mind of their section for more than thirty years . . ." To this Lincoln is reported to have replied, "Well, Defrees, if you think the time will ever come when people will not understand what 'sugar-coated' means, I'll alter it; otherwise I think I'll let it go." Like his many homely but effective figures of speech this one demanded simple and idiomatic language, and it was Defrees, rather than Lincoln, whose feeling for diction was awry.

In this first "Message to Congress" Lincoln gave a new statement of his philosophy of government as contained in the "First Inaugural Address," but without the pleading and palliation of that address and with a vigorous statement of courage and conviction in the task of preserving the authority of the national government. On the whole the message is nearer in purpose and effect to his speeches and addresses than are his later messages. This is in part, perhaps, the result of the fact that it was delivered on July 4, and was an address to the nation as well as to Congress. In all his major messages, however, Lincoln tends to keep a tone of public speech, though they were not delivered in person, and in fact generally preserves the architecture of the oration, especially in the peroration. The conclusion of this message, though not so memorable as the peroration of the "Annual Message," December 1, 1862, is effective and somewhat reminiscent of the short peroration of the "Address at Cooper Institute."

The "Annual Message to Congress," December 3, 1861, aside from discussion of specific problems of government, has as its central theme the importance of free labor in a democracy. The student may well compare Lincoln's discussion of labor and capital, as well as his recommendations in regard to a department of agriculture, with the ideas propounded in the "Address before the Wisconsin Agricultural Society" in 1859. In spite of its factuality, the second half of this message contains several inspired passages, and is consistently of high literary merit, though its opening and its close are rhetorically less striking than those of the next "Annual Message."

The "Annual Message to Congress," December 1, 1862, is Lincoln's finest composition of this type. In many respects it is his masterpiece, approximating both of the "Inaugural" addresses in depth of conviction and even surpassing them in breadth of conception and height of imagination. Perhaps no American living at the time save Walt Whitman ever expressed so large a vision of the future of American democracy, the magnitude of its geographic and economic potentialities, and the infinitude of its social destiny in the quest for human liberty. In this huge scope Lincoln saw the immediate problems underlying the Civil War — Union and Emancipation — in their true perspective as subordinate to the necessity of preserving not merely the words of the Declaration of Independence, but its prophetic truth. In the largest sense Lincoln sought not simply to preserve the Union or to free the slaves, but rather to keep open the way to future amelioration in the lot of all humanity and to the progressive achievement of democracy in all human society.

The message reveals how truly Lincoln appreciated the dramatic course of human events. Of all his prior speeches, only the "House Divided Speech" of 1858 approaches it in the clairvoyance with which Lincoln states the meaning of his era as a turning point in the long quest for human dignity. From the opening paragraph to the splendid peroration, the message is charged with an electric feeling for the drama of a crisis in which the citizens of the United States "shall nobly save, or meanly lose, the last best hope of earth."

In spite of its formidable array of facts and figures and the gray steel of its logical armor, the whole message is alive with the dignity of the inspired word. If one thinks only of the "Gettysburg Address" and a few other short, lyrical passages, it is hard to estimate the man's literary stature in comparison with the great orators of other times; for these lyric speeches are scarcely comparable, being unique. But in judging this message the student may with reason bring as a touchstone the best of Edmund Burke, or Cicero, or Demosthenes, and yet find Lincoln's metal too pure to assay by such a test. If one would try, let him select his touchstone and then assay the concluding paragraph of this message:

> Fellow-citizens, *we* cannot escape history. We of this Congress and this administration, will be remembered in spite of ourselves. No personal significance, or insignificance, can spare one or another of us. The fiery trial through which we pass, will light us down, in honor or dishonor, to the latest generation. We *say* we are for the Union. The world will not forget that we say this. We know how to save the Union. The world knows we do know how to save it. We — even *we here* — hold the power, and bear the responsibility. In *giving* freedom to the *slave,* we *assure* freedom to the *free* — honorable alike in what we give, and what we preserve. We shall nobly save, or meanly lose, the last best hope of earth. Other means may succeed; this could not fail. The way is plain, peaceful, generous, just — a way which, if followed, the world will forever applaud, and God must forever bless.

X

Lincoln's numerous addresses, beginning with the "Farewell Address" and continuing through the "Second Inaugural Address," display little in the way of stylistic traits which differs essentially from the characteristics of his earlier work, except in beauty. As has already been noted, it is not in technical command of style so much as it is in power of feeling and imagination that the addresses of this last period surpass by all odds those of his middle period.

The new intensity seems to have been more the result of internal experience than of external influence. It was a common observation among Lincoln's friends that he was cold and unemotional. Also it is true that no other orator of his time was more coldly logical, more careful of a self-imposed restraint, than Lincoln was from 1854 to 1861. Upon his departure from Springfield in 1861 a note of fathomless emotion, at once heroic and simple, sounded for the first time in his "Farewell Address." This note was sounded again in the prose poem which he made of Seward's suggested peroration for the "First Inaugural Address": and thenceforth, restrained but full, it suffused the more important lyric utterances of his years in Washington, but above all the "Gettysburg Address" and the "Second Inaugural Address."

It has been said that Lincoln's art is always applied art, utilitarian in purpose and held strictly to the matter in hand. If this implies that it does not therefore reach the heights of imagination to which we conventionally expect only belletristic art to attain, nothing could be further from the truth. And yet, perhaps, even in the deep-moving cadence and high imagination of the "Gettysburg Address" and the "Second Inaugural Address," he considered his prose chiefly as a means to an end, recognizing that in an emotional crisis of national scope the truest appeal could not be made to the intellect alone. And because he had early learned to eschew the illusion of emotionalism, he was able in his great hour to plumb depths hitherto rarely fathomed by oratory.

The emergence of this new feeling was significantly coincident with his assumption of what he seemed to consider his supreme task — the preservation of the Union, and with it democracy. His utterances regarding slavery, in fact, his words on all other subjects, fine as many of them are, fall into place near or far from the high words in which he defended and pleaded for democracy as symbolized in the Union. Alexander Stephens once said that the Union with Lincoln rose in sentiment to the "sublimity of a religious mysticism." The "Gettysburg Address" is excellent literary evidence in support of Stephens' opinion, for it reveals Lincoln's worship of the Union as the symbol of an ideal yet to be realized.

Lincoln's problem at Gettysburg was to do two things: to commemorate the past and to prophesy for the future. To do these things he took the theme dearest to his audience, honor for the heroic dead sons and fathers, and combined it with the theme nearest to his own heart, the preservation of democracy. Out of this double theme grew his poetic metaphor of birth, death, and spiritual rebirth, of the life of man and the life of the nation. To it he brought the fervor of devoutly religious belief. Democracy was to Lincoln a religion, and he wanted it to be in a real sense the religion of his audience. Thus he combined an elegiac theme with a patriotic theme, skillfully blending the hope of eternal life with the hope of eternal democracy.

Above all Lincoln believed that "all men are created equal," in the only way that a mind as coldly logical as his could believe in it. Just how he believed it, is indicated by his use of one word, *proposition.* This word has proved a stumbling block for some readers of the "Gettysburg Address." Matthew Arnold is reported, probably inaccurately, to have read as far as "dedicated to the proposition" and stopped. Charles Sumner said that at first he did not like the word, but that he later decided it was satisfactory. Yet the word *proposition* was inevitable for Lincoln. He often tried to use his words as exactly as a mathematician uses his formulae. By his own account he had "studied and nearly mastered" Euclid, and hence we may be sure that he used the word naturally in the logician's sense: a statement to be debated, verified, proved. Thus democracy, as an active, living thing, meant to Lincoln the verification or the proving of the proposition to which its very existence was in the beginning dedicated. Eighty-seven years had gone into the proving, the Civil War had come at a critical stage in the argument, the Union armies at Gettysburg had won an immediate victory, and the affirmation that "all men are created equal" was still a live rather than a dead issue. It was still a proposition open to argument and inviting proof, but not on any account one that had already been proved. The further proof was for "us the living, to be dedicated here to the unfinished work which they who fought here have thus far so nobly advanced."

It was thus that Lincoln believed in democracy, as a living thing striving toward truth, not as an accomplished fact nor as a meaningless form of words incapable of proof. He had said some years before, "the Declaration of Independence contemplated the progressive improvement in the condition of all men." And again, "I say in relation to the principle that all men are created equal let it be as nearly reached as we can." Down through the years, again and again, there had appeared in his speeches and letters this central concept of progressive improvement in the condition of mankind. And at Gettysburg he took the occasion to reaffirm his belief in the necessity of striving on.

So it was no accident that, as he thought on the past life of American democracy, his words and allusions began, in his very first sentence, calling to mind a haunting phrase out of the Old Testament: "the days of our years are three score and ten," and with it the symbolic act of consecration traditionally observed of old by Hebrew and Christian, dedicating their children to the service of God. And thus he wrote, "Fourscore and seven years ago our fathers brought forth on this continent a new nation, conceived in liberty, and dedicated to the proposition that all men are created equal."

But the "new nation" had in eighty-four years grown old. It was already thinking too much in terms of the past. The proposition to which the founding fathers had dedicated it must not mean anything new. Although the proposition had specifically stated *all men,* the laws of the nation had insisted that it had not meant *ALL* men; it had meant only white men; it must not mean *ALL* men. The war had come, and with it the death of that old nation, and the birth of a new. Its death was at Gettysburg, symbolized in the graves of those "who here gave their lives that that nation might live." Its life, too, was at Gettysburg, symbolized in Lincoln's audience; "It is for us the living, rather, to be dedicated here . . . ."

The key words of the "Gettysburg Address" are three simple ones, two pronouns and an adverb: *they, we, here*. With his usual practice Lincoln repeats them, emphasizing again and again what he wanted his audience to carry away. "It is for us the living to be dedicated here to the unfinished work which they who fought here have thus far so nobly advanced."

Repetition of sounds, as well as of words, is a marked characteristic of Lincoln's style throughout his works. He often employs in poetic flashes alliteration, assonance, and even rhyme sounds. But in the "Gettysburg Address" these several varieties of repetition provide an effect unique in Lincoln's prose. With these devices indicated by italics, the oral pecularities of the first sentence of the address become apparent: *"Four score* and *seven* years ago our *fathers* brought *forth* on this *continent* a *new nation, conceived* in liberty and dedicated to the *proposition* that all men are *created* equal." The reader may, if he is interested, verify for himself the remarkable extent to which Lincoln employs these devices with fine effect in the remainder of the "Gettysburg Address" as well as in many other passages.

Another variety of repetition, grammatical parallelism, is equally characteristic of Lincoln's general style. He uses this device with such frequency and variety that it seems to have been a consistent habit of his mind to seek repetitive sequences in both diction and sentence structure for the alignment of his thought. That this was the result of his deliberate seeking for an emphasis and simplicity which would prove effective with the common man is implied in the often repeated testimony given by Herndon: "He used to bore me terribly by his methods, processes, manners, etc., etc. Mr. Lincoln would doubly explain things to me that needed no explanation. . . . Lincoln's ambition in this line was this: he wanted to be distinctly understood by the common people. . . ." Herndon might have added that Lincoln's favorite ideas — those which appear again and again in his works, and which he turned over and over in his mind through months and even years—and his most memorable phrases almost invariably betray this repetitive pattern.

On this basic pattern of parallelism in thought, Lincoln often elaborates a distinctly poetical cadence, suggesting comparison with the cadenced prose of the seventeenth century. Although balanced rhythms with caesuras are indigenous to English poetry and perhaps to English prose, Hebrew literature through the King James Bible probably provided the literary examples which Lincoln knew best; and from his fondness for Biblical phraseology he may have derived his mastery of the technique.

In his lyrical passages balance becomes most striking, as it enriches his melancholy reflections or his fervent appeals to the hearts of his audience. Within single sentences it occurs in two forms: in a balanced sentence of two parts with a caesura approximately midway; and in a series of phrases or clauses separated by caesuras and grouped in balanced staves of two or more phrase units. Within an individual phrase or clause internal balance and parallelism often occur. A fine example of the first type, with a pointed use of antithesis, is the following sentence from the "Letter to J. H. Hacket," November 2, 1863: "I have endured a great deal of ridicule without much malice; and have received a great deal of kindness, not quite free from ridicule." An example of the second type is the concluding sentence of the "Second Inaugural Address":

> With malice toward none; with charity for all; with firmness
> in the right, as God gives us to see the right, let us strive
> on to finish the work we are in; to bind up the nation's
> wounds; to care for him who shall have borne the battle, and
> for his widow, and his orphan—to do all which may achieve
> and cherish a just and lasting peace, among ourselves, and
> with all nations.

Sometimes this rhythm pattern extends over an entire group of sentences, or even the whole of a short address: the "Farewell Address" for example. In this address there are two parallel patterns, of thought and of rhythm. Within and between some sentences they become identical. In others they merely coincide. Between others there is a compensating balance of phrases and pauses, although the sentence movement is reversed from periodic to loose structure, and the rhythm pattern is varied. The only sentence which appears without a compensating rhythm is the first, standing alone as a topic statement. Within this general pattern of close parallels there is enough variety in individual sentences to avoid monotony but sufficient regularity of rhythm to produce distinct cadence, in some phrases approximating loose metrical effect:

> My Friends: No one, not in my situation, can appreciate my feeling of sadness at this parting. To this place, and the kindness of these people, I owe everything. Here I have lived a quarter of a century, and have passed from a young to an old man. Here my children have been born, and one is buried. I now leave, not knowing when or whether ever I may return, with a task before me greater than that which rested upon Washington. Without the assistance of that Divine Being who ever attended him, I cannot succeed. With that assistance, I cannot fail. Trusting in Him who can go with me, and remain with you, and be everywhere for good, let us confidently hope that all will yet be well. To His care commending you, as I hope in your prayers you will commend me, I bid you an affectionate farewell.

As these balanced rhythms sometimes approach meter in their regularity, Lincoln tends to heighten their effect with an occasional metrical phrase or sentence. Such phrases occur most frequently in perorations or passages of high emotional content: as for example, in a phrase of the "Second Inaugural Address": ". . . to do all which may achieve and cherish a just and lasting peace among ourselves . . ."; or in a phrase of the "Gettysburg Address": "The world will little note nor long remember what we say. . ."

Although Lincoln was without doubt consciously deliberate in attention to sound, his choice of words seems to have been guided primarily by other values: meaning more than sound or connotation, concrete words more than abstract words, current idiom more than authoritarian nicety. So much has been written on the qualities of exactness, clarity, and simplicity in his style that it seems unnecessary to stress them further. They are, however, the qualities of prose excellence wherever it is met with, and as such hardly set Lincoln's style apart from that of Edmund Burke, though they do, in their degree, set his style apart from that of Stephen A. Douglas or that of William H. Seward. Important and obvious as these qualities are, one may wonder if Lincoln's memorable passages are not remembered today for their unique effects of arrangement, rhythm, and sound as well as for the intrinsic value of their thought. What Lincoln's own answer might have been we may infer from the following comment in one of Herndon's letters to Jesse W. Weik:

> Mr. Lincoln's habits, methods of reading law, politics, poetry, etc., etc., were to come into the office, pick up book, newspaper, etc., and to sprawl himself out on the sofa, chairs, etc., and read aloud, much to my annoyance. I have asked him often why he did so and his invariable reply was: 'I catch the idea by two senses, for when I read aloud I hear what is read and I see it; and hence two senses get it and I remember it better, if I do not understand it better."

There is an old Arabian proverb which holds that "that is the best description which makes the ear an eye." In his use of figures of speech, sound, and rhythm, Lincoln illustrates again and again the truth of the old saying, which he probably had never heard.

Lincoln's composition has so much the stamp of these peculiarities even in the first draft of such a piece as the 'Gettysburg Address" that his revisions do little more than accent them. In his revision of Secretary Seward's suggested peroration for the 'First Inaugural Address," however, he demonstrates the deliberate artistry of his style, bringing his own peculiar pattern of thought and rhythm to another man's ideas, substituting his own exact and concrete words for orotund and vague terms, removing redundant and useless words, bringing closer together words that will enhance through assonance and alliteration the sound effect of the whole, and finally, changing a vague, transcendental metaphor into a homely but poetic figure which will be understood by every man who hears or reads it.

To label one of the following as Lincoln's is superfluous. Every sentence declares its creator:

I close.

We are not, we must not be, aliens or enemies, but fellow-countrymen and brethren.

Although passion has strained our bonds of affection too hardly, they must not, I am sure they will not, be broken.

The mystic chords which, proceeding from so many battlefields and so many patriot graves, pass through all the hearts and all the hearths in this broad continent of ours, will yet again harmonize in their ancient music when breathed upon by the guardian angel of the nation.

I am loth to close.

We are not enemies, but friends. We must not be enemies.

Though passion may have strained, it must not break our bonds of affection.

The mystic chords of memory, stretching from every battlefield, and patriot grave, to every living heart and hearth-stone, all over this broad land, will yet swell the chorus of the Union, when again touched, as surely they will be, by the better angels of our nature.

The study of Lincoln's works reveals the dignity of a great mind and heart that seeks for rightness in principle, fairness in act, and beauty in utterance. He is a creative consciousness in whom the reality of nineteenth century America yet lives and breathes. As this reality is in Lincoln intrinsic, and his communication of it inimitable, so his words endure, representative and symbolic with singular completeness of the epoch which nurtured him. And so it is that he becomes as we study him, like the classic literary figures of the past, something more than a man. Time may dissipate the factual significance of his deeds, both as private citizen and as President, but we must always know and acknowledge the shining spirit that illumines his words.

THE AUTHORSHIP OF THE
"REBECCA" LETTERS*

I

The "Rebecca" letters which appeared in the *Sangamo Journal* in
August and September 1842, Lincoln's unfortunate entanglement
with James A. Shields which ensued, and the correspondence leading up to a duel which never came off, have never been adequately
studied by any biographer of Lincoln whose work I have read.
Albert J. Beveridge in his *Abraham Lincoln:* 1809—1858 gave perhaps the most adequate treatment to date, but he also contributed
considerable confusion and inaccuracy to the facts as well as to
the interpretation of this material. What follows is a criticism of
Beveridge's handling of this material and a re-examination of the
question of Lincoln's authorship.

To summarize the essential facts of the whole affair: The first
of these letters, dated August 10, 1842, purporting to come from
"Lost Township" and signed "Rebecca," was published in the
Sangamo Journal of August 19, 1842. It was largely a lament for
the sad predicament in which the people of Illinois found themselves following the failure of the State Bank in February 1842.
The worthless State Bank currency had driven good money out of
circulation, and such transactions as were carried on were largely

*The Abraham Lincoln Quarterly, June 1942.

by barter. Of course, "Rebecca" blamed the Democratic office-holders and commented on the report circulating throughout the state that "the Governor was going to send instructions to collectors, not to take anything but gold and silver for taxes." This was the peak of perfidy: the state refusing to honor the currency of its own institution.

Such instructions were sent out in a circular letter dated August 20, 1842, signed by the state auditor, James A. Shields, which letter was published in the *Journal* of August 26, 1842. The furor which ensued was an opportunity that Whig politicians took care not to neglect, and first among them was Lincoln, avid for the political scalp of James A. Shields. Perhaps Lincoln disliked Shields personally, but even if he had not disliked him, the implications of personal corruption and chicanery which he proceeded to heap upon the unfortunate auditor were more or less to be expected as part of a political technique long practiced by politicians of both parties.

The second "Rebecca" letter, which Lincoln later admitted writing, dated August 27, 1842 (the day after the publication of Shields' circular letter), was published in the *Journal* of September 2, 1842. Unlike the first letter, which contained only a mild condemnation of Democratic office-holders in general, the second letter made Shields as state auditor the butt of ridicule and contumely.

A third brief letter from "Rebecca" dated August 29, 1842, enclosing a letter purporting to come from her sister, appeared in the *Journal* of September 9, 1842. These two communications were mild in nature and apparently of the same vintage as the first letter, but in the same issue of the *Journal* appeared a fourth letter dated September 8, 1842, also signed "Rebecca," which in attacking Shields' personal courage exceed the second letter in contumely, but was childishly amateurish in execution. Then, in the *Journal* of September 16, 1842, appeared some doggerel signed "Cathleen," again ridiculing the "Irish" blarney of Shields.

Upon learning from Simeon Francis, the editor of the *Journal,* that Lincoln was responsible for these anonymous tirades directed against himself, Shields wrote Lincoln a letter that assumed Lincoln to be the sole author, demanded a retraction of "all offensive allusions" in all the letters, and concluded with the following sentence: "This may prevent consequences which no one will regret more than myself." To this letter Lincoln replied in a note which took particular notice of the threat implied in the concluding sentence, and pointed out that there was in Shields' letter "so much assumption of facts, and so much menace as to consequences," that he could not "submit to answer that note any further. . . ."

From this point onward the whole affair was so "honorably" mismanaged by Shields' friend Whiteside and Lincoln's friend Merryman that a duel seemed imminent. Fortunately, however, Lincoln finally made, and Shields accepted, the admission: "I did write the 'Lost Township' letter which appeared in the *Journal* of the 2d inst., but had no participation in any form, in any other article alluding to you."

Beveridge's account of the "Rebecca" letters and the ensuing correspondence with Shields is occasionally inaccurate as to facts, and somewhat unfair to Lincoln as to implications. In the first place, Beveridge gets mixed up about the sequence of the respective letters, and consistently refers to the *second* letter as the "third" and the *third* as the "second." Hence, his statement that Lincoln admitted writing the "third" but not the "second" letter, is precisely opposite to the facts.

In the second place, Beveridge states that Shields and Whiteside had not broken the state laws against dueling, which prohibited even the sending of a challenge or a verbal agreement to fight, while Lincoln and Merryman had at least "ignored the law." The words on which Beveridge's bias turns are "ignored" and "technically"· "Technically, neither [Shields or Whiteside] had yet broken these sweeping laws, although Lincoln and his friends had ignored them. In view of Lincoln's public appeal for observance of law, the fact that he was the offender and his insistence on fighting rather than apologizing unless Shields would withdraw his demand for retraction, it is not easy to determine his state of mind at the time." If this statement were fairly put as to both parties involved, it would read that both Shields and Lincoln had *ignored* the state laws, but that neither of them had *technically* broken them. Shields in his first letter to Lincoln demanded a retraction of all the

"Rebecca" letters without knowing that Lincoln had written them all. Lincoln in turn demanded that Shields retract his menacing letter before he (Lincoln) would consent to state the facts of his involvement. Now, admittedly, this unbending stiffness on Lincoln's part has in it a suggestion of the cockpit, and no one can make Lincoln out to have been either gracious or kindly in his reply to Shields' first letter. On the other hand, one cannot fail to see in Shields' demand a good deal of the menace and presumption that Lincoln saw and resented. In short, neither man seems to have been imbued with as much meekness and mildness as either might well have afforded had each not let his "honor" stiffen prematurely. Lincoln shows badly enough without Beveridge's biased interpretation to make him appear worse. It seems, in view of the plain words of the correspondence, most difficult to determine Beveridge's state of mind as he twists his interpretation all *for* Shields and all *against* Lincoln.

It is true that Shields' first letter did not "technically" challenge Lincoln, but one can hardly fail to understand Lincoln's inferring that, unless he retracted, a challenge would be issued. For Shields wrote: "I will not take the trouble of enquiring into the reason of all this, but I will take the liberty of requiring a full, positive and absolute retraction. . . . This may prevent consequences which no one will regret more than myself." This concluding sentence in Shields' letter was unmistakable in its implications to Lincoln.

Lincoln's reply, dated September 17th, questions Shields' assumption of facts, but does not "technically" challenge Shields any more than Shields had challenged Lincoln. It merely implies, in its turn rather stiffly, that Lincoln will not be frightened by any menacing implications. Shields' second letter, according to both Merryman's account and Whiteside's account, Lincoln would not receive unless Shields first withdrew his menacing first note. At this point negotiations hung, Lincoln presuming, naturally, that if Shields refused to withdraw his first note, then a challenge could be expected. Apparently Whiteside, Shields' friend, did his verbal best to impress Lincoln with this probability, and Lincoln's instructions to Merryman concerning the duel were drawn up merely in anticipation of receiving a challenge, not as an acceptance of a challenge. In short, Beveridge seems, because of his apparent bias against Lincoln and Lincoln's friend Merryman, to wish the reader to see Lincoln as forcing the fight. The correspondence does not bear Beveridge out.

In the third place, Beveridge's bias seems to have led him to overstep the facts in his attempt to make Lincoln responsible for the first and third "Rebecca" letters. He implies that Lincoln's plain and clearly stated admission—"I did write the 'Lost Township' letter which appeared in the *Journal* of the 2d inst., but had no participation in any form, in any other article alluding to you"—dodges the authorship of the first letter and also the third letter, the latter of which Beveridge mistakenly calls the "second"; and further, Beveridge states categorically that an editorial which appeared in the "same issue of the *Journal*" attacking "the pompous proclamation of Shields and Carlin" was "either written or inspired by Lincoln." Neither part of this "either. . . or" statement is substantiated by any facts which Beveridge adduces, and in the light of my investigation of his other statements it seems likely that this one is equally without foundation in fact.

II

In regard to the authorship of the first "Rebecca" letter, in which there is no allusion to Shields, Beveridge is again categorical in his statement that Lincoln wrote it. Although it is true that Lincoln's statement of authorship already quoted would not absolutely rule out the first letter, inasmuch as Shields is not mentioned in it, the statement signed by Merryman, Bledsoe, and Butler does rule it out, specifying that Lincoln had written the letter in the *"Journal* of the 2d, and that only. . . ." Lincoln would scarcely have allowed this statement to stand if he had written more than one letter. Furthermore, Beveridge states that the style of the first letter is "plainly Lincoln's work" and that the third letter (which he calls the "second") is "in the peculiar style and vein of all Lincoln's other Rebecca letters. If Lincoln did not write the second [third] Rebecca letter, it is puzzling to speculate who did write it, since, so far as is known nobody in Springfield was master of the distinctive style in which all the Rebecca letters, except the last,

were written." When one realizes that the phrase "all Lincoln's other Rebecca letters" presumes the very thing that is unproven, then
the whole statement becomes worthless. There is in Beveridge's
statement so much assumption of facts which do not exist that one
can only point out that the facts which do exist concerning the style
of the letters do not justify his statement.

The style of none of the other three letters is precisely that of
the one Lincoln admitted writing. In easy use of vernacular, in
humor, in character portrayal, and in conception as well as handling of dramatic situation and dialogue, Lincoln's letter is wholly
different from and more vivid than any of the other three. The
first letter is nearest to it in merit, but is not clearly and
indisputably in the same style. However, the style of the first is
in quality, it is true, not far beneath Lincoln's style. The use of
some of Lincoln's favorite arguments and one illustrative story
about the man with patent legs does suggest a possibility of his
authorship. Such things, however, are not sufficient evidence to establish even a conjecture of probability. The circumstance of the
arguments against the State Bank being much the same as those
in Lincoln's "Sub-Treasury Speech" is slight evidence, for
Lincoln's arguments were not copyrighted and had been made
locally common knowledge by numerous public debates, which
could have provided many anonymous pens with the gist of the
argument in the first letter. As a matter of possibility, it is quite
likely that the author of the first letter shared the common arguments of the day, not only with Lincoln, but with most of the Whig
politicians of the time. As to there being no one else in Springfield
capable of writing the letters, suffice it to say that Beveridge had
either a very low opinion of the other Whigs in Springfield, or a
very exalted opinion of the style of the first and third letters.

In general conception and style the first and third letters are
discursive, garrulous, and mildly droll in satire and humor where
the second is lively, to-the-point, and very sharp in satire and
humor. In the first letter, Rebecca is conceived as an old woman
with considerable culture as well as a sense of humor. In the second
she seems not only younger, but also a bit crude and a little
masculine, if not down-right rowdy. Whereas in the first and third

letters the style is idiomatic and colloquial only to a limited degree, in the second it is not merely colloquial but even dialectal; and whereas the colloquial figures of speech are rather commonplace in the first and third letters, in the second letter they are, though equally colloquial, far more vivid and original.

In more specific details of style the contrast is just as striking. The grammar of the first and third letters is colloquial, but goes no further than an occasional double negative in violating standards. The second letter is not simply colloquial but is largely dialectal in its grammar *(run* for *ran, chaw* for *chew, seed* for *saw, kivered* for *covered,* etc.). There are no parallels in the first and third letters to such dialectal usage in the second. The spelling of the first and third letters is standard except for typographical errors, whereas the spelling of the second letter is dialectal and even illiterate. For example: *knick-knacks* and *girls* are spelled correctly in the first letter, but in the second we find *"nick-nacks"* and *"galls."* The second letter is filled with such spellings as *ax* (for ask), *mought, desarnin', 'spose, conceity,* etc. Also, the final *g* of participles is regularly omitted in the second letter, but not in the first and third letters.

In diction the contrast is no less striking. In the first and third letters the diction is predominantly formal and even literary, with a few homely words and phrases interpolated, rather obviously, for effect. These interpolations of homely diction are the more striking evidence in that they occur in the more formal context of the first and third letters, but not in the second where one might expect them. For example, the several uses of the phrase "this end of the timber," or "the upper end of the timber," and the "Kikapoo timber," occurring in both the first and third letters do not appear in the second. There are several other examples of diction peculiar to the first and third letters, but perhaps specific mention need be made of only one other very curious example. Lincoln writes often in the second letter of the Democratic party in power as "the democrats," but in the first and third letters the term is "the democracy": for example, "they. . .would then vote just as the democracy wanted them." Such curious and specific diction, appearing in both the first and third letters, is ground for strong suspicion that they were written by the same hand, and their absence in the second letter is ground for doubting that they were written by Lincoln.

Another point perhaps worth mentioning is the fact that the fourth letter, written by Mary Todd and Julia Jayne, has more in common with Lincoln's letter in several points of style than Lincoln's letter has in common with the other two. It lacks, however, the skill and dexterity of handling, the vividness of imagery and diction, and the sharp sense of the ridiculous which marks Lincoln's letter. It is a crudely amateurish attempt to imitate what Lincoln had done with a fair degree of skill, and as such it has literally nothing in common with the first and third letters. The verse signed "Cathleen," which appeared in the *Journal* on September 16th, was possibly also the work of the two women. Certainly, Lincoln's statement rules out all possibility of its being his.

In summary, the facts concerning the style of the "Rebecca" letters, seem to me to indicate conclusively that the first and third letters were written by some person other than Lincoln. Beveridge's opinion to the contrary, in spite of its unqualified positiveness, seems to have been based on a very cursory and even careless reading; and like his study of the correspondence between Lincoln and Shields, and Whiteside and Merryman, seems to have been biased by a desire to picture Lincoln in a more unfavorable light than the facts warrant.

My opinion is that possibly Simeon Francis, the editor of the *Journal,* wrote the first letter and also the third, since these two have so much in common. Thus, when Shields inquired concerning the authorship of the whole series, the editor named Lincoln and probably made no mention of the authorship of the other two letters, because Shields' name had not even been mentioned in the first and had barely been mentioned and not at all ridiculed or defamed in the third. Lincoln had written the second letter and had been responsible for the publication of the fourth, written by Mary Todd and Julia Jayne, and hence when Shields demanded to know the author of the letters defamatory to himself, Lincoln's name was properly given. It is difficult otherwise to understand Lincoln's statement of authorship, except we assume with Beveridge, that he dodged the authorship of the first and third letters. Since there is nothing in either that would seem to be worth dodging, one cannot conclude, even if one supposes Lincoln would not have hesitated to do so, that he would have had sufficient motive for dodging the responsibility for writing them.

My guess that the editor of the *Journal* may have written the first, and possibly the third, letter is based on the several sly, but not very subtle, allusions to paying for subscriptions with produce, which were hints to rural subscribers that the editor would appreciate some payment in produce from those subscribers who were in arrears but had no money to pay. To strengthen this assumption there is the fact that the editor was running in the identical column with the first letter a notice "To our Subscribers," which suggests that those in arrears should pay up. "Our farmer friends can pay us in wheat, or produce at the market price." With such a notice in view, immediately following the second postscript, the hand of an editor is not improbable in this statement from the first letter: ". . .we want your paper, and times are getting so hard I shall have to send you a pot of butter instead of the money." Even better is the second postscript:

> 2d. P.S. If I should send you a jar of pickles this fall and some nice apples, I hope you will accept of them. I wonder people don't think more than they do, how gratified you would be to receive such presents. It is a fact, if they would only think so, they would enjoy as much pleasure in making you such little presents of the very best apples, and peaches, and such things, as you would in receiving them. R.

It is perhaps not necessary to suggest that the present writer does not wish to appear positive in identifying the author of the first and third letters on this slight bit of evidence. If the question of Lincoln's authorship of the first and third "Rebecca" letters is hereby laid to rest, the purpose of this study has been accomplished.

WHO WROTE THE
"LETTER TO MRS. BIXBY"?*

As is well known to most students of Lincoln, the purported facsimiles of the "Letter to Mrs. Bixby" have been judged to be
forgeries, and the original manuscript has never been found. Furthermore, the opinion has been somewhat widely held that Lincoln
never wrote such a letter at all. Of course, the myth that Lincoln
was a semiliterate country lawyer gave rise even before his death
to much guessing as to who wrote his speeches and letters, and in
spite of Herndon's testimony to the contrary and the official editing
of Lincoln's works by his former secretaries John G. Nicolay and
John Hay, the rumors continued that Herndon, Seward, Nicolay,
and Hay, among others, had written this or that particular item
or passage. But apparently only John Hay lent his own personal
testimony to these suppositions, and it is exceedingly difficult today
to determine just *what* Hay's testimony, written and oral, meant.
The following resumé will give the essential facts of the controversial story concerning his authorship of the famous letter.

In his book *Across the Busy Years* (1940) Nicholas Murray
Butler related the following:

> Theodore Roosevelt admired the Bixby letter greatly and had a
> framed photograph of it in one of the guest rooms at the White
> House. John Morley occupied this room while the guest of

The Lincoln Herald, February 1943. F. Lauriston Bullard *(Abraham Lincoln and
the Widow Bixby,* 1946) greatly amplified the known facts about Mrs. Bixby and
her sons, but added little or nothing to the facts about the composition of Lincoln's
letter.

President Theodore Roosevelt in 1904. His attention was attracted to the Bixby letter, of which he had never heard, and he too admired it greatly.

One morning during his visit to Washington, Morley called on John Hay, then Secretary of State, whose house was on the opposite side of Lafayette Square from the White House. Morley expressed to Hay his great admiration for the Bixby letter, to which Hay listened with a quizzical look upon his face. After a brief silence, John Hay told Morley that he had himself written the Bixby letter and that this was the reason why it could not be found among Lincoln's papers and why no original copy of it had ever been forthcoming. Hay asked Morley to treat this information as strictly confidential until after his (Hay's) death. Morley did so, and told me that he had never repeated it to any one until he told it to me during a quiet talk in London at the Athenaeum on July 9, 1912. He then asked me, in my turn, to preserve this confidence of his until he, Morley, should be no longer living.

Butler is not content to have reproduced this story, with all its pious observation of promises kept, but goes even further in casting doubt on a majority of the letters which bear Lincoln's signature from 1861 to 1865. He claims that:

As a matter of fact, Abraham Lincoln wrote very few letters that bore his signature. John G. Nicolay wrote almost all of those which were official, while John Hay wrote almost all of those which were personal. Hay was able to imitate Lincoln's handwriting and signature in well-nigh perfect fashion.

Another version of John Hay's authorship of the Bixby letter is that given by the Reverend Gildart Arthur Jackson in a letter written to E. V. Lucas on January 16, 1922, and published by Lucas in *Post-Bag Diversions* (1934). The prior date of this story makes the claim of secrecy in the Morley—Butler story not a little improbable. In its essential part the Jackson story is as follows:

When I lived at Knebworth, Cora, Lady Strafford—an American—occupied for a time Knebworth House, Lord Lytton's place, and the late Mr. Page, the American

Ambassador, used to spend week-ends there. On one occasion, Lady Strafford told me, he noticed a copy—framed, I think—of Lincoln's letter and asked her if she knew the true history of it. He then related that John Hay had told him that when the news of the mother's bereavement was given to Lincoln he instructed Hay to write a suitable reply of condolence. This Hay did, and handed it to Lincoln. Lincoln was so surprised that Hay had so perfectly captured his style of composition that he had the letter exactly as Hay wrote it sent to the mother as coming from himself.

That is Mr. Page's story to Lady Strafford of Lincoln's famous letter, and I suppose he was a man who knew what he was talking about; nor do I suppose that Hay was the man to say what was untrue. I feel sure that I have given this as Lady Strafford gave it to me, and as she is still in the land of the living she can corroborate it if the matter interests you sufficiently.

Although there may be no doubt concerning the integrity of Butler, Morley, or Page, the story has not likely gained in accuracy by reason of being kept for so many years in the fallible memories of men. John Hay, we may admit, told Morley that he (Hay) had written the letter, but what did he mean when he used the word *wrote?* Did he mean simply that he had *penned* the letter, or that he had *composed* it? There is no doubt in Butler's mind that Morley understood Hay to mean *composed,* but one may wonder whether Hay even tried to make himself completely accurate and clear in this statement, when, as we shall see, he was not so careful on previous occasions when he discussed the authorship of Lincoln's letters.

In a letter written from Paris on September 5, 1866, Hay answered W. H. Herndon's specific inquiry concerning the letters which Lincoln wrote as President, in the following language: "He [Lincoln] wrote very few letters. He did not read one in fifty that he received. At first we tried to bring them to his notice, but at last he gave the whole thing over to me, and signed without reading them the letters I wrote in his name. He wrote perhaps half-a-dozen a week himself—not more."

Executive Mansion
Washington, Nov 21. 1864

To Mrs Bixby, Boston, Mass,
Dear Madam,

I have been shown in the files of the War Department a statement of the Adjutant General of Massachusetts that you are the mother of five sons who have died gloriously on the field of battle. I feel how weak and fruitless must be any word of mine which should attempt to beguile you from the grief of a loss so overwhelming. But I cannot refrain from tendering you the consolation that may be found in the thanks of the republic they died to save. I pray that our Heavenly Father may assuage the anguish of your bereavement, and leave you only the cherished memory of the loved and lost, and the solemn pride that must be yours to have laid so costly a sacrifice upon the altar of freedom.

Yours very sincerely and respectfully,
A. Lincoln

Facsimile of the Bixby Letter, once widely circulated as genuine, but now believed to be a clever forgery of the original which has been lost.

Executive Mansion
Washington, Nov 21, 1864

To Mrs Bixby, Boston, Mass.
      Dear Madam,
                    I have been shown in the files of the War De-
partment a statement of the Adjutant General of
Massachusetts that you are the mother of five sons who have
died gloriously on the field of battle I feel how weak and
fruitless must be any word of mine which should attempt to
beguile you from the grief of a loss so overwhelming But I
cannot refrain from tendering you the consolation that may
be found in the thanks of the republic they died to save I
pray that our Heavenly Father may assuage the anguish of
your bereavement, and leave you only the cherished memory
of the loved and lost, and the solemn pride that must be yours
to have laid so costly a sacrifice upon the altar of freedom
             Yours very sincerely and respectfully

A. Lincoln

Transcription of the Bixby Letter. See facsimile on the facing page.

This statement may be generally true[1]. Perhaps after 1861
Lincoln wrote few letters. It is interesting to note that Hay's estimate of "half-a-dozen a week," whether it be occasionally a little
high or a little low for all the genuine compositions of Lincoln,
amply covers the really significant letters, of which there are rarely
ever that many dated during the same week. There are, however,
several inadequacies and inaccuracies in the statement as a whole.
When Hay states that "he gave the whole thing over to me," he
hardly does justice to Nicolay, who, as numerous manuscripts
show, penned many of Lincoln's letters. Furthermore, when Hay
states that Lincoln "signed without reading them the letters I wrote
in his name," he presumes quite a bit. If he had looked over a
number of such letters as he did pen for Lincoln, he would have
found a number with corrections and emendations written in by
Lincoln before he signed them. Then too, Hay's statement implies

[1]The statement was proved not even "generally true" by publication of *The Collected Works* in 1953.

that all of the letters thus signed by Lincoln were composed by Hay himself. This is demonstrably not the case in the "Letter to General H. W. Halleck," July 29, 1863, which is in phraseology and style distinctly Lincoln's, and is emended and corrected as well as signed in Lincoln's handwriting, though penned by Hay. Some letters Lincoln apparently dictated to Hay, others to Nicolay, and still others to secretaries who relieved and assisted Nicolay and Hay from time to time. And often Lincoln emended them before signing his name. Finally, Hay's statement fails to take into account the many letters he did write in his own person (and in his own handwriting!) and signed with his own name as the President's secretary.

Another interesting example of how loosely Hay used the word *wrote* is contained in two references in his Diary to Lincoln's "Response to a Serenade," November 9, 1864.[2] The first of these is as follows: "The President answered from the window with rather unusual dignity and effect and we came home. (Added later: 'I wrote the speech and sent it to Hanscum.')" This statement might readily be misinterpreted, if detached from its setting, to mean that Hay had composed the Response, when as a matter of fact he merely *penned* what Lincoln *said,* perhaps polishing a bit according to his own light. It is interesting that this speech as printed in the *Complete Works* is far inferior to the other "Response" of November 10, 1864, which Lincoln took the trouble to write out himself. Hay's second comment is as follows: "The speeches of the President at the last two serenades are very highly spoken of. The first I wrote after the fact, to prevent the 'loyal Pennsylvanians' getting a swing at it themselves."

Furthermore, it is a curiously interesting fact that of the only two letters which Hay states in his Diary that he *wrote* (implying *composed*) one is omitted from the *Complete Works* (1894) and the other is so utterly without personal style and without significance as to be of little worth. Of the first of these two letters Hay notes: "Today I induced the President to sign a letter to Col. Rowland approving his proposed National Rifle Corps. I think

[2]Hay also misdated it November 9 in *The Complete Works,* when it was actually delivered on November 8.

Rowland himself rather a humbug but his idea is a good one." This "induced the President to sign" sounds far different from the tone of Hay's statement to Herndon and probably indicates far more accurately the limit to which Hay's authority and function as secretary extended. The second of these letters is the "Letter to G. H. Boker," October 26, 1863, which may be consulted in the *Complete Works* as an example of the colorless and inconsequential style of Hay's compositions as secretary to the President, most of which Hay signed in his own name with the notation "A.P.S." appended.

If one were to take Hay's statement to Herndon as complete and accurate, one would get just such an impression as Nicholas Murray Butler records when he states categorically that Hay wrote "almost all" of the personal letters. In a letter to the author, Dr. Butler gives the following explanation of his statement: "All I can say in response to your question is that it was Robert T. Lincoln himself, Abraham Lincoln's son, who told me that it was the custom of John Hay to write in the name of Lincoln all letters of a non-political kind and that he, Hay, imitated Lincoln's handwriting admirably. Robert T. Lincoln certainly knew what he was taking about." If one could agree with Dr. Butler's belief in Robert T. Lincoln's authority, there would be no argument, but unfortunately no evidence has been uncovered that will substantiate this belief. Perhaps, after all, Robert T. Lincoln "knew" only what John Hay had told him, and what Hay had told him was probably much the same as the statement to Herndon.

In regard to the specific question of Hay's ability to imitate Lincoln's handwriting, one must doubt Dr. Butler's belief. There is still some study to be done on this matter, and there is the bare possibility that a number of letters among those included in the *Complete Works* of Lincoln may prove to have been written by Hay in imitation of Lincoln's handwriting. That there can be no large number, however, is a foregone conclusion. In the first place, Hay would not have had time to painstakingly imitate Lincoln's scrawl in any number of letters without entailing an enormous amount of labor beyond his usual duties as secretary. The business of imitating handwriting *(forging* is the less polite word for it) is

no easy task for an expert, and Hay certainly had his hands full
without undertaking such an utterly useless task. Secondly, the
author has never seen among the several hundred Lincoln
manuscripts which he has studied either in the original or in
photostatic copy any letter in which Lincoln's handwriting could
have been imitated by Hay, without demonstrating beyond all doubt
that he was a very poor imitator. There are numerous letters which
are not in Lincoln's handwriting, but they are clearly in Hay's
handwriting, or Nicolay's, or that of one of the other scribes who
did copy work in the White House. Furthermore, the author has
queried a number of authorities who know a great deal more about
Lincoln manuscripts than he does, and not one of them has ever
admitted having seen such a letter. In only one instance known
to the author is there even a possibility that Hay might have been
attempting to imitate Lincoln's handwriting, and that is the
"Telegram to Mrs. Lincoln," December 21, 1864, which is in the
Brown University Library. That Hay penned this telegram seems
certain. Perhaps he was trying to imitate Lincoln's scrawl in order
to get the telegram sent free, though that would not have been necessary. In any event, the telegram is not in Lincoln's hand, and
if it is an imitation it is an exceedingly poor one that anybody can
detect by comparing it to genuine Lincoln manuscripts.

In another instance Hay had an opportunity to imitate Lincoln's
handwriting when there would have been a real need for it. In the
"Letter to Henry W. Hoffman," October 10, 1864, Lincoln
originally wrote the phrase "better posted." After Lincoln has finished the letter Hay carefully scraped out the word *posted,* as he
records in his Diary, and wrote in the word *informed*. Here, if
anywhere, Hay had reason to imitate "in well-nigh perfect fashion"
Lincoln's script, and yet the manuscript clearly attests that the word
is in Hay's penmanship. In short, if there is any evidence that Hay
ever did imitate Lincoln's handwriting, it is still in hiding.

Of the numerous letters which are in Hay's handwriting, or
Nicolay's for that matter, the only criteria which will serve in most
cases to determine the President's composition from that of the
secretary are those of style, characteristic expressions, and content.
Such criteria are not infallible, but they serve better than one who

has never studied Lincoln's style might suppose. Regardless of the handwriting, there can be no doubt that Lincoln composed such letters as the "Letter to James C. Conkling," August 26, 1863, or the "Letter to General Rosecrans," November 19, 1864.

We may conclude concerning Hay's function as secretary to President Lincoln, therefore, that Dr. Butler is probably incorrect in stating that Hay could and did imitate Lincoln's handwriting, but certainly incorrect in the opinion that the imitation was "well-nigh perfect." Further, we may conclude that Dr. Butler is correct in his belief that as one of Lincoln's secretaries Hay wrote a good many letters, but incorrect in believing that many of the better letters were composed by Hay. Concerning Hay's statement to Herndon, we may conclude that it is inadequate, inaccurate, and incorrect, in certain particulars.

Returning to the question of just what Hay may have told John Morley, one wonders whether in the statement that "he had himself written the Bixby letter" Hay meant any more than he did in the statement to Herndon. Of course, the whole story as told by Dr. Butler is mere hearsay at third hand, carried in the memory of John Morely for seven years, and in the memory of Dr. Butler for twenty-eight years, but the distinguished character of the bearers of this gossip must lend it a certain credence. One may reflect , especially in view of Hay's letter to Herndon, that "to err is human." If we assume that Morley remembered verbatim what Hay told him, then we may assume that Hay used the word *write* in some form when discussing his own participation in the Bixby letter. But, did he mean that he wrote it from Lincoln's dictation, or copied it from Lincoln's first draft, or that he composed it entirely himself and submitted it for Lincoln's signature, or that he composed it and penned it and signed it in imitation of Lincoln's handwriting?

It is obvious from Dr. Butler's account that the occasion of Morley's discussion of the letter with Hay was brought on by the facsimile which Morley had seen in the White House. It is likewise obvious that Hay meant to inform Morley that he (Hay) knew the facsimile to be a forgery. In this case his use of the word *write* would not necessarily imply that he had composed the letter. As the Reverend Mr. Jackson tells the story, of course, it is elaborately detailed that Hay meant to claim the composition as well as the penning of the letter. One cannot help wondering, however, whether Jackson's version as given by E. V. Lucas is not so largely a matter of British tea-table gossip that it should be entirely disregarded. It seems that it may even be a garbled account of the same story told by Dr. Butler. In any event, both stories are mere hearsay, and, though they raise questions, they answer none.

When, and only when, the manuscript of the Bixby letter is produced can we hope to sift the whole truth from the whole untruth in these claims. Since the original has been sought diligently for more than half a century, one must doubt that it is now in existence. In view of these circumstances, we can only rely on the circumstantial evidence surrounding the composition of the letter and the internal evidence of style in the letter, both of which point conclusively to Lincoln's authorship.

The circumstances which occasioned the writing of the letter make it seem improbable that Lincoln would have "instructed Hay to write a suitable reply." Governor Andrew of Massachusetts sent the supposed facts in the Bixby case to the War Department and specifically stated in his endorsement, "I really wish a letter might be written her by the President of the United States, taking notice of a noble mother of five dead heroes so well deserved." The case received the approval of various officials in the War Department and was referred to President Lincoln. After the letter was written, it was sent to the Adjutant-General of Massachusetts, William Schouler, an old acquaintance of Lincoln's, who had first called Mrs. Bixby's case to the attention of Governor Andrew and who delivered the letter to Mrs. Bixby in person and released a copy of it to the press. It is conceivable that Lincoln might have dismissed such a request as Governor Andrew's by turning it over to one of his secretaries, but in view of his practice in obliging numerous other requests for testimonials, letters of introduction, etc., it seems strange that he should have dismissed an opportunity such as this. It was just the sort of opportunity for publicly recognizing patriotism that Lincoln gladly seized in other instances, and in addition was an opportunity to oblige his old friend Schouler and the governor of Massachusetts.

Finally, the internal evidence of style seems to mark the letter as Lincoln's. It has been claimed that Hay could easily have imitated Lincoln's style. Perhaps he could have, but the author has yet to see in any of the letters which Hay wrote as Lincoln's secretary, including those discussed here, or in any of those that are published in the biographies of Hay, any evidence that Hay could or did imitate Lincoln's style or that of any other writer. Some of Hay's poetry is imitative (pretty sadly!), but his letters are invariably in his own peculiar idiom and are wholly unlike Lincoln's.

If the student will read aloud the best of Lincoln's lyrical passages in the "Fairewell Address," "Gettysburg Address," or "Second Inaugural Address" and then read aloud the "Letter to Mrs. Bixby," he will find it exceedingly difficult to believe that anyone other than Lincoln composed such sentences as: "I feel how weak and fruitless must be any word of mine which should attempt to beguile you from the grief of a loss so overwhelming . . . I pray that our Heavenly Father may assuage the anguish of your bereavement, and leave you only the cherished memory of the loved and lost, and the solemn pride that must be yours, to have laid so costly a sacrifice upon the altar of freedom." Then if one wishes to be further assured, let him procure a copy of Thayer's *Life and Letters of John Hay* and read a few of Hay's compositions.

In conclusion it may be said that discovery of evidence in the form of *demonstrable examples* of Hay's imitation of Lincoln's handwriting and style would bolster Dr. Butler's exceedingly weak claim. At present there seems to be nothing to it. Out of the welter of improbabilities in the claim one can see a single logical possibility that would embrace most of the evidence at its face value. John Hay may have told John Morley that he (Hay) wrote the Bixby letter, meaning merely that he penned it either from Lincoln's dictation or from a first draft, and submitted it to Lincoln for signature. But why, in this event, would Hay have sworn Morley to secrecy? One concludes by wondering whether there may have been in John Hay a touch of mild chicanery that permitted him to enjoy with a knowing smile the perpetuation of the forged facsimiles, so long as the popular sale and distribution of those facsimiles added to the fame and glory of his idol.

AS ONE SOUTHERNER TO ANOTHER

Concerning Lincoln
*and the Declaration of Independence**

Is it possible for human beings to live permanently at peace and in amity, and at the same time hold absolute beliefs totally divergent and conflicting when translated into human activity? An article in *The South Atlantic Quarterly* (October 1942) raises again this question which seems to me to lie in one form or another at the root of all human conflict. If more than eighty years after the Civil War Mr. Archibald Rutledge, "the Poet Laureate of South Carolina," and those Southerners who believe with him, can still find it profitable to twist words for the sake of justifying a dead mythology, and, presumably, can believe what they say, what hope have we that our contemporaries in Japan and Germany can be persuaded, even at the point of a bayonet, to abandon the beliefs which motivate them in this present conflict? "The South not only *believed* her cause was just; but what she believed to be true *was* true," says Mr. Rutledge. If the quality of truth is absolute and determined merely by the willingness of people to believe in it, then the South indeed fought and lost the Civil War in vain, and the Union, in some measure, lost in winning. Unfortunately, the fight, which Mr. Rutledge is carrying on merely verbally after all these years, is still being carried on politically against the entire principle

*The South Atlantic Quarterly, January 1943.

of human equality, and when Mr. Rutledge sneeringly designates a portion of the Declaration of Independence as "the idiotic sentence that all men are created equal," he reveals the well from which certain Southern politicians draw the tainted water they are pouring into the cups of Southern democracy in their fight against political equality for the disfranchised white man as well as the Negro in the Southern states. None of these men, apparently, believes in what was to Abraham Lincoln the essential "proposition" to which this country was dedicated at its birth, and each in his way works his intellectual machinery overtime to rationalize a fetish of "white supremacy" that is indeed psychopathic.

I propose to discuss the tenability of belief in the "idiotic sentence" which Lincoln held and so memorably expressed, and which is to a large part of the people of this globe not an idiotic phraseology devoid of practical sense, but the statement of an ideal toward which practical human effort can and must be directed. Before I undertake this, however, I wish to analyze, for the benefit of those who may think that Mr. Rutledge and his ilk are the guardians of absolute veracity, certain ideas and words which seem to me to display a singular disregard for even relative truth.

To begin with, Mr. Rutledge's main purpose in this article seems to be to damn Lincoln's effort to preserve the Union as the machination of a shrewd politician and demagogue who seized an opportunity to trick the South out of her divine right of secession and to consolidate his own power. Mr. Rutledge quotes the famous passage from Lincoln's "Mexican War Speech" of 1848, that "Any people anywhere, being inclined and having the power, have the right to rise up and shake off the existing government and form a new one that suits them better," as proof that Lincoln regarded "*secession* as a vital privilege of any people." Perhaps there are those who would quibble that *secession* and *revolution* are not precisely the same thing, but Mr. Rutledge insists that they were, and I do not believe Lincoln himself would care to argue much about that. I do believe, however, that Lincoln would insist that his phrase "having the power" be given full weight. At no time, so far as I know, did Lincoln ever concede that the South had the power, for he saw clearly that only a small minority of the nation's people were undertaking, not so much to "shake off the existing government," but rather to refuse to obey it. In other words, secession *began* not as revolution, but as rebellion. Perhaps it *became* revolution, but that is a matter of small consequence here.

Up to the time when armed force was employed at Fort Sumter, Lincoln insisted that all issues could, so far as he was concerned, be settled by ballots rather than bullets, and was even then reluctant to employ the latter until such action was forced upon him. Then, of course, it became purely a question of whether the South or the Union *had the power*. From Lincoln's point of view, secession was a mistake because it did not have the power to separate from, much less to overthrow, the existing government, and this point of view he took pains to develop in his "First Inaugural Address." But when Southern leaders blindly insisted that they did have the power, the only proof of the bloody pudding was in the eating. There was not, as Mr. Rutledge implies, any notable shift in Lincoln's fundamental belief in a people's right to overthrow the existing government, if they had the power. And I am sure that Mr. Rutledge knows that a considerable portion of the people of the South never believed in the power of their states to secede.

There is still another factor concerning Lincoln's belief in revolution which Mr. Rutledge conveniently overlooks, perhaps because of its being connected with the "idiotic sentence" in the Declaration of Independence. Anyone who knows Lincoln's political philosophy, or will take the trouble to study it, can verify that his belief in revolution was specifically the belief which Thomas Jefferson formulated in the Declaration of Independence. Jefferson's words ought not to require quoting, but one wonders if the following words are familiar:

> We hold these truths to be self-evident, that all men are cre-
> ated equal, that they are endowed by their Creator with cer-
> tain unalienable Rights, that among these are Life, Liberty
> and the pursuit of Happiness— That to secure these rights,
> Governments are instituted among Men, deriving their just
> powers from the consent of the governed,—That whenever any
> Form of Government becomes destructive of these ends, it is
> the Right of the People to alter or abolish it, and to institute
> new Government, laying its foundation on such principles, and

organizing its powers in such form, as to them shall seem
most likely to effect their Safety and Happiness.

This was the right of revolution which Jefferson claimed and which
Lincoln recognized. Lincoln admitted the right of a people to revolt
against government "destructive of these ends." Perhaps Mr.
Rutledge thinks that the Union was "destructive of these ends" and
that therefore secession was justified, but he is patently twisting
Lincoln's words when he contends that Lincoln thought so. From
Lincoln's point of view, it was not the Union, but the government
of the state of South Carolina, that was "destructive of these ends."
To claim support for secession in Lincoln's early statement of belief
in revolution is sheer sophistry.

Then Mr. Rutledge goes over again the old, old question of responsibility for the employment of force. "It was Lincoln who
made the South secede; it was he who, by dispatching a formidable
fleet against Charleston, compelled South Carolina to fire on the
flag." It is amusing to see in the pitiable little collection of ships
sent to reinforce and provision Fort Sumter the "formidable fleet"
of Mr. Rutledge's sentence, but what can one say about the
psychology behind it? No doubt some descendant of Mr. Tojo will
be able eighty years hence to reason with himself that the pitiable
forces which reinforced so belatedly the Philippines, Guam, and our
other Pacific outposts "compelled" Japan to attack them. Without
making invidious comparisons, there is just this much worth in the
analogy—in both instances the President of the United States resolved to attempt to keep what the armed forces of the United
States held, and to give no inch further under the threat of
consequent war. Both Lincoln and Roosevelt gave notice by the
act of reinforcement that they did not propose to back down without a fight. One may question the ultimate wisdom of either action,
but one cannot reasonably maintain that the man who stood his
ground and reinforced his position was the aggressor, simply because
he refused to get out. Mr. Rutledge implies that Lincoln could have
backed down, but he does not seem to recognize that Jefferson
Davis might also have had that possibility. Here is the crux of the
matter: when two political forces are at loggerheads, each with
armed force at its back, armed force is the only solution to the

impasse   unless one is willing to back down. Backing down, or
"appeasement" as it has come to be known in our day, solves no
problem   and brings no peace when the motivations of the two
political forces are absolutely in conflict. To Lincoln the Union was
worth maintaining even by force of arms, to Jefferson Davis the
Confederacy was worth it—only the power, and with it the belief
of the two opposing factions could decide the issue. As Lincoln
had the power, so I believe he had the belief which alone can sustain
power until, and after, the culmination of victory.

There is insufficient space here to attempt to refute all of Mr.
Rutledge's misrepresentations of fact. One example should suffice
to illustrate his almost psychopathic determination to distort data
to fit his purpose of damning Lincoln and justifying Southern
political leadership:

> The South had no reason to doubt then what is now generally
> accepted by the impartial historian as a fact: that Lincoln con-
> tributed to the fund which John Brown was raising for his
> Harper's Ferry venture. Horace Scott Knappe, in his *History
> of the Wabash Valley,* thus relates the circumstances: "A
> wild-looking man came into a store at Ashland, Ohio, where
> H.S.Knappe had taken his son, Trivette, to buy a pair of
> shoes, and asked for the proprietor. Trivette pointed to the
> desk in the back of the store. The wild man, who was John
> Brown, said to the proprietor that he was raising money to
> buy pikes to arm slaves. The proprietor said he was in favor
> of freeing the slaves, but that he was not in favor of any
> violence. John Brown, pointing to the paper, said, 'Why,
> look here!' And there was Abraham Lincoln, of Springfield,
> Illinois, on the list for $100."

Now, any fair-minded reader must see that the little episode as given
by Mr. Knappe is merely a recounting of an old man's story, a bit of
local folklore in all probability, and that there is no justification for
stretching this into the statement that "it is now generally accepted
by the impartial historian as a fact." On the contrary, not even Mr.
Knappe would seem to imply that the possible fact that Lincoln's
name appeared in a list of contributors would justify such a claim as
Mr. Rutledge makes. The fact is that there is no reputable evidence
that Lincoln ever contributed, and there is quite sufficient evidence

that he did not (cf. "Letter to J. C. Lee," Lincoln, *Works*, VI, 64; and Karsner, *John Brown, Terrible Saint*, p. 193). Lincoln's attitude toward John Brown is so pointed in its application to secessionists that perhaps his own statement of it should be considered:

> Old John Brown thought slavery wrong, as we do; he attacked slavery contrary to law, and it availed him nothing before the law that he thought himself right. He has just been hanged for treason against the State of Virginia; and we cannot object, though he agreed with us in calling slavery wrong. Now if you undertake to destroy the Union contrary to law, if you commit treason against the United States, our duty will be to deal with you as John Brown has been dealt with. We shall try to do our duty.

Surely Mr. Rutledge must have overlooked this statement in his blind wish to justify secession in Lincoln's own words.

What is the source of the contemptuous attitude which Mr. Rutledge manifests toward Lincoln and toward the Declaration of Independence because of that most significant of phrases — "the idiotic sentence that all men are created equal" — unless it is a psychopathic desire, frustrated but potent, to rule by virtue of birth, distinction of race, family, name, or any of the other shibboleths by which his ilk would test the right of men to rule others? Some of the best minds of the South have been frustrated for eighty years by this decadent medievalism which inhibits Southern political progress, and although the last decade has seen a notable advance in the social philosophy of a large majority of Southern political leaders, there seems just recently to be a recrudescence of the old, old fear and hatred which may split the Democratic party, and thereby so impair the United States in its struggle for democratic principles all over the world, that victory of arms over fascism may be empty indeed. It is manifest in the pronouncements and actions of such men as ex-Governor Dixon of Alabama, ex-Governor Talmage of Georgia, and Senator Bilbo of Mississippi, leaders of the "white supremacy" phalanx among Southern Democrats, who are opposed not only to repeal of the poll tax, but to all New Deal social legislation and policy which gives anything like an equality of treatment to the Southern Negro.

Is the philosophy of American democracy, including the idea

that "all men are created equal"—which we may be sure is waging as great a part in the present war as the General Sherman tank or the Flying Fortress, and without which our nation would be spiritually bankrupt— a philosophy that some Americans cannot accept as applying to Negro, Hindu, or Chinese? Even Mr. Rutledge, I think, might find it profitable to consider Lincoln's rationalization of faith in democracy as it is stated over and over in his works and as it is so potently and beautifully worded in the "Gettysburg Address."

Above all, Lincoln believed that "all men are created equal," in the only way that a mind as coldly logical as his could believe it. Just how he believed it is indicated by his use of the word *proposition* in the "Gettysburg Address." This word perhaps provides a stumbling block for some readers, and yet it was the inevitable word for Lincoln. By his own account he had "studied and nearly mastered" Euclid, and hence we may be sure that he used the word in the logician's sense: a statement to be debated, verified, proved. Thus democracy, as an active living thing, meant to Lincoln the verification or proving of the proposition to which its very existence had in the beginning been dedicated. Eighty-seven years had gone into the proving, the Civil War had come at a critical stage in the argument, the Union armies had won an immediate victory at Gettysburg, and the affirmation that "all men are created equal" was still a living rather than a dead creed. It was still a proposition open to argument and inviting proof, but not on any account one that had already been proved. The further proof was for "us the living, to be dedicated here to the unfinished work which they who fought here have thus far so nobly advanced." It was thus that Lincoln believed in democracy as a living thing striving toward accomplishment, and not either as an accomplished fact or a meaningless form of words incapable of proof. He had said some years before, "the Declaration of Independence contemplated the progressive improvement in the condition of all men." And again, "I say in relation to the principle that all men are created equal let it be as nearly reached as we can." Early in life he had recognized the practical truth phrased by Mr. Julian Huxley in an essay which appears in the same issue of *The South Atlantic Quarterly* with Mr. Rutledge's: ". . . human individuals are the democratic yardstick. The satisfaction of the needs of individual human beings is one side of the picture; the other is their free and active participation in the life of the society to which they belong." Down through the years, again and again, there had appeared in Lincoln's writings this central concept of progressive improvement in the condition of all mankind, measured by the well-being and freedom of the individual, and it guided not only his war aims but also his peace aims. At Gettysburg he merely took the occasion to reaffirm in memorable words his belief in striving on.

So it was no accident that, as he thought on the past life of American democracy, his words and allusions began, in his very first sentence, calling to mind a haunting phrase out of the Old Testament: "the days of our years are three score and ten," and with it the symbolic act of consecration traditionally observed of old by Hebrew and Christian, dedicating their children to the service of God. And thus he wrote, "Fourscore and seven years ago our fathers brought forth on this continent a new nation, conceived in liberty, and dedicated to the proposition that all men are created equal."

But the "new nation" had in eighty-seven years grown old. It was already thinking too much in terms of the past. The *proposition* to which the Founding Fathers had dedicated it must not mean anything new. Although the proposition has specifically stated "all men," it had not meant ALL men; to some it had meant only white men, and to them it must not mean ALL men. The laws of the nation were hardening; its vision was dim. The war had come, and with it the death of that old nation and the birth of a new. Its death was at Gettysburg symbolized in the graves of those "who here gave their lives that that nation might live." Its life, too was at Gettysburg symbolized in Lincoln's audience: "It is for us the living, rather, to be dedicated here. . . . "

The key words of the "Gettysburg Address" are three simple ones, two pronouns and an adverb: *they, we, here*. With his usual practice Lincoln repeated them, emphasizing again and again, what he wanted his audience to carry away—"It is for us the living to be dedicated here to the unfinished work which they who fought here have thus far so nobly advanced."

It was because the Union meant this to Lincoln that he could not recognize the right of secession. Alexander Stephens, the Vice President of the Confederacy and the only Southerner who knew Lincoln personally and his political philosophy well enough to understand his motive, said that with Lincoln the Union rose in sentiment "to the sublimity of a religious mysticism." The truth of this comment is borne out by the poetic symbolism of the "Gettysburg Address." The Union was for Lincoln the symbol of living democracy, which sought to verify the basic principle of its existence, a democracy yet to be realized in perfect form, but still "the last best hope of earth." To have recognized the right of secessionists to destroy that Union would have been for Lincoln completely incompatible with his basic faith.

It is perhaps something more than an interesting coincidence that some fourscore years have again elapsed since the Civil War began, and we find our nation engaged in a great global war, "a people's war" in which the principle of democracy, "government of the people, by the people, for the people," must again be kept alive by heroic effort. Surely we must recognize today that what Mr. Huxley calls "the democratic yardstick" is one and the same with Lincoln's "last best hope of earth." In this we have our greatest tradition, established by Jefferson and his fellow signers of the Declaration of Independence, and given added dignity by the profound belief of such men as Abraham Lincoln and Franklin D. Roosevelt. It is a tradition of men, not things; of belief, not systems; of ideas, not forms; of change, not status quo. Only in this has our past a living meaning for the present, and the test of the noblest words Jefferson ever wrote or Lincoln ever avowed lies today in what they mean to us "the living." It remains to be seen who will rule our country in the future, and who will give to the government of the world its principle of guidance, but we may hope that to them as to Thomas Jefferson and Abraham Lincoln the proposition that "all men are created equal" may be something more than Mr. Rutledge's "idiotic sentence."

LINCOLN IN POLITICS, 1948*

That Lincoln is still in politics is evident to anyone who has kept up with the political speeches, editorials, and feature stories during the recent campaign. Being a subscriber to a national news-clipping service, for the purpose of keeping informed on Lincoln manuscripts which are occasionally found in safety deposit boxes and attic trunks, the editor has been deluged in recent months, with items having to do with Lincoln's part in "the present crisis." Such bounty of unwanted news items suggested the summary that follows.

General comments from editors, columnists, and feature writers gave the customary review of political campaigns of the past, the 1856 and 1860 campaigns of course playing a large part in the journalists' effort to condition the public for extravagance and pageantry, if not for violence. One columnist recalled that many delegates to conventions "used to carry guns and knives," and that while Seward's followers staged fancy parades, Lincoln's managers "packed the convention hall with rooters."[1] Another writer noted that the Grand Old Party was telling the common people it "has had their interest at heart ever since the days of honest Abe," and

---

*The Abraham Lincoln Quarterly, December 1948.

[1]Alexander George, Kalamazoo, Michigan, Gazette, June 20. Citations of sources do not mean necessarily that the article or editorial originated in the paper cited. "Boiler-plate" editorials, unacknowledged quotations and excerpts, as well as syndicated articles, are the rule in contemporary journalism, and not an article in a hundred came to our desk as the individual contribution of the paper from which it was clipped.

129

that "the Presidential Follies of 1948 won't be too bad."[2] Writers reflected on the significance of the fact that the names of patron saints Lincoln and Jefferson were on every political tongue, and several commented that one would be led to think them up for election again.[3] Other writers attempted to counteract cynicism by insisting that it is "politicians who keep democracy alive," and that contemporary candidates are not the first to speak as liberals to liberals and as conservatives to conservatives—"Abraham Lincoln did the same thing—only more so. He was an ardent liberal in the West. . . but went to New York. . . and was so conservative he practically repudiated his western doctrine."[4] Such is American history as purveyed by journalists. A widely printed editorial encouraged readers to remember that "In spite of talk, next president will be okay. . . . Abraham Lincoln is almost canonized now but almost the kindest thing said by his opponents in 1860 was that he was an uncouth, semi-literate backwoodsman with a flair for obscene stories."[5] Another recalled that Lincoln was reported to have said, "If I were to try to read, much less answer, all the attacks made on me, this shop might as well be closed for any other business."[6]

Dorothy Thompson, recalling that "Lincoln. . . received his nomination in deep melancholy," wondered why candidates were so avid for nomination in 1948.[7] Other writers reflected that some of Lincoln's humility would grace the seekers for office in 1948,[8] or lamented that "the kind of liberalism so easily recognized in Jefferson and Lincoln. . . has an artificial look in today's political circus."[9]

A mingling of sarcasm and humor is apparent in comments on the techniques of modern campaigning. The ghost writers who "produce. . . a large part of the torrent of words" can never "tug

[2]Daniel Sands, Ft. Smith, Arkansas, *Times Record,* September 5.
[3]Washington, Missouri, *Missourian,* July 8; Arthur Edson, Associated Press, June 26.
[4]Malcolm W. Bingay, Kansas City, Missouri, *Star* (et al.), July 11.
[5]Monroe, Louisiana, *News-State* (et al.), July 2.
[6]Union Town, Pennsylvania, *Independent,* April 30.
[7]"On the Record," June 18.
[8]W. E. A., Burlington, Vermont, *Free Press,* September 11.
[9]Brattleboro, Vermont, *Reformer,* June 29.

at the heartstrings of America more effectively than 'Honest Abe' "[10] Newsreels "What would Lincoln . . . . have thought of that?"[11] Television—"Could Lincoln have made it with television?"[12] No, "Lincoln would have flopped on television."[13] Considering "the unhappy appearance of Clare Luce on video," another writer asked, "What chance would Abraham Lincoln . . . have enjoyed under the handicap of this new campaign apparatus?"[14] Surveying such a campaign, one editor was moved to exclaim, "Gosh, all this and the circus, too, next week!"[15]

As was to be expected the Republican party made what use it could of Lincoln. For the convention hall there was the huge reproduction—the Gardner photograph made on November 15, 1863 (Meserve 59). Governor Dwight Green of Illinois in his keynote address quoted "of the people, by the people" with implications of Republicanism's 1948 discipleship. The Associated Press noted that Governor Green's quotation "was the third time that Lincoln's famous words were echoed on the platform today."[16] The Republican platform quoted solemnly from Lincoln's Annual Message to Congress, December 1, 1862, "The dogmas of the quiet past are inadequate to the stormy present. The occasion is piled high with difficulty and we must rise with the occasion. As our case is new, so we must think anew and act anew."

In commenting on Governor Green's keynote address, Arthur "Bugs" Baer observed that it might have gone further in quoting and paraphrasing the Gettysburg Address by saying " 'Sixteen years ago our forefathers' and so on until evaporated."[17] Walter Lippmann opined concerning the platform's quotation of Lincoln that it was "unusual in view of the tenor of the Reece, Green, Hoover, and Martin orations"[18] Within a few weeks Republican editors were beginning to wonder if, perhaps, the implication of

[10]Larston D. Farrar, Kansas City, Missouri, *Times,* September 10.
[11]Cheyenne, Wyoming, *Eagle,* September 21.
[12]Arthur Edson, Associated Press, June 26.
[13]Malcolm W. Bingay, Omaha, Nebraska, *Evening World Herald* (et al.), July 19.
[14]Ray Tucker, Rapid City, South Dakota, *Journal* (et al.), June 26.
[15]Phoenix, Arizona, *Times,* September 17.
[16]June 21.
[17]King Features Syndicate, August 4.
[18]"Today and Tomorrow," June 24.

the Lincoln quotation might be true. One observed, somewhat startled, that "No greater fulfillment of such a promise ever came in United States history than 16 years ago with the accession of Franklin D. Roosevelt. . . . Is Governor Dewey—we are assuming his election—going to startle the country with a similar New-New Deal?"[19] Billy Rose confidently predicted that when Dewey "walks into the room which Abe Lincoln once used as an office, the new president may very well wonder why one man is remembered and another forgotten. . . . Marse Tom is going to carry the ball way left of center."[20] Eleanor Roosevelt replied that this "could be said of any president. . . . Any president who hopes to become a figure in history. . . will have to calculate today what interests and policies will give him that position. The bankers won't do it. The industrialists won't do it. It can be done only when a man evokes a response in the heart of the average man and woman."[21]

Looking back on the Republican, the Democratic, and the Progressive conventions, one editor suggested that politicians of all parties "file away for recalling in 1952 the entire nominating speech in behalf of Abraham Lincoln at the Chicago GOP Convention in 1860. On that occasion, Norman Judd said: 'I desire on behalf of the delegation from Illinois to put in nomination as a candidate for president of the United States, Abraham Lincoln, of Illinois.' Just 26 words. But Lincoln, it may be noted, was nominated and elected."[22]

Following the Republican convention, there seems to have been little inclination on the part of the Republican candidates for president and vice president to quote from or refer to Lincoln, but editors and feature writers made their best effort to keep Lincoln in the campaign.

Governor Warren's speech at Springfield, Illinois, was naturally an exception. Maintaining that "Abraham Lincoln would be greatly disturbed by the elements of dissention [sic] and confusion among our people which he would find today," Governor Warren stipulated that "we want to bring back within our country a kind

[19]Gloucester, Massachusetts, *Times* (Independent Republican), July 12.
[20]"Pitching Horseshoes," July 14.
[21]"My Day," July 16.
[22]Birmingham, Alabama, *Age-Herald,* August 2.

of good feeling to which the patron saint of our party was devoted," and maintained that Governor Dewey was a man after Lincoln's own mold.[23] The ribbing which this speech took in the press from coast to coast was stupendous. But that Dewey was Lincoln's legitimate heir was a favorite, even if occasionally an extravagant, claim. "Not since Abraham Lincoln has such a voice been heard in this land," editorialized William Loeb.[24] Dewey's moustache, "the first facial foliage in 35 years" on a presidential candidate, went right back to Lincoln for authentic Republican precedent.[25] An old timer who had voted for Lincoln was photographed shaking hands with Dewey and pledging his vote.[26]

Of course, when the Dewey—Stassen debate was taking place, all good Republican papers were reminded of the Lincoln—Douglas debates, but at least one dissident opined that "The Dewey—Stassen debate was of no particular consequence. The subject for debate was not earth-shaking in importance and debaters were not particularly steamed up," and admitted, "We fought desperately to stay awake."[27] Yet when Dewey called Stassen to conference after the convention, the event again recalled a Lincoln angle: "The nearest parallel is to be found in the case of Abraham Lincoln. When elected he put his chief rivals for the nomination into his cabinet."[28] One citizen, Sigmund Pollack, found a means to place on record his uncertainty of Dewey's Lincolnesque stature; he picketed the White House bearing a sign which read "Is that man Dewey fit to sit where Lincoln sat?"[29]

Long before the Democratic convention assembled in Philadelphia's convention hall (minus the portrait of Lincoln), the press had been prophesying further development of the historical analogy between the Democratic party in 1860 and in 1948. It was recalled almost daily that division among Democrats had elected Lincoln in 1860, but it was likewise noted that, the South being

[23] Associated Press (et al.), August 19.
[24] Burlington, Vermont, *News* (et al.) June 25.
[25] Arthur Edson, Associated Press, June 29.
[26] Detroit *Free Press*, May 7.
[27] David V. Felts, Decatur, Illinois, *Herald*, May 19.
[28] Boston *Globe*, July 21.
[29] United Press, August 11.

what it was in 1948, there was no likelihood of avoiding the similar fission over a similar issue with its roots in racism. Hardly a columnist or an editor failed to point up the parallel, and numerous news stories sent over the wires of all news services were slanted to the historic parallel. Out of this deluge of copy, one gleans President Truman's similarity to Lincoln in his stand on civil rights on the one hand, and his similarity to Stephen A. Douglas in losing the South on the other. And on all hands the press portrayed the GOP as exulting over the fierce conflict in the ranks of an erstwhile invincible opposition.

Senator Barkley's "old time eloquence" brought rousing cheers when he took notice of the Republican platform's quotation from Lincoln and recalled that "This is the precise description of the conditions which faced this country 16 years ago, when the Democratic party accepted the responsibility of charting a new course." According to the Senator, the Republicans had nothing new to offer, and in his opinion, "Republican politicians and leaders have not been closer to Lincoln in two generations than to quote him."[30] Parenthetically, as has already been noted, even Republican papers began within a few weeks, after Dewey's campaign speeches were well under way, to wonder if indeed the platform quotation were not an unsuspected prophecy. Representative Sam Rayburn followed Barkley's lead by charging that the Republican party "has been penny-wise and pound foolish. . . ever since the party of Abraham Lincoln was hijacked by Joe Grundy and the Pennsylvania Association of Manufacturers."[31] Commenting on the Democratic allusions to Lincoln, Walter Kiernan dryly observed that "the Democrats spoke well of Lincoln. . . . They're not against him or any other Republican who has been dead as long."[32]

The remoteness of the Republican party's interest in the common man and liberal legislation remained a favorite theme with Democratic party candidates and editors throughout the campaign. Typical is the following editorial comment: "With the exception

[30]Associated Press, July 13.
[31]Associated Press, July 14.
[32]Salt Lake City, Utah, *Salt Lake Telegram* (et al.), July 15.

of the Theodore Roosevelt administration. . . . the Republican party has done naught, since Abe Lincoln, but play into the hands of Wall Street financialism. . . ."[33] In his speech at Springfield, Illinois, President Truman likewise voiced the opinion that the Republican party had "departed from the fundamental principles" of Abraham Lincoln. "The masters of the Republican party today would have been the bitter enemies of Lincoln in his time, just as they are the enemies of his principles today."[34] The President had had occasion to hark back to Lincoln earlier, when he alluded to the campaign as "the most important. . . since the Lincoln-Douglas debates."[35] Although the Republican press endorsed the analogy in the Dewey-Stassen debate, Truman's love of historical analogy brought considerable patronizing or sarcasm. One editor tut-tutted, "How public men love to compare their own situation with some historic crisis in the past!"[36]

But historical analogies will appear! An editorial in the Springfield, *Illinois State-Register* (October 12) was able (with some helpful suggestions from The Abraham Lincoln Association) to print a notable passage from Lincoln's last speech in the campaign of 1858, which had overtones for President Truman's campaign: "As I have not felt, so I have not expressed any harsh sentiment towards our Southern brethren. . . . I have meant to assail the motives of no party, or individual; and if I have, in any instance (of which I am not conscious) departed from my purpose, I regret it. . . ."

Of course, good Democrats took their occasion to compare President Truman to Lincoln, just as Republicans were doing with their candidate. In the Democratic convention, Illinois delegate Ben Adamowski made a seconding speech for Truman comparing him to the immortal son of Illinois. The most amusing comparison of all, however, called upon the fact that both Lincoln and Truman once served as U.S. Postmasters.[37] Perhaps the truest comparison called attention to the similar circumstances of 1864 and 1948. In

[33]South Bend, Indiana, *Mirror,* September 10.
[34]Associated Press, October 12.
[35]United Press, September 7.
[36]Holland, Michigan, *Sentinel,* September 20.
[37]Boston *Post,* August 22.

1864 a convention of dissatisfied Republicans nominated Frémont, and as numerous editorials and columnists concluded in 1948, "Probably never since Abraham Lincoln's second term has a President of the United States been so discredited within his own party as is President Harry Truman."[38] And it was hopefully noted that Lincoln's fortunes rose between his nomination and the November election. One editor admitted that "President Truman lays no claim to being a Lincoln, but he would not be human if he did not take comfort from the turn in Lincoln's luck."[39] It was likewise recalled that Lincoln had said in June 1864, "It is not best to swap horses while crossing the river."[40]

As President Truman's campaign swept toward election day, even observers in predominantly Republican states were remembering Lincoln's effectiveness in speaking to the common man. On September 23, the Knoxville, Iowa, *Express* commented on Truman's speech at Dexter, Iowa, "He could speak to them [the farmers] in their own language. . . . No doubt. . . a few. . . would have made the remark that President Truman was just a common man . . . but many Americans also remember another common man, a plain man of the people who had homely ways—his name was Abraham Lincoln."

The revolt of the southern wing of the Democracy which came to a head at Philadelphia had been promised by leading "Dixiecrats" from the moment of President Truman's announcement of his civil rights program. Governor Jester of Texas was representative of old-time Southern Democrats who hoped to keep unity in the party, but at the same time to eliminate the civil rights statement from the party's platform. On April 20, he addressed a large gathering of Texas Democrats, elaborating on his opposition to the Truman program: "Bad laws do not make good neighbors. Enforced associations create strife and resentment. Legislation cannot make friends more friendly, nor neighbors more neighborly. Social equality cannot be legislated. Abraham Lincoln,

[38]Seaton, Illinois, *Independent* (et al.), July 22.
[39]Big Rapids, Michigan, *Pioneer*, April 29.
[40]Moline, Illinois, *Dispatch*, July 20.

the Great Emancipator, opposed efforts to create social equality by law."[41]

At this point Governor Jester admitted that the advancement of the Negro in the South had been short of what might have been done in particular instances, but he recounted the undeniable advancement in the South as a whole and praised the friends of the Negro race for what had been accomplished. In general, it seemed that all but the hide-bound among Southern Democrats were willing to permit, and even to facilitate, the gradual improvement of the social and political status of the Negro and to encourage the necessary education of white men in the South to the idea of advancement for the colored race. But, dictation of means and methods from outside the South would not be acquiesced in, even though a Democratic president were the moving force.

The southern press, of course, carried all the features and press stories which played up the analogy between 1860 and 1948. In them, the emphasis on the position of Abraham Lincoln and Stephen A. Douglas in 1860 gave both an analogy and a contradiction to Truman's position. As Douglas tried to find ground on which he could hold both Northern and Southern Democrats and, inevitably, lost the southern minority through holding to the minimum which would be acceptable to liberal Northern Democrats, so it seemed Truman was striving in 1948. Truman's stand in 1948 was perhaps no more advanced than that of Douglas in 1860, and yet it was too strong for the stomach of the Southern Democrats. Lincoln's position in 1860—to limit the spread of slavery, but not to interfere with the institution in the South—curiously enough, was cited as historical precedent for the position being taken by the southern wing of the party in 1948. The relative silence of candidate Dewey on the issue of civil rights suggested that Republicans were willing to let their past sponsorship of the Negro garner what votes it could in the North, and at the same time leave it to be inferred that Lincoln's position of non-interference in the South was the candidate's position in 1948. There was a good chance that the split among Southern Democrats might allow Dewey to gain the electoral votes of a few

[41]Amarillo, Texas, *News,* April 23.

doubtful states. Even as early as July, Democratic newspapers in the South were coming out for Dewey.[42]

The thinking of the Dixiecrats is indicated in the address of Gessner T. McCowey of Alabama at the Thurmond—Wright notification ceremony at Houston, Texas. "We of the South do much more for our colored friends than their great Emancipator Abraham Lincoln was willing to do. Here is what he said at Charleston, Illinois [September 18, 1858]: 'I will say that I am not, nor have I ever been, in favor of bringing about in any way the social and political equality of the white and black races; that I am not, nor have I ever been, in favor of making voters or jurors of Negroes, nor qualifying them to hold office. ' "[43] This quotation was widely used in the southern press throughout the campaign. Of course, the fact that Lincoln later, after secession was a fact and bloody battles had been fought, did advocate the very things denied in the Charleston debate, was not mentioned by any Dixiecrat. However, there were southern editors who quoted Lincoln to better effect: "Let us discard all this quibbling about this man and the other man—this race and that race being inferior, and therefore they must be placed in an inferior position. . . ."[44] And there were columnists widely read in the South who reiterated that "Today's heated discussion of civil rights needs the spirit of Abraham Lincoln. . . ." Lincoln believed in "the growth of moral sentiment which he did so much to promote. . . . 'Why should there not be a patient confidence in the ultimate justice of the people?' That spirit could be used today."[45]

That neither Abraham Lincoln nor any other political leader of the past is the exclusive property of any political party became even more evident with the adoption of the platform of the Progressive party, which announced, "We are the political heirs of Jefferson, Jackson, and Lincoln—of Frederick Douglass, Altgeld and Debs—of fighting 'Bob' LaFollette, George Norris and Franklin Roosevelt." In accepting the nomination of the Progressive party,

---

[42]Editorial, Phoenix, Arizona, *Gazette,* July 17.
[43]Montgomery, Alabama, *Journal,* August 12.
[44]Rector, Arkansas, *Democrat,* September 16.
[45]Samuel B. Pettingill, San Antonio, Texas, *Express* (et al.), July 27.

Henry Wallace took pains to develop in detail this political inheritance from Jefferson and Lincoln: "One hundred and fifty years ago, Thomas Jefferson took leadership in forming a new party . . . which overcame the odds of a hostile press, of wealth and vested interest. . . . The party Jefferson founded . . . was buried here in Philadelphia last week. . . ."

Likewise, "Fourscore and seven years ago, the successful candidate of another party took office in Washington. . . . The party of a Lincoln has been reduced to the party of a Dewey. . . . But we here tonight. . . dedicate ourselves to the complete fulfillment of Lincoln's promise; we consecrate ourselves to a second emancipation. . . ."[46]

The press greeted the Progressive party with a wide observation of historical analogy, surveying the failure of third parties in the past. Third parties were certainly in the American tradition, but failure was the chief characteristic which they held in common. It was noted, however, that initial failure sometimes led to ultimate success. Such was the record of the Republican party, organized in 1854 as a third party but becoming by 1860 the chief opposition to the Democratic party. Few editors or columnists outside the communist press indicated any expectation that there was even a remote possibility of the Progressive party's duplicating the Republican record in 1860. On all hands it was agreed that tradition held third party candidates to be certain losers.

Concerning one of the "splinter" parties of the past—the Radical Democracy party of 1864—it was recalled that when Lincoln heard of the convention numbering some three hundred and fifty persons, he picked up his Bible and opened to I Samuel, chapter xxii, and read aloud: "Everyone who was in distress and everyone who was discontented gathered themselves unto him; . . . and there were with him about 400 men."[47] And an Arkansas paper observed that "Americans tend to greet all third parties with rousing cheers of the Bronx variety."[48]

That Wallace was supported from the beginning by communists

[46]Associated Press, July 24.
[47]Kansas City, Missouri, *Times*, July 24.
[48]Little Rock, Arkansas, *Gazette*, August 15.

was his chief hindrance to an effective appeal to the electorate. When he undertook to defend his communist support, he drew upon himself a barrage of editorials. "He assures his audiences that American Communists are not 'as violent as Lincoln or Jefferson were in their day'. . . . There need be no doubt about the position of American Communists. They constitute a wing of the international communist party, which is subject to Soviet Russia discipline, and they believe in violent overthrow of all such governments as that of the United States. . . ."[49] Another widely printed editorial put it in a nutshell, "Perhaps to many, the democratic principles of Jefferson and Lincoln's anti-slavery stand seemed as radical as Marx's philosophy did to a later generation. But can Mr. Wallace forget that there were no secret police under Jefferson, or that the Lincoln administration conducted no purge trials and set up no one-party system?"[50]

Throughout the campaign the Progressives claimed the Lincoln tradition. Following Wallace's tour of the South, strewn with vegetables and bad eggs, the Progressive party's treasurer, Dr. Clark Foreman, termed the heroic-comic tour "the greatest single blow for freedom in this country since Abraham Lincoln's emancipation proclamation."[51]

Likewise, the platform of the Socialist Workers party claimed Lincoln among an assortment of political forefathers: "In 1860 William Lloyd Garrison and Wendell Phillips, John Brown and Frederick Douglass, Abraham Lincoln and Thaddeus Stevens personified the forces which waged merciless war against the slaveholders' attempt to perpetuate their outmoded system. . . . The Socialist Workers party, in these years of decision comes forward as the continuator of these revolutionary traditions. . . ."

As was to be expected, the labor press took many occasions to remind its readers of Lincoln's words on labor, and as usual neglected to accompany them by the companion passage on the rights of capital. (Both appear in Lincoln's Address before the Wisconsin State Agricultural Society, September 30, 1859; see also

---

[49]Kenneth G. Crawford, The Register and Tribune Syndicate, September 2.
[50]Bozeman, Montana, *Chronicle* (et al.), August 31.
[51]Associated Press, September 8.

the Annual Message to Congress, December 3, 1861.) One wonders whether the day will ever come when spokesmen for either labor or capital will quote the whole of Lincoln's pronouncements on the relationship existing between labor and capital in a democracy. A widely printed story emanating from the Federated Press stipulated that labor was "willing to bet a waste basket of old press releases against a copy of the Taft-Hartley act that none of the Republican star speakers" would remind their audiences of such Lincolnian axioms as the following: "There has never been but one question in all civilization—how to keep a few men from saying to many men: You work and earn bread and we will eat it."[52] Labor's attack upon the Republican sponsored Taft-Hartley bill, and upon Senator Taft's prolonged defense of it, quoted over and over, "Labor is prior to and independent of capital. Capital is only the fruit of labor";[53] but in replying to Senator Taft one labor editor introduced variety by taking a different text:

> There are two sides to every question. Even in politics. Abe Lincoln once explained this by showing that the word liberty has two meanings. "The Shepherd," Lincoln said, "drives the wolf from the sheep's throat for which the sheep thanks the shepherd as his liberator, while the wolf denounces him for the same act as the destroyer of liberty."
>
> When we listen to political speeches we try to figure out which side of the bread our margarine is on. In other words, are we sheep or wolf?
>
> Take Bob Taft's recent speech, presented as the official Republican view that labor is responsible for high prices. Here is what Taft said:
>
> "The situation which gives concern to members of both parties is the spiral of inflation resulting in constantly higher prices. But, of course, the higher prices are caused directly by the greatly increased purchasing power of the people competing for all kinds of food and other commodities."
>
> Prices, Taft believes, "have been chasing wages" ever since he helped kill OPA.[54]

[52]Toledo, Ohio, *Union Leader* (et al.) May 21.
[53]McCallister Coleman, Minneapolis *Labor Review* (et al.), September 2.
[54]Butte, Montana, *Labor News,* September 16.

When Don Loudon, national director of the Republican Party Labor Division, undertook to defend the GOP policy on labor, he ignored the quotations so favored by the labor press, and quoted instead Lincoln's belief that our nation "cannot endure half slave and half free," and cited "I believe each individual is naturally entitled to do as he pleases with himself and the fruits of his labor. . . ." Loudon further quoted, "Accustomed to trample on the rights of others, you have lost the genius of your own independence and become the fit subject of the first cunning tyrant who rises among you." By trading the "dictatorship" of the New Deal for a Republican regime under Dewey, Loudon implied, labor would enjoy a return to its ancient heritage of freedom.[55]

Similarly, other editors and columnists undertook to use Lincoln quotations to justify capitalism in 1948. In answer to the question: "What is capitalism?" one writer found that Lincoln had defined it to complete satisfaction in the following passage:

> The prudent, penniless beginner in the world labors for wages awhile, saves a surplus with which to buy tools or land for himself, then labors on his own account another while and at length hires another new beginner to help him. This is the just and generous and prosperous system, which opens the way to all, gives hope to all, and consequent energy and progress and improvement of conditions to all.[56]

Thus the game of political quotations always excerpted the half-truth rather than the whole, and misrepresented Lincoln as a spokesman for labor or for capital, rather than for democracy which recognizes and tries to mete justice to both. That Lincoln in his own day was worried about the attempt "to place *capital* on an equal footing with, if not above *labor,* in the structure of government," is proved by his denunciation of such effort in his Annual Message to Congress, December 3, 1861, but it is also historical fact that in his analysis of the proper relation between them, Lincoln was not a partisan of either, but rather an advocate of a democracy which would, although recognizing the priority of labor, guarantee the rights of both.

[55]New York *Post* (et al.), June 25.
[56]Duncan Wharton, Los Angeles *Forum*, July 9.

Thus far we have surveyed Lincoln's part in the national political campaigns. There remains the part he played in state and local politics. Since state and local candidates followed the trends already summarized on the national scene, there is little to be gained in repeating the incidents, analogies, and quotations. Republican candidates claimed to be Jeffersonians. Said Patrick J. Hurley, "I am as much a Jeffersonian as Lincoln was. I . . . expect to receive . . . the undivided support of the Jeffersonian Democrats of New Mexico."[57] Democrats claimed to be Lincolnians. Said Guy C. Williams, Democratic nominee for Porter County (Indiana) superior court judge, "Abe Lincoln was no more Republican than I am."[58]

In one state, however, there developed an analogy which played no small part in an important senatorial campaign. Illinois Republicans, as was to be expected, strove to represent their candidacies as the continuation of the Lincoln tradition. Richard Yates Rowe, state treasurer and Republican candidate for lieutenant governor, dedicated the Western Illinois Fair with a speech recalling the "heritage of heroes" and the "inspiring figure of Abraham Lincoln."[59] Other Republican candidates followed this pattern, simply recalling to the mind of the electorate the fact that Lincoln was a Republican, but little further use of Lincoln was attempted by his party. In fact, it seemed as if Illinois Republicans found Lincoln an asset only in his role of patron saint, and wished to avoid too close association with his ideas and his precedent. In particular, the Republican candidate for re-election to the United States Senate, C. Wayland Brooks, dodged, not too adroitly, the challenge issued by the Democratic candidate Paul H. Douglas to re-enact the Lincoln—Douglas debates.[60] When Brooks declined the challenge on the ground that he had no time for persons of no consequence, candidate Douglas commented, "In 1858 Abraham Lincoln did not think he was too big to debate with my distant kinsmen, Stephen A. Douglas. . . . Brooks must feel that he is

[57]Albuquerque, New Mexico, *Tribune,* August 19.
[58]Valparaiso, Indiana, *Vidette-Messenger,* September 27.
[59]Pittsfield, Illinois, *Republican,* July 7.
[60]Associated Press, July 6.

a bigger man than Lincoln."[61] Thereafter, candidate Douglas debated with an empty chair symbolizing his opponent, and made considerable capital of Brooks' refusal to meet him on the platform. What effect this device had upon the electorate is indicated by the fact that Douglas won the election.

Although a multiplicity of conclusions may be drawn from this survey of Lincoln's part in American politics in 1948, the editor wishes to draw only one, based upon familiarity with Lincoln's own use of the political past of the nineteenth century. No candidate in 1948, of any party, showed knowledge of America's political past, comparable to that which animated all of Abraham Lincoln's great speeches in 1858, 1859, and 1860, and his speeches and messages to Congress from 1861 to 1865. Ghost writers and political advisers have not demonstrated that many minds can think more acutely than one. Perhaps President Truman came to recognize this fact, for as his campaign wore to its close he repeatedly discarded his ghost-written text and spoke, for better or for worse, from his own mind and heart.

In the light of post-election knowledge, however, the chariness of Republican party candidates in avowing the principles of Abraham Lincoln, even when they were seeking to wear his aegis, invites speculation as a factor in unprecedented defeat under auspices of unprecedented favor. Furthermore, the paradoxical circumstance of an opposition, almost universally admitted to be without hope, not merely pledging allegiance to Lincoln's fundamental doctrine of human rights but also bearing as a result the brunt of internecine feud while waging battle for the liberal application of that doctrine, likewise invites speculation as a factor in unprecedented victory. No doubt the political analysts will find political and economic rationalizations in plenty for the "miracle" of November 2, 1948, but one cannot escape wondering whether the moral issue, all but obscured in the pre-election balloting which misled the public opinion polls, did not in the voting booths of the nation loom as a ghost which would not down. It was Lincoln who said that out of the "abundance of man's heart . . . his mouth will continue to speak," and it was Lincoln who believed that "right makes might."

[61]Metamora, Illinois, *Herald* (et al.) September 3.

"BEEF! BEEF! BEEF!"

LINCOLN AND JUDGE ROBERTSON*

More than one President of the United States has cracked momentarily under stress and dashed off a hot-tempered letter, which scarcely adds to his dignity as chief executive, but nevertheless enriches history with a minor episode of great human interest.

In November 1862, President Lincoln was confronted by numerous executive problems perhaps neither more nor less irritating than had been his customary fare during the eighteen months since his inaugural, but one of them seems to have roused his temper and prompted his writing of a sarcastic letter that would certainly have made the headlines had it been made public.

Lincoln had reason to be on edge. Plagued by an army which he described as "demoralized by the idea that the war is to be ended, the nation united, and peace restored, by strategy, and not by hard desperate fighting,"[1] he had in September dismissed one of General McClellan's ablest officers, Major John J. Key, for making a cynical remark to the effect that "The object is that neither army shall get much advantage of the other; that both shall be kept in the field till they are exhausted, when we will make a compromise

*The Abraham Lincoln Quarterly, September 1951.
[1]Memorandum on Furloughs, November 1862, Emanuel Hertz, *Abraham Lincoln, a New Portrait,* II, 888.

and save slavery."' And finally, on November 5, he had issued the
order   removing McClellan from command of the Army of the
Potomac.

There were other irritants in plenty. Observance by Union business men of their right to conduct "business as usual" in time of
war was creating a dangerous flow of war materiel away from
Union armies, ostensibly for such neutral countries as Canada, but
in reality for transshipment to the Confederacy. To put a stop to
this practice, Lincoln issued on November 21 an executive order
prohibiting export of arms and munitions.

But by far the most plaguing situation was the bickering among
Unionists in Kentucky and Missouri as to whether they would support the President's plea for state legislation providing gradual
emancipation. Lincoln's preliminary Emancipation Proclamation
of September 22 had been a dish that Union slave-owners could
not relish, for many of them regarded their constitutional right to
property in the form of slaves more highly than they regarded the
Union itself.

In the midst of these daily cares, Lincoln received a telegram
from his old friend of an earlier day, Judge George Robertson of
Lexington, Kentucky. Back on August 15, 1855, Lincoln had written Robertson one of his memorable letters in which he opined
sarcastically, "The fourth of July has not quite dwindled away; it
is still a great day— *for burning fire-crackers!!!*"' A good deal of
water was over the dam since those days when two old-line Whigs,
whose party had fallen apart and left them standing more or less
alone, could reflect calmly, if somewhat bitterly, on the irrational
progress of politics.

As of November 1862, the staunchly loyal Robertson was involved in a struggle with a fellow patriot, colonel of a regiment
of Wisconsin Volunteers encamped on the "Dark and Bloody
Ground" to protect Union Kentuckians from marauding troops of

'Record of dismissal of John J. Key, September 26-27, 1862, autograph document,
The Robert Todd Lincoln Collection, The Library of Congress (hereafter cited as
DLC-RTL).

'Autograph letter, The Library of Congress.

rebel guerrillas, largely composed of native Kentuckians led by the glamorous John Hunt Morgan. The soldiers from Wisconsin were as a rule enthusiastic for emancipation as well as the Union, and they often questioned the loyalty of Union slaveholders in Kentucky who seemed so concerned with keeping Negroes in bondage. On November 19, Robertson telegraphed President Lincoln:

> The conduct of a few of the officers of the army in forcibly detaining the Slaves of Union Kentuckians may provoke a conflict between Citizens & Soldiers; . . . we desire you to say as we believe you will that military force will not be permitted for the detention any more than for the restoration of such property & especially in resistance & contempt of the loyal process of a Civil tribunal.[4]

Upon reading this telegram, the President was reminded, not, as usual, of a story heard around the circuit in some hotel lobby, but of an episode in American history. Whereupon he penned the following letter:

> Private   Executive Mansion
>   Washington, Nov. 20. 1862
>
> Hon. George Roberston
>   My dear Sir.
>   Your despatch of yesterday is just received. I believe you are acquainted with the American Classics, (if there be such) and probably remember a speech of Patrick Henry, in which he represented a certain character in the, revolutionary times, as totally disregarding all questions of country, and "hoarsely bawling, beef! beef!! beef!!!"
>   Do you not know that I may as well surrender this contest, directly, as to make any order, the obvious purpose of which would be to return fugitive slaves?
>   Yours very truly
>   *A. Lincoln*[5]

[4]Telegram, DLC-RTL.
[5]Autograph letter, ibid.

William Wirt narrates how, after the Revolution, Patrick Henry defended in court an army commissary named Venable who had been sued by a suspected Tory, John Hook, for two steers commandeered by Venable to furnish beef for his troops. After magnificently depicting the scene of triumph following the surrender of the British at Yorktown, Patrick Henry concluded his speech to the jury: "But hark! what notes of discord are these which disturb the general joy, and silence the acclamations of victory—they are the notes of *John Hook,* hoarsely bawling through the American camp, *beef! beef! beef!"*[6]

As apt as was the allusion to Patrick Henry's speech, Lincoln seems to have thought better of sending the letter, possibly because in the meantime he had received another communication which indicated that Robertson was more personally involved than his telegram had indicated. While the telegram made an ardent plea for upholding the constitutional rights of the loyal slaveholders of Kentucky in general, it said nothing of Robertson's personal involvement with the officers of the army who were "forcibly detaining Slaves of Union Kentuckians," and whereas Lincoln's sarcastic allusion to Tory John Hook would have been a telling blow to Union slaveholders as a group, it would be certain, in the light of particular facts in the case, to alienate one whom Lincoln knew to be a sincere Unionist, as well as a legalist of adamant temper whose respect for the letter of the law might turn him away from the cause that was dearer to Lincoln than emancipation.

On November 17, Colonel William L. Utley of the Twenty-second Wisconsin Volunteers wrote to his friend Alexander W. Randall, recently returned to Washington from his post as U.S. minister to Rome. Although the letter is a classic piece of Americana, it is too long to quote in full and has been abridged to the pertinent passages, as follows:

> I am in a devil of a scrape, and appeal to you for assistance.
> . . . I am ahead yet, but they have taken a new dodge on
> me, they have got me indicted at Lexington under the Laws
> of Kentucky. The Warrant is in the hands of the Sheriff of

[6]William Wirt, *Life of Patrick Henry* (1841), pp. 389-390.

this county he finds the same difficulty that the rats did in getting the bell on the cat, it would be a good thing to have done, but a bad thing to do. they find it so in arresting me. they can never do it while there is a man left in the 22d Regiment. the Brig. Genl. in whose Brigade we now are, Refuses to assist in arresting me. Now what I want, is to have you use your influence with the President to have him retained in command of this Brigade. for he certainly will be removed . . . unless measures are taken to prevent, or we shall again be placed under some pro Slavery *Jcass* as we have been . . until we were placed under him. You know how we was hurried off without blankets, tents or anything. . . . Kentucky was howling like a set of d—d Hyenas (as they are) for help. the men left their grain standing . . . we all throwed down our impliments and . . . came directly to Kentucky. . . . We have been Brigaded under five or six diferent Genls all just alike all chosen for their adherence to the Kentucky policy. We have had to submit to the most degrading orders. . . . We have laid in the dirt five nights on an old Rebel ex Congressmans farm (with a large straw stack roting down within 40 Rods of us). . . . When we left there two or three of his nigers got in the Regt and claimed protection. I refused to be made a niger ketcher, as you have no doubt seen by the papers. . . . I have tryed to avoid trouble on the niger question, but I could not escape it, but I am just the boy to meet it when it comes. . . . There is no such thing as unionism in Kentucky . . . . . . I wish Abraham Lincoln could hear what the professed union men call him. I told the Governor (Robinson) that all Kentuckeyans were either d—d trators or cowards, that there was no loyalty in the state, that you might put it all in to one end of the scales, and a niger baby in the other end, and Loyalty and unionism would go up with a rush I have given them hell, and now they intend to give me h—l.

. . . What I want is. . . to be kept under Generals that acknowledge the power of the president, or be taken out of the state. there is a general understanding among the genl officers commanding in Kentuckey to ignore the proclimation. . . . I am the first man that has attempted to carry it out, and now I am indicted by *Loud mouthed Union men.* . . . "[7]

[7]Autograph letter, DLC-RTL.

With this letter, Colonel Utley enclosed the following letter addressed to the president:

> Permit me respectfully to appeal to you. . . . For a long time . . . enduring hardships and privasions of military life and of army marches . . . we penetrated the state of Kentucky, the devastating hords of rebels fleeing before us. . . .
>
> As a compensation for these sacrifices, hardships and exposures . . . I now find myself indited for *manstealing,* by a Kentucky court, and hunted by her officers as a fellon for her penitentiary.
>
> The facts in the case are few, simple, and easily understood . . . . On Friday last, Judge Robinson of Lexington, representing himself as a Union man of whose counsels . . . you have seen fit to avail yourself, came into my lines, and claimed and demanded as his property, a Negro boy found in the regiment. How, when, where, or by what means the boy came into the lines, or by whom he was claimed as property, I had previously no knowledge. . . . I refused to recognize his claims, to lead the boy, as he requested, beyond my lines, or to forbid the soldiers from interfereing should he attempt to do so. He was not, however, forbidden to take him. . . . The boy refused to go with him and *claimed* protection from the power of one whose cruel treatment, as he asserted, had already made him a *dwarf* instead of a man. . . . To you, I now appeal for . . . protection . . . for simply standing by the Constitution, obeying the laws of Congress and honoring the Proclamation . . . issued on the 23d day of September last. . . . Judge Robinson declared the President's proclamation of the 23d of Sept, to be unconstitutional, to have no bearing on Kentucky and that the state would never submit to it. . . . "[8]

Alexander Randall took both letters to the White House and presented Utley's case, possibly on, or near, November 21, the same day that Lincoln held an interview with Union Kentuckians on the question of emancipation. As reported in the New York *Tribune* for November 24, Lincoln told his visitors from Kentucky that "he would rather die than take back a word of the Proclamation of Freedom, and he dwelt upon the advantages to

[8]Autograph letter, *ibid.*

the Border States of his scheme for the gradual abolishment of Slavery, which he urged them to bring fairly before their people. . . . Mr. Lincoln also expressed his determination to enforce vigorous measures to rid the State of Rebel sympathizers, and for that purpose a new Provost-Marshal General who has his heart in the work will be appointed." From the temper of these remarks, we may infer Lincoln's frame of mind when Randall laid before him Colonel Utley's communications.

On November 26, Lincoln telegraphed Robertson, "I mail you a short letter to-day."[9] The letter stated:

> A few days since I had a despatch from you which I did not answer. If I were to be wounded personally, I think I would not shun it. But it is the life of the nation. I now understand the trouble is with Col. Utley; that he has five slaves in his camp, four of whom belong to rebels, and one belonging to you. If this be true, convey yours to Col. Utley, so that he can make him free, and I will pay you any sum not exceeding five hundred dollars. Yours, &c. A. Lincoln.[10]

On December 1, Robertson replied in a manner conclusively demonstrating Lincoln's wisdom in withholding his first letter of November 20. Robertson refused to acknowledge, as might any patriot concerned chiefly with preserving the constitutional rights of all loyal Kentuckians, that his personal affairs were the real issue. His letter put the case thus:

> In my late telegram to you I did not allude to either my boy Adam, or to Col. Utley, or to his case. Divining your information, as you must have done, from some other source, you have been misinformed, and . . . misconceived the motive of my dispatch. . . . I had put Col. Utley in the position which I preferred, and I neither intended nor desired to seek any . . . intervention in . . . my own case. . . . The citation in my civil suit against him having been served, I can certainly obtain a judgement for $1000, and perhaps more. . . . My object in that suit was far from mercenary—it was solely to

[9]Autograph telegram, Brown University Collection.
[10]Copy, DLC-RTL. The original letter has not been located.

try the question whether the civil or the military power is
Constitutionally supreme in Kentucky. . . . "

With this letter the case seems to have been closed so far as
Lincoln was concerned, with Robertson content that the "question
whether the civil or the military power is Constitutionally supreme
in Kentucky" had been satisfactorily settled, and the "mercenary"
object of the suit not worth Robertson's pursuing. After the war,
however, Judge Robertson seems to have changed his mind. On
October 6, 1871, he obtained judgment against Utley in the U. S.
Circuit Court for the Eastern District of Wisconsin, in the amount
of $908.06, plus costs of $26.40, for having stolen his slave.
The constitutional guarantees of property were finally and completely vindicated.

The conclusion of the story is briefly told in an act of Congress
approved February 14, 1873, which directed the Secretary of the
Treasury to pay $934.46, "together with interest from the date of
recovery," for the "relief of William L. Utley."

"Autograph letter, DLC-RTL.

AN APPRECIATION OF THE
GETTYSBURG ADDRESS, DELIVERED
BEFORE THE CHICAGO HISTORICAL
SOCIETY, NOVEMBER 19, 1950

There are occasions which we feel should be observed with words fitly spoken. Commemorations and anniversaries present the speaker with situations unlike those to which he is accustomed, for although his subject is one on which little or nothing new can be said, and his function is recognized as symbolic rather than literal, nevertheless both he and his audience pray that what is already well known to both of them may somehow be transmuted and endowed with larger truth. As Lincoln could not have asked for a nobler opportunity than the dedication service at Gettysburg, so we could not ask for a finer occasion than the four-score-and-seventh anniversary of the Gettysburg Address; and yet we must wonder what can be said that will be fitting.

By your presence here, you have confessed your interest in the occasion and your recognition that our gathering is a symbolic repetition, commemorating a commemoration. Therefore I ask that you bear with me while I repeat some things which are well known to you. Perphaps we may draw inspiration from the fact that, however memorably he said it, Lincoln spoke at Gettysburg nothing new either to himself or to his audience. As a public speaker, Lincoln was

Chicago History, Fall 1950.

one of the greatest repeaters in history, stating again and again some simple truths that needed repeating because, somehow, the American people were in his day, as in ours, great forgetters, who although they had often heard the truth, were unable to hold it fast much longer than an eighth-grader can remember the lines he has memorized for a graduation exercise. When Lincoln went to Gettysburg to deliver his little speech commemorating an event which he believed would live as long as history itself, he probably thought of the occasion as one on which he could say once more the one big thing which he believed politically and had been trying to say during something like thirty years of public speaking.

All his political life Lincoln had been saying that the soul of America's being was the proposition that all men are created equal. This proposition was what Lincoln had called on an earlier occasion, in 1858, ". . . the electric cord in the Declaration that links the hearts of patriotic and liberty-loving men together, that will link those patriotic hearts as long as the love of freedom exists in the minds of men throughout the world."

On his way to Washington to be inaugurated, Lincoln made a speech at Independence Hall in Philadelphia. In this speech he paid his personal tribute to the Declaration of Independence by saying: "I have never had a feeling politically that did not spring from the sentiments embodied in the Declaration of Independence. I have often pondered over the dangers which were incurred by the men who . . . framed and adopted that Declaration of Independence. I have pondered over the toils that were endured by the officers and soldiers of the army who achieved that independence. I have often inquired of myself what great principle or idea it was that kept this Confederacy so long together. It was not the mere matter of the separation of the Colonies from the motherland; but that sentiment in the Declaration of Independence which gave liberty, not alone to the people of this country, but, I hope, to the world, for all future time."

On yet another occasion he recalled the biblical proverb about "words fitly spoken" being like "apples of gold in pictures of silver," and described the Declaration as ". . . *the* word, *'fitly spoken'* which has proved an 'apple of gold' to us. The *Union,* and the *Constitution,* are the *picture of silver,* subsequently framed around it. The picture was made, not to *conceal,* or *destroy* the apple; but to *adorn,* and *preserve* it. The *picture* was made *for* the apple— *not* the apple for the picture. So let us act, that neither *picture,* or *apple,* shall ever be blurred, or broken."

As Lincoln never gave up in his attempt to remind America yet another time, on a different occasion he asked and answered an important question: "What constitutes the bulwark of our own liberty and independence? It is not our frowning battlements, our bristling sea coasts, the guns of our war steamers, or the strength of our gallant and disciplined army. These are not our reliance against a resumption of tyranny in our fair land. All of them may be turned against our liberties, without making us stronger or weaker for the struggle. Our reliance is in the *love of liberty* which God has planted in our bosoms. Our defense is in the preservation of the spirit which prizes liberty as the heritage of all men, in all lands, everywhere. Destroy this spirit, and you have planted the seeds of despotism around your own doors."

These quotations are really only a few of the many that Lincoln spoke on the same theme, and they illustrate how he recognized the truth that it is the spirit that makes a living nation. A society without spirit may be an aggregation of people, but it cannot be a living nation.

Have we ever asked ourselves the question: What is the United States? An aggregation of people? A confederacy of states? A nation? Does any one of these names have a being and a spirit? Is our nation a living reality, or a mere abstraction? Lincoln had pondered these questions and had formulated an answer—a concept which was for him more than a rhetorical statement. The United States is a being which projects in the large the soul and intellect of the individual free men who are its equal component parts. The United States exists only by and for its free citizens. Unlike the ancient tribe, or the nation dedicated to a tribal creed, in which the individual exists only for and by the grace of the divine tribe, the United States is no motherland or fatherland, and claims no myth of demigods on the horizon of history, supernatural progenitors of a peculiar and superior race. It is rather a projection of the *free man,* multiplied by the image of his fellowmen, who are like him in being different physically and mentally, in loving liberty, and in wanting to meet and be met as the equals of other men.

Have you ever considered how in the Gettysburg Address Lincoln spoke of the United States as conceived, born, and growing through childhood to maturity; of its having reached, as it were, a period of great sickness when it trod the valley of the shadow of death on a battlefield more gory than any in previous history; and of its rebirth to a new and more vital life? Call this a figure of speech if you will, such language reveals that to Lincoln the United States held a peculiar, living reality which no mere abstraction of government can hold.

Into Lincoln's concept was distilled the best thought of five hundred years of European civilization, striving to break the hold of tribal myth and superstition, to divest humanity of outworn social and political forms, and to create a new pattern in which men might live together without being either ruler or subject, master or slave. The concept was humanistic in that it projected the humanist's conviction that the mind of the individual man could give order and meaning to the impulse of the individual life. To understand was to be free to act in harmony with fate in the pursuit of happiness. So Lincoln conceived the nation as a being with conflicting drives, hopes, and fears, but guided by reason—not all-knowing, but capable of learning and growing, and capable of regeneration in the midst of decay. For this nation, conceived in liberty and perpetuating the free spirit that gave it birth, could not die so long as men lived who gave of their life, their liberty, and their happiness to preserve it.

Preservation of the United States came to be Lincoln's official task as President in 1861, but he had been laboring to this end for thirty years. Likewise, the fact that he took for his subject at Gettysburg the preservation of the Union, and with it the golden apple of freedom and equality, was no accident of the occasion. He had said more than twenty-five years before Gettysburg, "We find ourselves under the government of a system of political institutions, conducing more essentially to the ends of civil and religious

liberty, than any of which the history of former times tells us
. . . We toiled not in the acquirement or establishment of them
—they are a legacy bequeathed to us . . . 'tis ours only to transmit
these . . . to the latest generation that fate shall permit the world
to know."

Ten years before Gettysburg, he had pleaded with his fellow
Americans as they ran down hill toward civil war, "Let us re-adopt
the Declaration of Independence, and with it, the practices, and
policy, which harmonize with it. . . . If we do this, we shall not
only have saved the Union; but we shall have so saved it, as to
make and keep it, forever worthy of the saving."

And after war came, but still nearly a year before Gettysburg,
he had addressed Congress with these words: "Fellow-citizens, *we*
cannot escape history. . . . We *say* we are for the Union. The world
will not forget that we say this. We know how to save the Union.
the world knows we do know how to save it. We—even *we here*—
hold the power, and bear the responsibility. In *giving* freedom to
the *slave,* we *assure* freedom to the *free*— honorable alike in what
we give, and what we preserve. We shall nobly save or meanly lose,
the last best hope of earth. . . . "

Some men have professed astonishment at Lincoln's devotion to
the United States. Alexander Stephens, Vice President of the
Confederacy, said that Lincoln's devotion was a "religious
mysticism." And we may well ask why Lincoln believed the United
States to be worth preserving. Was it simply because he was born
in a log cabin, lived without many luxuries of life, had to work
hard for what he got, was disappointed often, but eventually became President? Or was it merely because he was born in America?
Certainly there was nothing sacred about the status quo of
American government for its own sake that held him, for if one
thinks political campaigns are bitter today, one should read some
of the things that Lincoln and Douglas said in 1858, not merely
about each other, but about the administration of President
Buchanan, to whom they were both opposed. If the United States
government was so bad, how could Lincoln speak of the United
States as "the last best hope of earth"?

It would certainly be wrong to think that Lincoln believed there could not be a better nation or government than the United States. Such a view implies a degree of smugness and chauvinism which never characterized Lincoln. When we ponder the Gettysburg Address, we know it was not the status quo of government as Lincoln knew it, or as we know it today, which was his "last best hope of earth." It was rather the ideal principle, to the achievement of which our government was dedicated, and must be continually rededicated, that inspired his poetic metaphor of birth, life, death, and rebirth of the nation at Gettysburg.

Like a few other truths of the past which have been memorized and inculcated from childhood, the Gettysburg Address and the Declaration of Independence are often mitigated, not so much by the ridicule of those who deny them, or scoff at them, as by the indifference of those who profess them without devotion to their meaning, or the zealotry of those who chant them as a ritual of protective charm for the chosen. Like the Sermon on the Mount, the Gettysburg Address was given to *all men* who can hear with more than their ears, and they do not have to come to us, the guardians of the creed, to perceive Lincoln's meaning. If we fail perpetually to strive toward Lincoln's symbolic goal, we may be sure that though people of other lands will continue to draw inspiration from Lincoln, they will not follow us. And it will not be through mere verbal appreciation and commemorative exercises, proper though they may be, but through actual achievement of freedom and equality, that the world will come to know that the Gettysburg Address and the Declaration of Independence are America's living creed.

As we look back to Gettysburg the same number of years that Lincoln looked back to the birth of the nation in Independence Hall, we may well repeat what he so nobly said for our grandfathers and great-grandfathers, but let us resolve anew for ourselves and for our children, that we shall be rededicated to the unfinished work.

"Four score and seven years ago our fathers brought forth on this continent, a new nation, conceived in Liberty, and dedicated to the proposition that all men are created equal.

"Now we are engaged in a great civil war, testing whether that nation, or any nation so conceived and so dedicated, can long endure. We are met on a great battle-field of that war. We have come to dedicate a portion of that field, as a final resting place for those who here gave their lives that that nation might live. It is altogether fitting and proper that we should do this.

"But, in a larger sense, we can not dedicate—we can not consecrate—we can not hallow—this ground. The brave men, living and dead, who struggled here, have consecrated it, far above our poor power to add or detract. The world will little note, nor long remember what we say here, but it can never forget what they did here. It is for us the living, rather, to be dedicated here to the unfinished work which they who fought here have thus far so nobly advanced. It is rather for us to be here dedicated to the great task remaining before us—that from these honored dead we take increased devotion to that cause for which they gave the last full measure of devotion—that we here highly resolve that these dead shall not have died in vain—that this nation, under God, shall have a new birth of freedom—and that government of the people, by the people, for the people, shall not perish from the earth."

LINCOLN COUNTRY*

During the first half of the nineteenth century the area bounded by the Great Lakes on the North, the Mississippi on the West, and the Ohio River on the South and East was perhaps the single dominant factor in American politics. It was also one of the dominant factors in the economic development of the nation, and it exhibited the representative, even symbolic, aspect of American civilization and culture which travelers from the Eastern Seaboard as well as from European countries recognized as a "New World." During the first twenty-five years this area, then called the Northwest, or simply the West, was a frontier of American civilization in one or the other of the two phases described by Frederick Jackson Turner: the hunter and trader frontier, and the farmer frontier. By the time of the Civil War, however, it had acquired, in comparison with the Eastern Seaboard and in terms of the economic and social structure then obtaining, a fully settled and relatively stable civilization. Though predominantly agricultural, it was not more so than the areas east of the Appalachians or south of the Ohio, with the exception of those mercantile-industrial areas centered in New England and the Middle Atlantic states which still had a slight lead on the expanding (almost exploding) mercantile-industrial centers along the Ohio and the shoreline of the Great Lakes. It had developed a characteristic system of public education which fostered not merely an average

*First published under the title "The Pioneering Period," *The Centennial Review of Arts & Science*, Spring 1958.

literacy equal to that of the older states, but also in its new and as yet scarcely world-renowned colleges and universities, an intellectual leadership which commanded the respect of cultivated foreign travelers and occasionally challenged the attention of Boston or New York. It had developed, if not precisely a classless society as has so often been claimed for it, at least a society in which class distinctions were so flexible as to be impossible even for the native initiates to keep straight, because the qualifications were so diverse as money, religion, education, family, and, above all, success—what kind of success did not matter too much so long as it was unmistakable. It had developed an audience which appreciated and was avid for literature, theater, music, and lyceum lectures of all kinds; although its first practitioners of the arts would not become recognized very widely for another two decades, they were developing. However, in politics—the one activity of which all Americans of that era were purported master practitioners—the Northwest had produced a national leadership which, although challenged, could not be turned aside.

I

In the best American tradition (one might say the only American tradition universally recognized at the time), the civilization of this area was to a considerable extent self-made, but like all things human it had causes, influences, and impacts. Aside from its physical geography there was one principal cause which more than any other determined what kind of civilization developed in the area: the Northwest Ordinance of 1787 which provided for the orderly settlement of the area and the rapid establishment of new states. In summary, it may be said that the Ordinance undertook to ensure to the people who settled the Northwest Territory not only the opportunity to form states equal to any others under the Constitution, but also the opportunity to escape, so far as possible under the Constitution and so far as the people's own wisdom would permit, from the vestiges of an aristocratic and feudal past which were firmly embedded in the society as well as in the constitutions of some of the older states—slavery, primogeniture, and limitations on suffrage in particular. The encouragement to public education in the Ordinance of 1787 was a mere statement of what ought to be done, in contrast with the concrete provision in the Land Act of 1785 which had reserved the sixteenth lot of every township for maintenance of public schools in the township. In the long run, however, it was perhaps the general philosophical tone of the Northwest Ordinance, deriving from Jefferson's Report and the Ordinance of 1784 which was based on it, that influenced the frame of society and government adopted by the new states in the Northwest Territory.

Prior to the passage of the Northwest Ordinance, England's cession of her claims to this territory by the Provisional Treaty of 1782 and the action of the several Seaboard states in ceding their claims to the federal government had set the stage for the young republic's first experiment in colonization by making it the first territory under jurisdiction of the federal government. These were important acts. To the south of the Ohio two new states had been admitted to the Union, Kentucky in 1792 and Tennessee in 1796. In both, settlement had been retarded and early attempts at self government had been frustrated by the parent states of Virginia and North Carolina from which these new States were formed. Although the majority of the pioneers who flooded into this western Virginia and North Carolina through the Appalachian valleys were not natives of either, and although they were for the most part politically and socially unsympathetic to the plantation system and to slavery in particular, such was the hold of the Tidewater society on the government of the parent states that it was able to frustrate the effort in the West to adopt a radically different society or government. Land was disposed of in lots of tremendous acreage in such a way as to encourage both speculation and the establishment of large plantation holdings and to discourage small farmers without slaves or to force them to become "squatters" without title. It is notable that although the constitutions of both Kentucky and Tennessee, unlike their parent states, granted suffrage to free men without property qualifications, both perpetuated slavery, and in addition Tennessee required property qualifications for members of its legislature and governor and also established a system of taxation favoring the wealthy plantation owner by limiting the taxation on slaves and setting the tax on land at a uniform rate without regard to the land's quality.

In contrast with this experience, as the first federal territory the Northwest enjoyed not only the benefits of the Ordinance of 1787 but also a modicum of physical protection. It was federal troops under Anthony Wayne and William Henry Harrison, debatably assisted by frontier militia, that won the battles of Fallen Timbers and Tippecanoe. This protection so telescoped the first and second frontiers in the development of the Northwest that, unlike Kentucky and Tennessee (and western Pennsylvania as well), there was never in the Northwest a clearly established period of first settlements (except of course the French) entirely on their own against the wilderness and the savages. As a result, it must be recognized that the rapid population of the Northwest by small farmers of modest means, who were from the beginning more or less permanent settlers rather than squatters or hunters, was to a considerable extent fostered if not actually subsidized by the federal government.

That this fact colored the political complexion of the people is evident from the peculiar blend of Republicanism and Federalism which became apparent first in Ohio, then in Indiana and Illinois. This blend may be described as being Jeffersonian in philosophy and Hamiltonian in allegiance. The typical political philosophy of the area—espoused by Buckeye, Hoosier, or Sucker—recognized both the will of the people and the need for a strong federal rather than a state government to carry out that will. This is not to say that the settlers of Ohio or Illinois during the period of territorial government were of the opinion that the federal government could govern them better as territories than they could govern themselves as states. Rather, they recognized from the beginning that their power as a people derived from the nation rather than from the state. The citizenship they held in common both before and after achieving statehood was U.S. citizenship. The popularity of internal improvements as a political issue can be accounted for on the basis of local benefits, but the equal popularity of the protective tariff as a means of fostering industry cannot be accounted for in these states, which had as yet developed but little industry, except as an evidence of the philosophy that what would be good for the nation would be good for the state and for the individual. Both issues were viewed as the sort of thing that the federal government should legislate for the benefit of the nation as a whole.

II

The essential goal of life in the West during the first half of the nineteenth century has been pretty well agreed upon by historians of the period, as indeed it was pretty well agreed upon by the citizens of the area themselves, to have been the attainment of the greatest material prosperity, scientific advancement, and social progress that the world had ever known, a prosperity and progress for all, albeit any man who could lawfully attain more than another would be entitled to what he attained. There was enough for everybody and more for those who could get it. If the farm in Indiana was not as good as a man wanted, he could get a better one in Illinois. If the condition of laborer was not congenial, a man could read the law and go to practicing, or save a nest egg and become a capitalist himself. Abraham Lincoln's advice on both possibilities was brief and to the point. In 1858 he wrote to a friend who had recommended a young man to study law with him: "When a man has reached the age that Mr. Widmer has, and has already been doing for himself, my judgment is, that he reads the books for himself without an instructor. That is percisely the way I came to the law." In an 1859 speech, while discussing the virtues of free versus slave labor, he admitted with pride: "Twenty-five years ago, I was a hired laborer. The hired laborer of yesterday, labors on his own account today; and will hire others to labor for him tomorrow. Advancement—improvement in condition—is the order of things in a society of equals." It was just as simple as that to an ambitious man who had then lived forty-three of his fifty years in the Northwest. If one should object today, "But there were few men of Lincoln's calibre in the Northwest or anywhere else at that time," the answer is that there were hundreds, perhaps thousands, who thought they were not merely equal to but, in the phrase of the time, "a damned sight better than" Lincoln. As Professor Buley has put it, "The Andrew Jacksons, Abraham Lincolns and Andrew Johnsons were, to one way of looking, not unique, not even strikingly exceptional; like Daniel Boone they became known because they later got into conspicuous spots. In every western community of any size were other men just as able, men who in all probability would have accredited themselves just as well, had the accidents of history happened differently,"[1] The important thing was that men thought it was so, and seldom missed a chance, whether in politics or other activities, to try to prove it.

In one of the campaign biographies of Abraham Lincoln, known as "the Wigwam Edition," published in New York in 1860, the anonymous biographer introduced his subject as a backwoodsman.

> If there is any one peculiarity of American nationality, any phase of American character by which it is distinguished in the eyes of discerning foreigners, any trait that will make it preeminent in history, it is that singular sort of energy, half physical and half intellectual, nervous, intense, untiring, which has achieved all of greatness that America has yet attained; . . . . it is not delicate nor dainty, but tremendous and terrible; it is successful. This energy is manifested in many ways and by various characters, but by none more emphatically than the backwoods-man. . . .
>
> The backwoods-man represents this individual American character. Abroad, the backwoods-man is looked upon, and rightly, as the representative American.

Continuing in this vein the anonymous author sets up as his thesis for the biography of Lincoln essentially the same thesis that Frederick Jackson Turner would use twenty-three years later in establishing his bench mark for surveying American history. If for "backwoodsman" we understand "frontiersman," this early biographer of Lincoln may be said to have anticipated the native Wisconsin historian who was born nine months and ten days after Lincoln was inaugurated president.

The only trouble with this designation of Abraham Lincoln as "backwoodsman" or "frontiersman" is that after his twenty-fifth year it was wholly inapplicable, and what was true of Lincoln was likewise true of most of his contemporaries in the Northwest; few of them were ever backwoodsmen for more than a short period of their lives, and the period of the frontier in the Northwest Territory was so fleeting as almost to seem a historical myth if one

[1]Roscoe Carlyle Buley, *The Old Northwest; Pioneer Period,* 1815-1840 (Bloomington: Indiana University Press, 1951), 2 vols., II, 328.

looks steadily at the life of any one man or at the life in a particular community. Cincinnati, for example, was never a frontier community in a strict sense of the term after 1790, the year that Governor St. Clair changed its name from Losantiville, and by 1810 it was a flourishing town of twenty-three hundred, much like the towns of the same size east of the Appalachians.

The communities which provided the cultural matrix of civilization in the new states of the Northwest, were from the beginning well supplied with brains and an appreciation of the cultural ingredients which lent savor to civilization. Anyone who has studied the early history of a single community in the area, whether it be a community like Cincinnati which rapidly became and remained the leading metropolis of the area until overtaken after the Civil War by the younger cities on the Great Lakes, or a community like New Salem, Illinois, which disappeared within ten years after it was founded in 1829, cannot escape the evidence on every hand of the enormous energy referred to by the anonymous ,biographer of Lincoln. Although material necessities and comforts of life claimed a large share of this expenditure of energy, nevertheless intellectual and spiritual activities flourished from the very beginning of each settlement. Churches, schools, subscription libraries, debating societies, lyceums, historical societies, museums, scientific societies, newspapers, and literary magazines were established as soon as, and in many instances earlier than, the mills, factories, and commercial establishments which largely supplanted frontier home manufacture and handicraft almost before it became an established economy. In the intellectual sphere the product was first of all for local consumption, of course, and was an insufficient fare which had to be supplemented by large importations from the East and from abroad, but there was an occasional item for export, such as abolitionism, which shook the nation to its foundations.

What the citizen of the West thought of himself is abundantly recorded by the documentation in Professor Buley's great work, *The Old Northwest,* but two short and typical comments may suffice for our brief examples. An anonymous Illinois correspondent of a Philadelphia newspaper wrote in 1837: "Assuming this fact as granted [that everyone must be the architect of his own fortune] I would refer to the superiority of the western portion of our continent over the eastern, as regards the *acquisition of wealth—professional eminence—political distinction,* and the opportunity offered of *exercising influence on society* and the *destinies of our common country.*" In the same vein spoke editor James Hall, whose *Illinois Monthly Magazine* (later, *Western Monthly Magazine),* though certainly not the literary equal of *The North American Review,* was yet quite able to hold its own with other literary and intellectual organs of the East during the years 1830-1835. He stated bluntly: "The fact is that persons who emigrate to the west, have to learn from our people here, a vast deal more than they can possibly teach them." This confidence may have appeared to the Easterner, who frequently confused sophistication with education, as being somewhat overblown, but the emigrant to the West could ignore the advice only at great peril to his own success. The Bostonians as well as the Charlestonians had to "acknowledge the corn," to use a favorite contemporary Western phrase of the period, when men like Lincoln and Douglas went east to represent their state in the Congress and the Senate during the next two decades.

III

The story of the development of civilization in the Northwest Territory has been told excellently and at length in a number of scholarly works which should be so well known that any summary so brief as this may seem an impertinence.[2] I should like, however, to illustrate by reference to the two communities I have mentioned what happened in a relatively short space of time to transform a wilderness into the dominant section of the United States which the Northwest had become when Lincoln was elected president in 1860.

[2] In addition to Buley's *The Old Northwest,* two books may be mentioned in particular: John Donald Barnhart, *Valley of Democracy: The Frontier versus the Plantation in the Ohio Valley,* 1775-1818 (Bloomington: Indiana University Press, 1953); Beverly Waugh Bond, *The Civilization of the Old Northwest; A Study of Political, Social, and Economic Development,* 1788-1812 (New York, 1934).

In January 1790, Governor Arthur St. Clair found on the north bank of the Ohio "a small settlement" of cabins known as Losantiville, which he promptly renamed Cincinnati. Twenty years later Cincinnati had become a flourishing town of 2,300 which would remain the leading metropolis of the Northwest until overtaken by the younger cities on the Great Lakes after the Civil War. In 1825 its population reached 16,000, and by 1836 it was 30,000. As the manufacturing center of the West it boasted by the year 1832 cotton mills, machine carding mills, paper mills, type foundries, book binderies, machine shops, tinplate and sheet iron works, rope walks, coachmaking shops, saddletree factories, tanneries, tobacco factories, plow and ax factories, barrel factories, and shops manufacturing pianos and harps! Cincinnati had in 1833, twenty-four private schools, twenty public schools, and a college, Lane Seminary, founded in 1829 and already a flourishing hotbed of abolitionism. Cincinnati University, incorporated in 1809, folded up when its single building was blown down the same year, was revived in 1819 and conferred one M.A. and three A.B. degrees in 1821, whereupon it continued by fits and starts until it folded again in 1826, not to be revived until the present institution opened in 1835. There was also the Medical College of Ohio established by Dr. David Drake in 1818 (chartered in 1819), which would be competing within a decade with two additional medical colleges, the Worthington Reformed Medical College, which moved to Cincinnati from Worthington in 1840, and the College of Physicians and Surgeons which moved from Columbus to Cincinnati in 1841. These were abetted by the dental college founded by Dr. James Taylor in 1841. Cincinnati's public circulating library was established in 1814. In addition to a continuing assortment of newspapers which flourished from the year 1793 (when *The Centinel of the North-Western Territory* began publication) and which, as in other communities of the Northwest in this era, frequently provided more literate as well as more literary fare for their readers than do their counterparts in our own day. Cincinnati was the home of a remarkable number of periodicals of considerable literary and intellectual distinction, the most notable being Timothy Flint's *Western Monthly Review* (1827-1830) and James Hall's *Western Monthly Magazine,* a continuation of the *Illinois Monthly Magazine* which moved to Cincinnati in 1833 and continued publication until 1835. It is less significant, it seems to me, that these journals were not tremendously successful financially and ran for half a dozen years at best, than that they were established at all and maintained a relatively proud, if imitative, literary and intellectual level. In this era as in any other, the advancement of literature, science, and culture in general was spearheaded by a small portion of the population, and the names of James Hall, Timothy Flint, and Dr. Daniel Drake (brother of David) are found in the forefront of several varieties of cultural activity, whether literary society, antiquarian society, scientific society, circulating library, lyceum, museum, or school. By the 1830s an English visitor, Harriette Martineau, viewed the people and culture of Cincinnati "with high respect" and at no distinct disadvantage in comparison with the citizens of older cities which she visited in the East. Nor was Cincinnati exceptional. Within the same space much the same story can be told for Detroit, Cleveland, Vincennes, or three dozen other communities, with but little change except in names and dates.

At the other extreme from the community which thrived, let us look at New Salem, Illinois, which failed, or to use Abraham Lincoln's phrase, "winked out." Benjamin P. Thomas' *Lincoln's New Salem* (1934), a minor classic of its kind, gives an intimate picture of what this frontier community meant to a raw youth twenty-two years of age, who arrived as a laborer with less than a year of formal schooling, became a store clerk, store owner who went broke, postmaster, and surveyor, and was elected to his first political office as representative in the legislature, which success whetted the appetite that motivated his political activity until he landed in the White House a quarter of a century later.

New Salem was founded in 1829, flourished for six years, and became a ghost town in ten. During its six flourishing years, however, it provided Lincoln with the social, intellectual, and cultural matrix which developed his adult capacities and molded his mature mind. Beginning with a dam on the Sangamon River, a saw and gristmill, New Salem developed a modestly sufficient manufacturing economy for its immediate farming area in a period of three years, with a blacksmith shop, cooper shop, wheel and carriage shop, machine carding mill, cabinet and furniture shop, tannery, still house (no community was without one, legal or extralegal), half a dozen general stores, a respectable tavern, a "grocery" or saloon, etc. The population of New Salem probably never exceeded 150 souls (about the size of Chicago at that time), and the entire precinct including the neighboring farmland polled only 300 voters when Lincoln first stood for the legislature in 1832. But New Salem had a good subscription school run by Mentor Graham, whose claim to fame is that he also is purported to have tutored Lincoln. And although a public library was not achieved in six years, a good many books were available to borrowers in the private libraries of such citizens as the town's founder James Rutledge, a native of South Carolina, late of Georgia, Tennessee, and Kentucky; Dr. John Allen of Vermont, who held his medical degree from Dartmouth; and Dr. Francis Regnier, who came from Marietta, Ohio. A debating society flourished, if one may judge from the minute book which survives, with more serious discussion of intellectual, religious, and cultural subjects than one can readily discover in much further developed communities in our day. It was at this New Salem debating society and at the Lyceum which flourished at Rockville within walking distance that devotees of Tom Paine's *Age of Reason* and Volney's *Ruins* crossed intellects with Baptist, Presbyterian, or Methodist dogmatists. There was also the Temperance Society and the nonsectarian Sunday School founded by Dr. John Allen, which, though primarily moral and religious in purpose, were not of small consequence in the intellectual fare provided to effect that purpose. Although more time was spent, and large attendances gathered, at the cockfights, ganderpullings, horse races, wrestling matches, shooting matches, and Kentucky barbecues which New Salem provided in common with other frontier villages, time spent and numbers occupied were not then any more than now the sole indicia of cultural attainment. At any rate, it was during these years 1831—1836 at New Salem that A. Lincoln purportedly learned something of Shakespeare and Robert Burns from his friend Jack Kelsoe, studied Kirkham's *Grammar* and the six books of Euclid, read Paine, Volney, and

Jefferson, as well as all the newspapers which came to subscribers through the Post Office.

It was this community culture of the new states, whether in Ohio, Illinois, or Wisconsin, which provided the cultural matrix of Northwestern civilization, and the settlement of the Northwest was from the beginning predominantly a settlement of communities. In New Salem and Cincinnati, as in most communities in the southern half of the Northwest Territory, the family settlers were largely from south of the Ohio, while the bachelors came largely from New England and the Middle Atlantic, sometimes bringing wives later or marrying the local girls. European migrants also came in family or in community groups. In the northern half of the Territory, New England and Middle Atlantic settlers in family groups were the rule, particularly in the Western Reserve of Ohio and in Michigan. Throughout the area and in the midst of differences in origin, differences in religion, and differences in mores—which although they probably seemed large at that time are now diminished in historical perspective by comparison with the political, economic, and social interests which they shared in common—the settlers of the Northwest quickly came to believe that their transplanted and federally fostered civilization was the common denominator for the nation as a whole. Their first allegiance was to the nation rather than to the state. They did not consider the Declaration of Independence to have served its purpose as a justification of revolution long since a matter of history, but regarded it as a political creed to which their society and government were dedicated for the perpetual future. Although they believed that they were the nation's best achievement as of that date, they were so optimistic, almost without exception, as to regard the nation's future and their place in that future as one of unlimited development, improvement, and perfectibility.

ABRAHAM LINCOLN:

AN IMMORTAL SIGN*

One approaches any anniversary with a sense of mystery and of ritual, for every anniversary is a reminder that something which began long ago is yet unfinished. And the questions of portent and meaning which confronted our fathers, and their fathers before them, remain with us, if not identical, still recognizable variations on a theme which neither they nor we have fully comprehended. So, on the sesquicentennial of Abraham Lincoln's birth one recognizes that repetition cannot be avoided, and seeks to make a virtue of necessity, citing Lincoln's own practice for justification. As a public speaker, Lincoln was one of the greatest repeaters in history, stating again and again some simple truths that needed repeating because, somehow, people were in his day, as in ours, great forgetters, who although they had often heard the truth, were unable to hold it fast much longer than an eighth grader can remember the lines he has memorized for a graduation exercise. We remember, or should remember, in this age of conflict so similar in some respects to the age in which Lincoln lived, the memorable words of Lincoln, not because they bring ready-made answers to

*First published in *The Enduring Lincoln,* edited by Norman E. Graebner (University of Illinois Press: Urbana, 1959), this lecture was delivered a number of times to various audiences commemorating the Lincoln Sesquicentennial, including the English Speaking Union, London, November 17, 1958, and the University of Illinois, February 11, 1959.

our problems, but because they may help us find our own answers and perhaps may even help us to phrase them.

I

It is a real temptation to do nothing on such an occasion but quote Lincoln, and perhaps one could do worse than merely read, with critical appreciation, the sculptured logic of his argument, savoring the poetic imagery and rhythms of his style. But, while not neglecting Lincoln's own words, perhaps it would be better, if one could do it, to try to formulate in brief the image of Lincoln which has become one of the enduring symbols in human history. Hence, what follows is an attempt to outline the major contribution which Lincoln made, not merely to the realm of thought and letters, but in a broad scope to human life itself, as a man once flesh and blood and brain, but long since become a symbol and a myth, a story in the annals of humanity which runs as an unfailing spring for whoever thirsts for truth.

I must ask indulgence, at this point, for a personal note, because I do not see how I can proceed without admitting that I am to some extent retracing my own steps in the study of Lincoln, and reaffirming some of the convictions which this study has established. More than twenty-five years ago I concluded the writing of a doctoral dissertation on the subject "Lincoln in Literature" (published in 1935 as a book entitled *The Lincoln Legend)* with a quotation from Emerson's "Essay on History," which at that time seemed to me to summarize the forces which I thought I had identified at work in the many accounts of Lincoln's life—in biographical and historical writing no less than in the folklore, fiction, poetry, and drama with which I was chiefly concerned. Emerson had said the ultimate understanding of history demands that the student

> attain and maintain that lofty sight where facts yield their secret sense, and poetry and annals are alike. The instinct of the mind, the purpose of nature, betrays itself in the use we make of the signal narrations of history. Time dissipates to shining ether the solid angularity of facts. No anchor, no cable, no fences, avail to keep a fact a fact. Babylon, Troy, Tyre,

Palestine, and even early Rome are passing already into fiction. The Garden of Eden, the sun standing still in Gibeon, is poetry thenceforward to all nations. Who cares what the fact was, when we have made a constellation of it to hang in heaven an immortal sign?

At the sesquicentennial of Lincoln's birth, Emerson's philosophical and poetic comment furnishes not a conclusion but rather a point of departure for certain observations about the place which America's most representative historical figure has achieved in the story of mankind. The American people and the people of the world at large have adopted Lincoln as a symbol and have placed him as a star of the first magnitude in the firmament of historical heroes. Not a few writers, as well as artists in other media, have produced major works of art inspired by and assisting in the perpetuation of the symbolic myth of Lincoln. What is this symbol and what does it imply as one traces it in Lincoln literature? It is in broadest terms the myth of a folk hero, noble in intellect, morally inspired, and imaginatively gifted, whose success was thwarted by the tragic flaw of ambiguity in the human nature which was his and his people's heritage. The myth itself is ambiguous, shifting and changing in its meaning as perceived and treated by different minds, but always revolving around the poles of a human nature that is dually free and constrained, right and wrong, good and bad. This mystery has been phrased and rephrased in every age and all languages, but nowhere more succinctly than by the Psalmist's question addressed to the Divine Being: "What is man that thou art mindful of him?" The gamut of human dilemmas in a moral universe is unrolled throughout the life and personality of Lincoln, in the broadly ambiguous terms which may be similarly traced in the more or less legendary heroes of the deep past from Adam to Arthur or from Caesar to Cromwell. And a primary lesson of history may be learned from the extent of a multitude of facts which do nothing to diminish, but rather enforce, the symbolic import, as read in the factual record, of the hero whose life has been more rather than less rigorously recorded and studied.

Thus the figure of Lincoln represents the American people. The questions, who was Lincoln, how did he happen, where was he going, what did he mean, why was he so, was he good or bad, did he achieve or fail—these are the questions we ask of ourselves. Who are we, how did we happen, where are we going, what do we mean, why are we so, are we good or bad, will we achieve or fail? The truth about Americans is the consistency of our contradictions, a practical and materialistic people but given to mysticism beyond measure, a selfish people whose largess has been demonstrated to surpass the richest myths of antiquity, a self-reliant people who are so filled with self-doubt that we crave more than anything else to be understood and appreciated—like a youth who believes in himself but wonders if after all he may not be a failure—an honest people who are shocked to discover our self-deceit and who strive to redefine our honesty to prevent self-deception. In Lincoln we have an epitome of what we are, we like to think, at our highest and best, as well as at our most ambiguous, and we would believe that the world could know us better by studying his life and works.

All of this may sound mystical, and it is. In an individual human being or in a society, it is the mystical, artistic, creative intelligence which seeks to make something more than a sequence of facts out of the experience of human life. Even when this search goes by the name of "seeking to understand," the dual process is in truth "making it thus," and philosophically "knowing" and "creating" become one. It is for this reason that the study of biography and history is ultimately much the same study as the study of poetry and fiction, and to some people perhaps, the more fascinating of the two disciplines. To know the truth of history is to realize its ultimate myth and its inevitable ambiguity.

If the development of this theme appears to be following a line of thought which has been overworked somewhat in recent years by a school of literary criticism, it may be noted that most new ideas are old ones in new dress, and that both Emerson and Lincoln developed their similar philosophies of history before "symbolism," "myth," and "ambiguity" had become the shibboleths of twentieth-century academic criticism, but long after Plato and Socrates had pondered many of the same problems. In any case, the validity of this interpretation must stand on its own feet, albeit indebted to many thinkers besides Emerson, and including Lincoln, who have recognized that factual reality may be, after all, but a symbolic representation of a mystery, the meaning of which remains yet to be solved.

II

To illustrate, let us consider two key incidents, each with its set of circumstances amply if incompletely documented (there never has been complete documentation, of course, for any historical event). The first is the so-called beginning of the Civil War at Fort Sumter, and the second is the emancipation of the slaves. These are only two of many key incidents in the history of the Civil War and in the public life of President Lincoln which illustrate the ambiguity of the historical myth, but they are chosen because they are well known and may thus represent the problem better than several hundred less known or even minor incidents in Lincoln's life which could equally well illustrate the theme.

The question of who started the Civil War has obviously not been settled to date, as anyone who is willing to read more than one book can demonstrate to his own satisfaction. Even though the preponderant number of opinions, if one counts opinions, or the preponderant weight of opinion, if one weighs opinion, may seem to indicate that the South started it by firing on Fort Sumter, rather than that the North started it by "invading" Charleston Harbor with armed ships. When this question comes down to individuals, it is whether Lincoln started the war by ordering the expedition to relieve Fort Sumter, or whether any one of several assorted Confederates, ranging from General Beauregard, who certainly must have authorized the notification of intention to fire "within one hour," which bears the signatures of his Aides-de-Camp Chestnut and Lee, to Edmund Ruffin who is recorded as having fired the first gun. It is tragically humorous to reflect on the symbolic dispersal of even a "perhaps" assignment of final responsibility on the Confederate side. Every participant was *somewhat* responsible, but no individual was *finally* responsible in the Confederacy, least of all President Jefferson Davis, who was after all the President of a mere Confederacy. But on the Union side the symbolism is precisely the opposite; Lincoln was the final

human authority, and he never questioned the fact himself, although he understood clearly that this was a symbolic authority
vested in him by the ballots of the American people. He made it
clear, even though he did not expect agreement from the
Confederates, that his intention. to hold Sumter (as a symbol, be
it noted, for its value as a base of operations was negligible) was
not regarded by him as an act of aggression. The penultimate
paragraph of his First Inaugural Address stated the position from
which he could not retreat.

> In *your* hands, my dissatisfied fellow countrymen, and not in
> *mine*, is the momentous issue of civil war. The government will
> not assail *you*. You can have no conflict, without being your-
> selves the aggresors. *You* have no oath registered in Heaven to
> destroy the government, while *I* shall have the most solemn one
> to "preserve, protect and defend" it.

In his annual message to Congress, December 6, 1864, he
reiterated in his final paragraph what he had said three and a half
years earlier: "In stating a single condition of peace, I mean simply
to say that the war will cease on the part of the government, whenever it shall have ceased on the part of those who began it."

Thus the mystery of who started the Civil War centers in the
mind of Lincoln. Did he order the expedition to relieve Fort Sumter
as a cunning trick to solicit the first blow from the Confederacy
in order to pretend that he was attacked when in fact he was
attacking? This is the implicit premise of many and the affirmed
premise of some members of a school of thought which remains
active, though in a minority, today. A more charitable as well as
more philosophical way of putting the question would be: Did
Lincoln order the expedition to relieve Fort Sumter as a symbolic
force to illustrate to the secessionists that he did not recognize a
symbolic sovereignty which most of the citizens of those states
claimed to reside in fact in the state as opposed to the nation under
the Constitution? There is this difference in the two questions. The
first implies moral obliquity on the part of Lincoln, just as a similar
obverse would imply moral obliquity on the part of Jefferson Davis
and other secessionists; that is, did secessionists sponsor state
sovereignty and the act of secession as a cunning trick in the guise

of a moral right in order to perpetuate a ruling slavocracy in the South when it could no longer extend its power in the whole Union? The second question — did Lincoln order the expedition as a symbolic force to illustrate the symbolic sovereignty of the Union which he refused to abandon or to admit that the secessionists could abandon — not only implies but recognizes the political ambiguity of the Constitution itself on the matter of state versus federal sovereignty, as being the ultimate ambiguity which Lincoln hoped, if possible, to try to diminish gradually, if not to resolve finally, by ballots rather than bullets.

The whole question of who started the Civil War is thus a symbolic rather than a merely factual question, and it runs back, politically, psychologically, morally, and philosophically, to Cain and Abel and their distraughtly responsible father and mother. Who shall rule whom? Only the self-righteous, it seems to me, can read in Lincoln's Second Inaugural Address a statement of hypocrisy rather than a confession of sin and a prayer for absolution.

> Both parties deprecated war; but one of them would *make* war rather than let the nation survive; and the other would *accept* war rather than let it perish. . . . Both read the same Bible, and pray to the same God; and each invokes His aid against the other. . . . The Almighty has his own purposes. "Woe unto the world because of offences! for it must needs be that offences come; but woe to that man by whom the offence cometh!" . . . Fondly do we hope — fervently do we pray — that this mighty scourge of war may speedily pass away. . . .

Where is the tragic ambiguity of the human condition more poignantly set forth than in the record of the Civil War, where more poetically symbolized than in Lincoln, the hero who recognized this ambiguity in himself and in the people whom he represented, or where more memorably expressed than in his words?

III

The second incident chosen to illustrate the symbolic ambiguity of the Lincoln myth is the promulgation of the Emancipation

Proclamation. Did Lincoln free the slaves? At the time, his antagonists were quick to attack the Proclamation as a hoax, because its language limited emancipation specifically to those areas which were under Confederate control, and hence where Lincoln had no operational authority. Here again we are confronted with a symbolic action, as ambiguous in its meaning as is the language of the Proclamation itself, and yet it is the turning point in Lincoln's presidency. In promulgating the Proclamation, Lincoln burned a bridge behind him. Until September 22, 1862, the data on which the preliminary proclamation was issued stipulating January 1, 1863, as the date on which emancipation would take effect, Lincoln had not advanced much beyond the position he had stated in collaboration with his colleague in the Illinois legislature, Dan Stone, in a set of Resolutions entered in the *Illinois House Journal* under date of March 3, 1837, namely, "that the institution of slavery is founded on both injustice and bad policy . . . but that the Congress of the United States has no power, under the Constitution, to interfere with the institution of slavery in the different States." As late as August 22, 1862, he had written Horace Greeley, "If I could save the Union without freeing *any* slave, I would do it; and if I could save it by freeing *all* the slaves, I would do it; and if I could save it by freeing some and leaving others alone I would also do that." One month later he issued the preliminary proclamation which pledged:

> That on the first day of January in the year of our Lord, one thousand eight hundred and sixty-three, all persons held as slaves within any state, or designated part of a state, the people whereof shall then be in rebellion against the United States shall be then, thenceforward, and forever free; and the executive government of the United States, including the military and naval authority thereof, will recognize and maintain the freedom of such persons, and will do no act or acts to repress such persons, or any of them, in any efforts they may make for their actual freedom.

This was a promise, the fulfillment of which required not only the winning of the war but also the later enactment of the Thirteenth Amendment and the Fourteenth Amendment, and yet it marked a turning point not only in American history but also in Lincoln's personal thinking about slavery — that armed force should be used to set the Negro free in the rebel states as a means to the end of saving the Union.

Thus a symbolic act and a purely symbolic document established whatever facts of freedom the Negro may enjoy in the South today, but if anyone supposes that the ambiguities of that act and that document have been finally clarified by any amendment to the Constitution, or by any court decision rendered to date, or by any executive action by the President of the present United States, he surely cannot have been reading the newspapers.

There have been no statues erected to Abraham Lincoln in the South, but if one were to be erected in recognition of this sesquicentennial it might well bear inscribed on its pedestal the passage which occurs in the second paragraph of Lincoln's opening speech in the fourth debate with Stephen A. Douglas at Charleston, Illinois, September 18, 1858. Segregationist literature has cited this passage so often that it is probably better known in the South today than anything else Lincoln wrote, including the Gettysburg Address. This is what Lincoln said:

> I will say then that I am not, nor ever have been in favor of bringing about in any way the social and political equality of the white and black races, [applause] — that I am not nor ever have been in favor of making voters or jurors of negroes, nor of qualifying them to hold office, nor to inter-marry with white people; and I will say in addition to this that there is a physical difference between the white and black races which I believe will for ever forbid the two races living together on terms of social and political equality. And inasmuch as they cannot so live, while they do remain together there must be the position of superior and inferior, and I as much as any other man am in favor of having the superior position assigned to the white race.

Of course, it would be expecting too much for the segregationists to quote the letter Lincoln wrote to Governor Michael Hahn of Louisiana on March 13, 1864, which indicates that Lincoln modified his views expressed at Charleston to some extent before he died. He wrote to Hahn as follows:

I congratulate you on having fixed your name in history as the first-free-state Governor of Louisiana. Now you are about to have a Convention which, among other things, will probably define the elective franchise. I barely suggest for your private consideration, whether some of the colored people may not be let in — as, for instance, the very intelligent, and especially those who have fought gallantly in our ranks. They would probably help, in some trying time to come, to keep the jewel of liberty within the family of freedom. But this is only a suggestion, not to the public, but to you alone.

Basically, we have in Lincoln's own words the unresolved ambiguity of freedom for the Negro. Is freedom the same for black as for white? Are all men created equal?

IV

All his political life Lincoln had been saying that the soul of America's being was the proposition that "all men are created equal." He had referred to this phrase in the Declaration of Independence many times during the campaign of 1858 in language which seems to be directly contradictory to the spirit and meaning of the language he used at Charleston; such as, for example, when he spoke at Chicago on July 10, calling it "the electric cord . .
that links the hearts of patriotic and liberty-loving men together, that will link those patriotic hearts as long as the love of freedom exists in the minds of men throughout the world." How, if at all, can we reconcile this apparent contradiction?

The Gettysburg Address is Lincoln's highest expression, in poetic, symbolic terms, of how he conceived of the Declaration of Independence, not as a statement of fact but as a symbolic proposition to the ultimate proving of which the nation was dedicated at its birth. Lincoln believed that "all men are created equal" in the only way that a mind as coldly logical as his could believe in it. Just how he believed it, is indicated by his use of the word "proposition." This word has proved a stumbling block even for highly literate readers who cannot conceive of the essential kinship of poetry and mathematics as creations of the human mind in the search for truth, and of both poetry and mathematics as theory providing a symbolic frame in which life may be understood. By his own account Lincoln had "studied and nearly mastered Euclid," and we may be sure that he used the word "proposition" naturally in the Euclidean sense of a statement to be debated, and if possible, verified or proved. Thus American democracy, as an active, living thing, meant to Lincoln the verification or proving of the proposition to which its very existence was in the beginning dedicated. In 1863, eighty-seven years had gone into the proving, the Civil War had come at a critical stage in the argument, the Union armies had won an inconclusive victory, and the affirmation that "all men are created equal" was still a live proposition, open to argument and inviting proof, but not on any account one that had already been proved. The further proof was for "us the living, to be dedicated here to the unfinished work which they who fought here have thus far so nobly advanced."

It was thus that Lincoln believed in democracy, not as an already proven principle, nor as a meaningless form of words incapable of proof, but as the most viable political proposition about human life which the human mind had been able to conceive in the long history of civilization. The Gettysburg Address suggests that Lincoln's understanding of history was not far from Emerson's: "Who cares what the fact was, when we have made a constellation of it to hang in heaven an immortal sign?"

Into Lincoln's concept was distilled the best thought of two thousand years of European civilization, striving to break the hold of tribal myth, to divest humanity of outworn social and political forms, and to create a political-social pattern in which men might live together without being either ruler or subject, master or slave. The concept was humanistic in that it projected the humanist's conviction that the mind of the individual man could give order and meaning to the impulse of the individual human life. To understand was to be free to act in harmony with fate in the pursuit of happiness. So Lincoln conceived the nation as a being with conflicting drives, hopes, and fears, but guided by reason — not all-knowing, but capable of learning and growing, and capable of regeneration in the midst of decay. For this nation, conceived in liberty and perpetuating the free spirit which gave it birth, could not die so long as men lived who gave of their life, their liberty, and their happiness to preserve it.

Hence Lincoln phrased one of the most memorable passages in the English language, as a symbolic statement of the meaning of facts long since laid to rest in the tomb of history, but resurrected in the bloody travail of civil war to live again in a new era:

> Four score and seven years ago our fathers brought forth on this continent, a new nation, conceived in Liberty, and dedicated to the proposition that all men are created equal.
>
> Now we are engaged in a great civil war, testing whether that nation, or any nation so conceived and so dedicated, can long endure. We are met on a great battle-field of that war. We have come to dedicate a portion of that field, as a final resting place for those who here gave their lives that that nation might live. It is altogether fitting and proper that we should do this.
>
> But, in a larger sense, we can not dedicate — we can not consecrate — we can not hallow — this ground. The brave men, living and dead, who struggled here, have consecrated it, far above our poor power to add or detract. The world will little note, nor long remember what we say here, but it can never forget what they did here. It is for us the living, rather, to be dedicated here to the unfinished work which they who fought here have thus far so nobly advanced. It is rather for us to be here dedicated to the great task remaining before us — that from these honored dead we take increased devotion to that cause for which they gave the last full measure of devotion — that we here highly resolve that these dead shall not have died in vain — that this nation, under God, shall have a new birth of freedom — and that government of the people, by the people, for the people, shall not perish from the earth.

This symbolic conception of the Declaration of Independence was not new with Lincoln at Gettysburg, for he had many times before stated his recognition of the "immortal sign." One of his most pointed statements occurs in his letter to H. L. Pierce, April 6, 1859, written to be read at a festival honoring the birthday of Thomas Jefferson.

All honor to Jefferson — to the man who, in the concrete pressure of a struggle for national independence by a single
people, had the coolness, forecast, and capacity to introduce
into a merely revolutionary document, an abstract truth, applicable to all men and all times, and so to embalm it there,
that to-day, and in all coming days, it shall be a rebuke and
a stumbling-block to the very harbingers of re-appearing
tyranny and oppression.

But Lincoln was fully aware of the ambiguity of equality and
freedom for all men, and of the symbolic role of the Constitution
as "the picture of silver" framing "the apple of gold." Freedom
and equality are completely ambiguous except under symbolic authority, and the symbolism of the Constitution undertakes to resolve this complete ambiguity by breaking it down into many symbolic parts, each of which contains its own ambiguity, and all of
which are collectively referred to, somewhat euphemistically, as "a
system of checks and balances."

Who shall rule whom? As there is no absolute answer possible
except an ambiguous one, so there can be no practical, wholly
unambiguous answer in any specific case. Lincoln pointed out in
his First Inaugural Address that "No organic law can ever be
framed with a provision specifically applicable to every question
which may occur in practical administration." And in differences
of opinion (based on ambiguities) arises the necessity that someone
must acquiesce. "If the minority will not acquiesce," Lincoln continued, "the majority must, or the government must cease. There
is no other alternative; for continuing the government, is
acquiescence on one side or the other." But acquiescence on one
side or the other, under constitutional government, cannot resolve
finally the ambiguity of the human condition in which "all men
are created equal" and " are endowed by their Creator with certain
unalienable rights." When Lincoln said on February 22, 1861, at
Independence Hall, Philadelphia, that he would almost rather be
assassinated than to give up that principle, he not only voiced recognition of the extreme to which a minority of one might go, but
also avowed, in the strongest language he ever used, his own
dedication to the most precious of all ambiguities, precious be-

cause, as he said, it gave hope "not alone to the people of this country, but, I hope, to the world, for all future time." Not in certainty but in ambiguity lay the hope which to Lincoln, as one man, gave scope and meaning to the individual's quest for identity. This is the ultimate truth of the myth of Lincoln which inspires the poetry, the fiction, the drama, the statues, and the factual biographies as well, and it is the ultimate truth likewise of the myth of the American nation whose people Lincoln represented and still represents.

V

So far we have dealt with the Lincoln myth in terms of the ambiguity of its meaning to those who have studied it, and who by trying to understand, have to some extent created its symbolic proportions as lasting truth. All this is preface to what remains to be said about Lincoln the artist — the creative spirit that molded out of the circumstances of daily life and the historical events of the era in which he lived, a personal myth that literature (including biography and history) has made of him. Lincoln's personal myth was the seed from which the historical myth has grown.

Lincoln's life was to him a quest for identity and a creation of identity, sparked by ambition so intense that no immediate failure could put it off and no success could satisfy its craving. This creative impulse, as with all men in some degree perhaps, took various channels, but two main currents — the political and the literary — run throughout his life and frequently blend into one. Lincoln seems never to have begun and never to have ceased to love to play with people and to play with words. This instinct was born with him. There is little reason to question the folk stories about his childhood oratory and versifying, or early proclivities for making friends and influencing people, when such activity produced the documented record of his maturity. The essential effort of his life was to identify himself, by words and in relationship to his contempories, as a representative, symbolic hero. He sought to play a role the action and words of which he would create for himself as circumstance and opportunity arose, but always with his mind's eye on the ultimate scene of the ultimate act, in which he would achieve his symbolic identity.

His first political address, dated March 9, 1832, announcing his candidacy for representative in the Illinois legislature, concluded with a candid statement of this mission:

> Every man is said to have his peculiar ambition. Whether it be true or not, I can say for one that I have no other so great as that of being truly esteemed of my fellow men, by rendering myself worthy of their esteem. How far I shall succeed in gratifying this ambition, is yet to be developed.

After a quarter of a century, Lincoln's concept of his role had not materially changed. He had no pat solution to the problem of slavery, he sought to lead no crusade, but he hoped that in time the terrible ambiguity of human freedom and equality would gradually, in increasing measure, be resolved of necessity by new laws expressing the will of the majority, not of one state or one section, but of the United States. As to slavery, at that time the most that Lincoln hoped for, as he expressed it in the famous House Divided speech on June 16, 1858, was that "the public mind shall rest in the belief that it is in the course of ultimate extinction." By the end of the campaign, however, Lincoln had recognized slavery as the nemesis of the personal role as hero which he had dreamed for himself. He concluded his last speech in the campaign on October 30, 1858, as follows:

> Ambition has been ascribed to me God knows how sincerely I prayed from the first that this field of ambition might not be opened. I claim no insensibility to political honors; but to-day could the Missouri restriction be restored, and the whole slavery question replaced on the old ground of "tolerance" by *necessity* where it exists, with unyielding hostility to the spread of it, on principle, I would, in consideration, gladly agree, that Judge Douglas should never be *out*, and I never *in*, an office, so long as we both or either, live.

But this could not be, because Lincoln refused to accept as his final identity the role of a defeated Illinois politician, and because his nemesis remained, still capable of dealing him, before the final retribution, an ambiguous success as President of a disintegrating nation. The ambiguity of his success was ever present to Lincoln's mind from the moment of his election onward. Of his many frank recognitions of this ambiguity none is more succinct than the statement in a letter he wrote on April 4, 1864, to A. G. Hodges, editor of the Frankfort (Kentucky) *Commonwealth*. "I claim not to have controlled events," Lincoln wrote, "but confess plainly that events have controlled me." This was his clear judgment of his role as President after three years of war.

Four months later, having achieved the major part of his heroic identity, he spoke in one of his briefest and best speeches to the 166th Ohio Regiment on August 22, 1864, as follows:

> I beg you to remember this, not merely for my sake, but for yours. I happen temporarily to occupy this big White House. I am a living witness that any one of your children may look to come here as my father's child has. It is in order that each one of you may have through this free government which we have enjoyed, an open field and a fair chance for your industry, enterprise and intelligence; that you may all have equal privileges in the race of life, with all its desirable human aspirations.

Such is the myth, from log cabin to White House, and lacking only the tragic denouement which Lincoln was further to live and create for himself down to the last scene in Ford's Theatre on a Good Friday night, to a large extent made probable, if not indeed inevitable, by every choice of action which led up to it — such is the myth which Lincoln created, in his quest for identity, out of the ambiguity of his human nature. It is his story, it is our story, it is the world's story. And what does it mean? Let us begin again to see if we can discover its meaning.

In a log cabin, on Nolin Creek, in La Rue County, Kentucky, on February 12, 1809 . . .

But time has indeed "dissipated to shining ether the solid angularity" of that cabin, and its meaning is purely symbolic, "a constellation to hang in heaven an immortal sign." We must begin elsewhere. Anywhere will do.

LINCOLN'S MEANING TO

NEW JERSEY AND THE WORLD

An Address before the Special Joint Session of the New
Jersey Legislature, commemorating Abraham Lincoln's visit
to the State House on February 21, 1861*

*Mr. President, Mr. Speaker, Members of the Joint Session, and
Fellow Citizens:*

It is most gratifying that we meet today, in commemoration of
an event one hundred years ago, under circumstances vastly different from those which confronted the men whom we honor. Without
detracting from the seriousness and solemnity of this occasion, may
I remind you of a humorous aspect of that time when Abraham
Lincoln addressed your predecessors. I quote from the account of
the ceremony printed in the *Philadelphia North American and
United States Gazette* on the following day: "Arrangements were
made by the State Legislature to admit only such parties as might
adorn, but not embarrass the ceremonies. Members of either House
were debarred from entering the other." Whatever the reasons may
have been for such vigorous attention to preserving the respective
autonomy of each chamber, both the Senate and the Assembly gave
Abraham Lincoln their unreserved pledge of the "continued
devotion of this state to the Constitution and the Union founded
by our fathers, and that our people will cooperate with you in all

Congressional Record, Appendix, March 2, 1961, p. A1427-28.

constitutional efforts for a speedy and peaceable settlement of the differences which now distract our country. . . . " Today it is gratifying that both chambers have met in joint session to commemorate the separate occasions of one hundred years ago.

Humbly reflecting on scenes invoked by Mr. Anthony Quinn's reading of the words spoken a century ago by the greatest American who ever appeared before the Senate or the General Assembly of this heroic and historic state, and proudly grateful for the spirit of the man that was Lincoln, let us renew his pledge and theirs of "devotion to the Union, the Constitution and the liberties of the people."

We should also be, as Lincoln said he was, anxious that the principle of freedom and equality, "that something more than National Independence; that something that held out a great promise to all the people of the world to all time to come. . . . " shall be perpetuated. We are human beings first, and Americans second. Whether consistently or intermittently, most of us are partisans only at third hand. As one whose traditions are divided in politics, I have at different times, I believe, voted for both good Democrats and good Republicans. Let this centenary remind us that the right to choose is, and always has been, the guarantee of continued freedom, and that responsibility is the guarantee of the right to choose. And let it remind us also that when the people have chosen, they have the right to change or corroborate their choice at succeeding elections, but that the choice of the majority must be honored until a succeeding election affords another opportunity to change. This is what your predecessors recognized a century ago by honoring the man who had been chosen by the people of most of the then states of the Union, even though a plurality of the people of New Jersey had at the same election voted for an opposing candidate, and had chosen a majority of state representatives and senators from the opposing party.

This is, in simple, what the Civil War was about. As Lincoln phrased it in his Message to Congress in Special Session on July 4, 1861, the Civil Was was to "demonstrate to the world, that those who can fairly carry an election, can also suppress a rebellion—that ballots are the rightful, and peaceful, successors of bullets; and that when ballots have fairly, and constitutionally, decided, there can be no successful appeal, back to bullets; that there can be no successful appeal, except to ballots themselves, at succeeding elections. Such will be a great lesson of peace; teaching men that what they cannot take by an election, neither can they take it by a war—teaching all, the folly of being the beginners of a war."

As a nation, we did not learn this lesson easily, but a century of peace among ourselves testifies that we learned it fairly well. In fact, we seem to have learned it so well that we are sometimes impatient as a nation with other younger republics that have not learned it yet. We forget that nearly a century intervened between the establishing of our government under Washington and the preserving of it under Lincoln. Shall we expect more rapid or more effective learning on the part of nations younger than ourselves? Let us remember that with the exception of the little Republic of San Marino, we are the oldest republic on the earth, and with the exception of England, the oldest country with a history of continuous constitutional government in any form. It is the hope of elders always that the young may learn without making the mistakes their elders made, but let us judge fairly and calmly those who are striving today to establish or maintain in other lands around the world the governments of their choice. As we did not learn quickly or easily, as we have not yet learned fully, that "all men are created equal"; and "that they are endowed by their Creator with certain inalienable rights," should we not try more earnestly than ever before, to set a better example at home after nearly two centuries of national existence? As we have required so much to teach us and so long a time to learn, should we not do all we can to aid those who are just beginning?

Abraham Lincoln was a problem to the party that nominated him for the presidency, as well as to the party that opposed him, and he has remained a problem to both parties for a hundred years. Both can quote him for their respective purposes, and either suffers the penalty for not living up to what is quoted. He was a conservative bent on conserving the state existing, as a means to the state becoming; a conservative bent on preserving a degree of permanence while making desirable change; a conservative bent on conserving above all else the right of individuals and of classes of people to improve their condition, even when that improvement required major adjustments in the condition and privileges of other people. This kind of conservative is not easy for a political party or a nation to live with, but both parties and the nation learn in the long run that this kind of conservative is the only kind they *can* live with.

Nine days before Abraham Lincoln addressed the Senate and Assembly of New Jersey, he addressed a group of representatives of eight German workingmen's societies at Cincinnati, Ohio. These immigrant laborers had left the country of their birth in quest of the freedom and equality for all men, which, Lincoln said, held out hope to "all the people of the world to all time to come." As new American citizens, they came to greet the President-elect and to pledge him their whole support in whatever lay ahead, because they knew, perhaps better than their native-born compatriots, what would be lost if the new President could not preserve it.

In responding to their pledge, Abraham Lincoln said this: "Mr. Chairman, I hold that while man exists, it is his duty to improve not only his own condition, but to assist in ameliorating mankind; and therefore, without entering upon the details of the question, I will simply say, that I am for those means which will give the greatest good to the greatest number."

Today, we should also remember this, in New Jersey and in every state of the Union, because the people of the world remember it, if we do not. The concept that the United States was created to preserve and extend freedom and equality to all men, which Lincoln believed and struggled for, was not a something "for Americans only," and if we today fail to remember this, we may expect to be judged accordingly. The United States is judged among the people of the world by the extent of our success or our failure to live up to the ideal of Jefferson and Lincoln, both at home and abroad. Men like Jefferson and Lincoln, and their ideal of freedom and equality, were and are our greatest asset in the eyes of the world, but when that asset is not put to work at home, and shared abroad, it becomes a liability. If Lincoln's commitment to "ameliorating mankind" is replaced by a commitment to "maintaining the status quo," we cannot expect people in search of amelioration to be so ignorant as not to know the difference. The image of Abraham Lincoln and the image of Uncle Sam are not by any means synonymous in the eyes of the world. I am reminded of a cartoon drawn by a French cartoonist in one of the Paris newspapers in 1873. In it, the figure of Abraham Lincoln holds in the palm of his hand a Tom Thumb figure of Uncle Sam. The cartoonist's message cannot be misunderstood, and we may well wonder whether the enormous expansion of our material power as a nation in the twentieth century has altered this relative assessment of Abraham Lincoln and Uncle Sam in the eyes of the world.

We do not have to "sell" Abraham Lincoln to the masses of the people in the world any more than we have to "sell" the ideal embodied in the Declaration of Independence. But we do have to show them that the people of the United States still believe in the principle embodied in our Declaration of Independence, as a principle for "all the people of the world," as Lincoln believed in it. This is seldom, if ever, easy, but it is particularly difficult when what we think is *our interest* comes in conflict with what people in other lands think is *their interest.* Apropos of our once *peculiar interest* in slavery, Lincoln said, "The plainest print cannot be read through a gold eagle." I trust that the disappearance of the gold coin, as well as the devaluation of the dollar, will not lessen the point Lincoln was making, if we substitute for "gold eagle" the twenty-dollar bill, or the hundred-ruble note for that matter, since the difficulty in reading truth through material wealth is by no means confined to citizens of the United States.

On our part at least, should we not continue most carefully to weigh this matter of our interest, in the conservative spirit of Lincoln, recognizing that "ameliorating mankind" is the only ultimate interest worthy of ourselves and our nation? Let us seek the best means today by which "that something that held out a great promise to all the people of the world to all time to come . . . shall be perpetuated." This is what Abraham Lincoln means to the world; this is what we should strive to make Uncle Sam mean to the world. Although it is "fitting and proper" that we should commemorate this day, we can do even better every day, by continuing to extend the principle upon which our nation was founded.

LAST BEST HOPE*

History teaches us how slowly, sometimes painfully, and frequently how ambiguously the milestones and bench marks in the development of human society and government are established. It also teaches us how mixed are the motives of the people who set them up, and how complex are the currents of force that move the men into the positions on which they take their stand and set up the milestones or bench marks from which later generations take their bearings. And finally it teaches us how illusory and inadequate in retrospect may seem the achievement of that milestone or bench mark to the people who hope perennially that a question can be settled, as the common phrase goes "once and for all."

The Thirteenth Amendment to the Constitution is such a milestone or bench mark, set up by the people of the United States one hundred years ago, in their quest for freedom and equality of opportunity for all men.

Although it was the collective achievement of the majority of the people of the United States in 1865, it had been brought about, to a large degree, through the advocacy and the leadership of one man, Abraham Lincoln, who only four years earlier had no such intention at all.

When Lincoln was inaugurated on March 4, 1861, he was committed to a single objective: to preserve the Union. He had been committed for years to another objective, to prevent the fur-

*Proceedings, Fourth Annual American History Workshop, New Jersey Civil War Centennial Commission, New Brunswick, 1964.

ther spread of slavery, but his very election as President had signalized the accomplishment of that objective so conclusively to the slave states that they seceded from the Union.

In his Inaugural Address, Lincoln tried his best to try to persuade the slave states to stay in the Union, and stated again his often repeated promise that in his administration no interference by the federal government with slavery in the states would be attempted.

More than this, he endorsed the amendment to the Constitution which had recently passed both Houses of Congress and had been signed by President Buchanan just hours before he went out of office. This amendment would probably have been the Thirteenth if the slave states had stayed in the Union. It stated: "No amendment shall be made to the Constitution which will authorize or give to Congress the power to abolish or interfere within any state with the domestic institutions thereof, including that of persons held to labor or service by the laws of said state."

Thus Lincoln committed himself, in effect, to an amendment which would, if passed and unless repealed, perpetuate slavery in the states where it existed, so long as the slaveholders who ruled those states should continue to rule. He considered at this point that he could not do otherwise, in his single purpose to persuade the slave states to stay in the Union and to avoid the armed conflict and bloodshed which would result if they did not. This was done by a man who had repeatedly stated his personal belief that if slavery was not morally wrong, then nothing was wrong.

It is not hard to understand why many abolitionists were disgusted with him as a man who, in their view, was without real dedication to the abolition of a great moral wrong.

Then the war began at Fort Sumter, and Lincoln bent all his efforts towards subduing the rebellion. His greatest task, as he saw it at this point, in 1861, was to keep the loyalty and fighting effort of the people who did not care whether slavery continued or not, but who did care whether the Union continued. Particularly, his primary effort was to keep the border slave states in the Union, while he raised and equipped an army to subdue the rebellion and to enforce the authority of the United States in the seceded states by invasion.

As the war progressed, it became gradually more and more clearly evident, that the power of the slave states to wage effective war rested to a considerable degree on the continuing productivity of the slave economy. Hence a succession of blows were struck. On August 6, 1861, Congress passed the First Confiscation Act, which took away from their owners slaves used in military service against the United States. This hit primarily the disloyal slave owners in the border states, but also encouraged slaves in the seceded states to defect when they came close to Union lines. The Union commanders made the most of the opportunity to seize slaves as contraband of war.

The second blow came a year later, when Congress passed the Second Confiscation Act on July 17, 1862, declaring "forever free" all slaves of owners who supported the rebellion. Also passed by Congress in 1862 were the acts abolishing slavery in the District of Columbia and in the territories and setting free all slaves and families of slaves who served in the Union armies.

But the heaviest blow in the attack on slavery in 1862 was Lincoln's Preliminary Emancipation Proclamation, issued on September 22, 1862. Not only in the Union but also across the Atlantic, where the people of Europe were taking sides in the struggle, and where moral and political support for the Union was not a negligible factor in the war, Lincoln's proclamation established freedom for the slaves as the foundation on which the Union would be reconstructed.

The Preliminary Emancipation Proclamation set January 1, 1863, as the date on which the Final Emancipation Proclamation would be issued and stated its terms, freeing all slaves in all areas in rebellion and pledging the armed forces to enforce their freedom.

In addition, during the year 1862 Lincoln tried, without success, to encourage the loyal slave states to enact legislation emancipating their slaves. His Message to Congress, March 8, 1962, recommended legislation promising pecuniary aid to any state which would adopt gradual emancipation with compensation to owners. On July 14, 1862, he submitted a bill which provided that the President would deliver to any state United States bonds equal to the aggregate value, at a figure per head to be set by Congress, of all the slaves in any state. Again in his Annual Message, December 1, 1862, he repeated this recommendation. The prevailing reverence for private property in human bodies, however, prevented the legislatures of the loyal slave states from adopting measures to free the slaves of loyal owners, even with compensation, and not until West Virginia was admitted to the Union on June 20, 1863, with a gradual emancipation clause in its constitution, was any action effected by a state to take away the slave property of loyal owners.

In 1864 several of the seceded states which had been successfully invaded by Union armies—Arkansas, Louisiana and Tennessee—were restored to the Union under loyal governments which proceeded to adopt new state constitutions which abolished slavery. Following Lincoln's overwhelming victory at the polls in November 1864, the loyal slave states, under continuing executive pressure from Lincoln, who had now an unquestionable popular mandate to abolish slavery, began to act. First Maryland repealed its slave code, and then Missouri on January 11, 1865, abolished slavery by an ordinance passed by a special state convention.

By this time, however, Lincoln's strategy to abolish slavery was centered on his effort to obtain adoption of an amendment to the Constitution of the United States. In his Annual Message of December 1, 1862, Lincoln had called upon Congress to enact his proposed amendment in the form of an inducement to the states to abolish slavery by compensating them with federal money. His logic was impeccable.

> Is it doubted, then, that the plan I propose, if adopted, would shorten the war, and thus lessen its expenditure of money and of blood? Is it doubted that it would restore the national authority and national prosperity, and perpetuate both indefinitely? Is it doubted that we here—Congress and Executive—can secure its adoption? Will not the good people respond to a united, and earnest appeal from us? Can we, can they, by any other means, so certainly, or so speedily, assure these vital objects? We can succeed only by concert. It is not can *any* of us *imagine* better?' but, 'can we *all* do better?' Object whatsoever is possible, still the question recurs, 'can we do better?' The dogmas of the quiet past, are inadequate to the stormy present. The

occasion is piled high with difficulty, and we must rise with
the occasion. As our case is new, so we must think anew, and
act anew. We must disenthrall ourselves, and then we shall
save our country.

If his logic is impeccable, his eloquence had seldom if ever been
exceeded.

Fellow citizens, *we* cannot escape history. We of this Congress
and this administration, will be remembered in spite of ourselves. No personal significance, or insignificance, can spare
one or another of us. The fiery trial through which we pass,
will light us down, in honor or dishonor, to the latest
generation. We *say* we are for the Union. The world will not
forget that we say this. We know how to save the Union. The
world knows we do know how to save it. We—even *we here*
— hold the power, and bear the responsibility. In *giving*
freedom to the *slave,* we *assure* freedom to the *free* —
honorable alike in what we give, and what we preserve. We
shall nobly save, or meanly lose, the last best hope of earth.
Other means may succeed; this could not fail. The way is
plain, peaceful, generous, just—a way which, if followed, the world
will forever applaud, and God must forever bless.

Neither Lincoln's logic nor his eloquence could obtain the necessary two-thirds vote in Congress, where the Democrats were nearly
unanimous in their opposition. Continuing conferences and discussions went on between the President and the leaders in Congress
as to the best means of placing pressure where pressure was needed
and of persuading the votes of the reluctant senators and representatives who nevertheless were personally favorable to the abolition
of slavery. A key figure was Senator John B. Henderson of
Missouri. He was what was called "a progressive Conservative,"
and was the leading advocate of emancipation in his state. On January 11, 1864, Henderson introduced a Joint Resolution into the
Senate proposing "that slavery shall not exist in the United
States." Senator Sumner of Massachusetts, however, preferred different language and introduced his own Joint Resolution on February 8, providing that "everywhere within the limits of the United
States, and of each State or Territory thereof, all persons are equal

before the law, so that no person can hold another as a slave."
The phrase "all persons are equal before the law," taken from the
Constitution of Revolutionary France, was particularly dear to
Sumner.

Personal rivalry with historical overtones developed when
Senator Trumbull of Illinois, chairman of the Judiciary Committee, reported a substitute Joint Resolution differing from both
Henderson's and Sumner's versions and following the language of
the Northwest Ordinance of 1787: "Neither slavery nor involuntary
servitude, except as punishment for crime, whereof the party shall
have been duly convicted, shall exist within the United States, or
any place subject to their jurisdiction." Sumner tried to reinsert
his "equal before the law" phrase, but Trumbull's resolution was
adopted by the Senate without change. In the House, however, it
failed to obtain the necessary two-thirds vote, when only four
Democrats joined the unanimous eighty-seven Republicans voting
for it on June 15, 1864.

Lincoln expected its defeat and saw that the proposal for complete abolition of slavery by amendment to the Constitution would
be the key issue of his campaign for reelection. Even while the
House was debating the resolution he called the chairman of the
National Republican Committee, Senator Edwin D. Morgan of
New York, to the White House, and asked him to make the
keynote of his speech opening the convention a plea for the amendment, and to place the amendment as a plank in the Republican
platform. Lincoln's wishes were followed, and the delegates
responded with great enthusiasm.

During the campaign that ensued, Lincoln stressed the necessity
of abolishing slavery in order to win the war, while McClellan, his
Democratic opponent, reiterated the unchanging Democratic slogan
of "The Constitution as it is and the Union as it was. " The
election in November brought Lincoln an overwhelming victory
with a majority of 191 electoral votes, to which New Jersey did
not contribute, but more important for the Thirteenth Amendment,
there were elected 138 Unionists to 35 Democrates.

The mandate of the people was clear, but in the normal course
of events the newly elected Congress would not assemble until a

year later in December of 1865, and even if called into special
session by the President immediately following his inauguration,
could not act on the amendment before March 1865. Therefore,
Lincoln's maneuvers began to try to persuade a sufficient number
of lame duck Democrats to vote for the inevitable and thus hasten
the end of the war.

In his Annual Message, December 6, 1864, the President pleaded
publicly for the amendment:

> At the last session of Congress a proposed amendment of the
> Constitution abolishing slavery throughout the United States,
> passed the Senate, but failed for lack of the requisite two-
> thirds vote in the House of Representatives. Although the
> present is the same Congress, and nearly the same members,
> and without questioning the wisdom or patriotism of those
> who stood in opposition, I venture to recommend the
> reconsideration and passage of the measure at the present
> session. Of course the abstract question is not changed; but
> an intervening election shows almost certainly, that the next
> Congress will pass the measure if this does not. Hence there
> is only a question of *time* as to when the proposed amendment
> will go to the States for their action. And as it is to so go,
> at all events, may we not agree that the sooner the better?
> It is not claimed that the election has imposed a duty on mem-
> bers to change their views or their votes, any further than,
> as an additional element to be considered, their judgment may
> be affected by it. It is the voice of the people now, for the
> first time, heard upon the question. In a great national crisis,
> like ours, unanimity of action among those seeking a common
> end is very desirable—almost indispensable. And yet no ap-
> proach to such unanimity is attainable, unless some deference
> shall be paid to the will of the majority, simply because it
> is the will of the majority. In this case the common end is
> the maintenance of the Union; and, among the means to se-
> cure that end, such will, through the election, is most clearly
> declared in favor of such consititutional amendment.

In addition to his public plea, he privately called to the White
House representatives like James S. Rollins, himself a slave owner
and Congressman from the strongest slave district in Missouri.

Rollins listened and replied that he had made up his mind to vote for the amendment if it was again brought up. He also agreed to try to persuade other Democratic members of the Missouri delegation to do likewise.

The delegation in Congress from New Jersey also figured in these private maneuvers, when representative James M. Ashley of Ohio, urged Lincoln's Secretary Nicolay on January 18, 1865, that the Camden & Amboy Railroad interest had promised Ashley "that if he would help postpone the Raritan railroad bill over this session they would in return make the New Jersey Democrats help about the Amendment, either by their votes or absence." Senator Sumner was the proponent of the Raritan bill, however, and when Ashley had asked him to drop it for this session Sumner did not agree, because, he said, he thought the amendment would pass anyway. Ashley thought Sumner had other motives; namely, that the amendment would fail and then Sumner's resolution containing the phrase "all persons are equal before the law" could be reintroduced and passed. Nicolay continued, "Ashley therefore desired the President to send for Sumner, and urge him to be practical and secure the passage of the amendment in the manner suggested by Mr. Ashley."

When Nicolay told Lincoln of Ashley's proposal, the President replied, "I can do nothing with Mr. Sumner in these matters. While Mr. Sumner is very cordial with me, he is making his history in an issue with me on this very point. He hopes to succeed in beating the President so as to change this Government from its original form and make it a strong centralized power." Then calling Mr. Ashley into the room, the President said to him, "I think I understand Mr. Sumner; and I think he would be all the more resolute in his persistence on the points which Mr. Nicolay has mentioned to me if he supposed I were at all watching his course on this matter."

Such were the business pressures, and private personal motives, of some representatives when the historic amendment came to a roll-call vote in the House of Representatives on January 31, 1865. Of the five New Jersey representatives, for example, the single Republican John F. Starr voted yea; two Democrats, Andrew J.

Rogers and George Middleton, abstained; one Democrat, William G. Steele, and one Constitutional Union Party representative, Nehemiah Perry, voted nay. The Amendment passed with 119 yeas, 56 nays, and 8 abstaining. Thus the eight members not voting, including the two from New Jersey, secured the amendment's passage in the House.

Concerning this amendment there is a unique matter — namely, the President of the United States put his signature to it. That caused a little trouble when the Senate had to pass a resolution saying it was not necessary and he should not have done it.

There has been speculation as to why and how this happened. My guess is that since it had been more than a half century since there had been an amendment, nobody knew, including Lincoln, that he wasn't supposed to sign it when it was passed. Since he signed everything else that both Houses passed, he thought he should also sign this. Also, as noted earlier in this talk, President Buchanan had labored under the same misunderstanding. There may be another supposition, that certainly there wasn't anything passed by Congress during Lincoln's presidency which he would more gladly have set his signature to, and which he probably wanted to set his signature to, more than the Thirteenth Amendment.

At any rate, on the following night Lincoln spoke from a window of the White House to a crowd which paraded to music and gathered on the lawn. His speech was reported in the *New York Tribune* as follows:

> The President said he supposed the passage through Congress of the Constitutional amendment for the abolishment of slavery throughout the United States, was the occasion to which he was indebted for the honor of this call. The occasion was one of congratulation to the country and to the whole world. But there is a task yet before us -- to go forward and consummate by the votes of the states that which Congress so nobly began yesterday. He had the honor to inform those present that Illinois had already today done the work. Maryland was about half through; but he felt proud that Illinois was a little ahead. He thought this measure was a very

fitting if not an indispensable adjunct to the winding up of the great difficulty. He wished the reunion of all the states perfected and so effected as to remove all causes of disturbance in the future; and to attain this end it was necessary that the original disturbing cause should, if possible, be rooted out. He thought all would bear him witness that he had never shrunk from doing all that he could to eradicate slavery by issuing an emancipation proclamation. But that proclamation falls far short of what the amendment will be when fully consummated. A question might be raised whether the proclamation was legally valid. It might be added that it only aided those who came into our lines and that it was inoperative as to those who did not give themselves up, or that it would have no effect upon the children of the slaves born hereafter. In fact it would be urged that it did not meet the evil. But this amendment is a King's cure for all the evils. It winds the whole thing up. He would repeat that it was the fitting if not indispensable adjunct to the consummation of the great game we are playing. He could not but congratulate all present, himself, the country and the whole world upon his great moral victory.

Ratification by the state legislatures proceeded in rapid succession, and with the ratification by Georgia's newly reconstituted loyal legislature, on December 9, 1865, the necessary two-thirds having been reached, Secretary of State Seward proclaimed the amendment ratified, without waiting for the last six states to ratify, New Jersey among them not ratifying until January 23, 1866, the third from last, with Iowa ratifying on January 24, 1866, and Texas not until February 18, 1870.

In retrospect, Senator Henry Wilson of Massachusetts summarized, in his *History of the Rise and Fall of the Slave Power,* the mixture of motives which led to the adoption of the Thirteenth Amendment. Some men were motivated, he said, by "religious obligation," some by "humane considerations," others by "resentment" against slaveholders for starting the war, but most men were motivated by what he called "prudential considerations merely."

He continues. "They accepted emancipation not so much from

any heartfelt conversion to the doctrine of anti-slavery as from the conviction that the removal of slavery had become a military, if not a political necessity." Furthermore, a very great many continued bitterly to oppose the fact after its accomplishment, and constantly sought to thwart its effect, with the result that the Negro, though legally thenceforth free, was seldom better off, and frequently worse off economically and socially than he had been before the war. The Fourteenth Amendment was necessary to protect his civil rights and the Fifteenth Amendment to guarantee his right to vote, but neither of these further amendments can suffice to this date to effect the specific purposes for which they were passed. What Henry Wilson called "the foul spirit of caste" has continued for a century to thwart the Negro constantly and the white man not infrequently as well, in the quest for government in which, for the first time in history, man might achieve the ideal posed in the phrase so dear to Senator Sumner, "all persons equal before the law."

But as we have been reminded so often of late, and so recently as our last political campaign, "you can't legislate human nature." True enough, perhaps, but individual men do change, even in the matters of their closest conditioning in the communities and homes in which they are reared.

The man who was President and who more than any other influenced the placing of the bench mark in our history which is the Thirteenth Amendment, was such a man. In his personal relationships with Negroes, Lincoln was never motivated by "the foul spirit of caste," but more than this, he learned to recognize the right to pride in a Negro's mind and heart and to apologize even for an unintentional hurt to that pride.

Henry Samuels related after the war how he and a group of other Negroes called at the White House in 1864 to protest the unequal pay which Negro laborers were receiving from the Army. Lincoln listened to them until they had stated their case, then "turned his head and jocularly said, with one of those peculiar smiles of his: 'Well, gentlemen, you wish the pay of "Cuffie" raised.' " The young Negro Samuels objected: "Excuse me, Mr. Lincoln, the term 'Cuffie' is not in our vernacular. What we want is that the wages of the American Colored Laborer be equalized with those of the American White Laborer." Lincoln apologized, "I stand corrected, young man, but you know I am by birth a Southerner and in our section that term is applied without any idea of an offensive nature. I will, however, at the earliest possible moment do all in my power to accede to your request." As a result, the War Department issued an order requiring that Negro laborers be paid at the same rate as white men doing the same work.

This little incident illustrates two things: 1) the beginning of the Negro's assertion of his right to one form of equality—equal pay for equal work, and 2) a reasonable white President's agreement to implement that equality by executive order.

In the hundred years that have elapsed since then, the Negro's advancement has been painfully slow, in part perhaps because too few Negroes have asserted their right to equality and pushed to achieve their equality, and in part because too few white men have been as reasonable as Lincoln in recognizing and agreeing to the Negro's right to the equality and in acting to implement it. There have been few Presidents in the White House since Lincoln who have been willing to use the executive power effectively to implement even the Negro's right to equal pay for equal work, much less this right to vote, even in national elections. The courts have been unwilling, the state governments have been unwilling, Congress. has been unwilling, and the Presidents have been unwilling, for the most part, because our government has been a government by white men primarily for white men. As most white men did not believe with Lincoln in 1862 that "in giving freedom to the slave we assure freedom to the free," so most white men apparently do not yet believe in assuring equality of opportunity for others they assure equality of opportunity for themselves.

Fortunately, as it turned out, Lincoln's "last best hope of earth" was not really the last, for either Negro or white. It was "nobly saved," it is true, but it turned out to be inadequate to our future. Today, a hundred years later, it is still more a hope than a possibility, not to say, a reality, and yet there are signs that a majority of white men and a majority of Negroes may be, for the first time, coming to recognize what the opening words of our Declaration of Independence really mean.

Injustice cannot be terminated by a formula of words. Legislation can be at most only the initiation, not the accomplishment, of democracy with order. Unless persistently enforced, at the insistence of the people who enacted it, legislation is mere words, nothing more.

LINCOLN AND SHAKESPEARE

It is a truism that from the seventeenth century, almost if not quite to the present, Shakespeare and the King James Bible have been the double well from which the literate have drawn the major portion of their common literacy. Even today, when one cannot assume much of anything as a common denominator in literacy, it is perhaps as likely that the viewers of a TV quiz program will recognize the names of Adam and Eve or Macbeth and Lady Macbeth as it is that they will recognize the names of Lil' Abner and Daisy Mae or Rhett Butler and Scarlett O'Hara. In Lincoln's day anyone who had learned to read in school much beyond the alphabet could not avoid knowing some Shakespeare, for the simple reason that passages from the plays made up considerable portions of the literary textbooks which were used in the grammar schools. Such a textbook was Scott's *Lessons in Elocution,* and some of the passages from Shakespeare which Lincoln is recorded as having quoted during his occupancy of the White House can be found in this textbook, studied during his boyhood in Indiana. It is difficult to avoid the conclusion that he may have first learned them by heart, in some instances at least, from this source rather than from his first reading of the plays themselves.

But Lincoln's reading of Shakespeare merely began with such books as Scott's, and he became a close and appreciative reader of many of the plays during his mature years in Springfield, Illinois, as is testified unanimously by those who knew him and recorded their knowledge either personally or in interviews given to Lincoln's earliest biographers. In fact, the copy of Shakespeare which Lincoln owned while living in Springfield, and which contains his autograph on the title page, is preserved in the Folger Shakespeare Library in Washington, D.C.

In Lincoln's day the Shakespearean fraternity was not limited to professors of English, actors, and poets, but embraced practically all formally or informally educated people and the majority of the more or less self-educated. For example, two of Lincoln's law partners, Lamon and Herndon, were almost as familiar with and able to quote from Shakespeare as he was, and Lamon prided himself as a critic of the finer points in the performance of Shakespearean actors whom he, as something of a theatre habitue, rarely missed the opportunity of seeing. Also, we should remember that American cities, and even towns like Springfield, Illinois, which in our day have not seen a Shakespearean play or any other kind of professional performance, except on television, for close to half a century, in Lincoln's day had a theater which presented touring players. In cities like Washington not one theater but three regularly offered the best actors of the day in their repertory of Shakespearean roles every season. When was the last time Shakespeare was presented at the only surviving theater in Washington? If it were not for the Library of Congress, the local university drama departments, and the summer performances at the Washington monument, there would not be any Shakespearean performances in the nation's capital. At any rate, I hope I have made my point — that common literacy of school children in Lincoln's day was not limited to texts written with limited vocabularies, and the common literacy of adults embraced more than newsprint and what is sometimes referred to as "contemporary literature."

Although Lincoln probably saw Shakespeare acted prior to his election to the Presidency, his fondness for Shakespeare on stage did not become a matter of notoriety until he had become a fairly frequent theatergoer in Washington. In fact, this notoriety stemmed from a "spontaneous visit" on the evening of March 13, 1863, to Grover's National Theatre to witness a performance by James H. Hackett of the role of Falstaff in *King Henry IV*. Not one to neglect the opportunity afforded by this mark of the President's interest, Hackett wrote Lincoln from New York on March 20, "I would respectfully ask your acceptance of a volume which I have recently published and the concluding portion of which refers particularly to the remarkable points of that renowned character Falstaff." Hackett's book, entitled *Notes and Comments on Certain Plays and Actors of Shakespeare, with Criticism and Comments* (1863), also contained as its first chapter a lengthy discussion and analysis of "Hamlet's Soliloquy on Suicide."

Five months later, Lincoln finally got around to replying.

> Executive Mansion
> Washington, August 17, 1863

My dear sir:

> Months ago I should have acknowledged the receipt of your book, and accompanying kind note; and I now have to beg your pardon for not having done so.
>
> For one of my age, I have seen very little of the drama. The first presentation of Falstaff I ever saw was yours here, last winter or spring. Perhaps the best compliment I can pay is to say, as I truly can, I am very anxious to see it again. Some of Shakespeare's plays I have never read; while others I have gone over perhaps as frequently as any unprofessional reader. Among the latter are Lear, Richard Third, Henry Eighth, Hamlet, and especially Macbeth. I think nothing equals Macbeth. It is wonderful. Unlike you gentlemen of the profession, I think the soliloquy in Hamlet commencing "O, my offence is rank" surpasses that commencing "To be, or not to be." But pardon this small attempt at criticism. I should like to hear you pronounce the opening speech of Richard the Third. Will you not soon visit Washington again? If you do, please call and let me make your personal acquaintance. Yours truly A. Lincoln

On September 4 Hackett acknowledged with thanks Lincoln's "frank, unaffected and courteous letter" and promised to avail himself of Lincoln's invitation to "call whenever again in Washington." He also promptly had the letter printed as a broadside, which bore the somewhat disingenuous notice, "Printed not for publication but for private distribution only, and its convenient perusal by personal friends." It is impossible to believe that an actor so publicity-wise as Hackett could think this broadside would escape notice in the press, especially in view of the fact that he had played precisely the same trick on former President John Quincy Adams in 1839, and had recounted the episode with relish in the very book which he had presented to Lincoln.

In a vein of patronizing sarcasm *the New York Herald* took notice of Hackett's broadside on September 17:

LINCOLN AND THE THEATER

Abraham Lincoln as a dramatic critic — The latest and greatest of Shakespere's Commentators. Mr. Lincoln's genius is wonderfully versatile. No department of human knowledge seems to be unexplored by him. He is equally at home whether discussing divinity with political preachers, debating plans of campaigns with military heroes, illustrating the Pope's bull against the comet to a pleasure party from Chicago, arguing questions of constitutional law with Vallandigham sympathizers, regulating political parties in Missouri, defending his policy before party conventions, or inditing letters to the philosopher in chief of the *Tribune* academy. In all these, and the disposition of the countless questions that have come up for his decision during the last two years and a half, he has displayed a variety of attainments, a depth of knowledge, a fund of anecdote, a power of analysis and a correctness of judgment that stamp him as the most remarkable man of the age. It only remained for him to cap the climax of popular astonishment and admiration by showing himself to be a dramatic critic of the first order, and the greatest and most profound of the army of Shakesperean commentators.

And this he has now done. The Falstaff of our stage has been honored with an autograph letter from the American autocrat, just as Shakespere himself was honored with an amicable letter from King James the First, and which, we are told, "that most learned prince and great patron of learning was pleased with his own hand to write." We have obtained a copy of the President's letter, and deem it of sufficient interest and importance to print it in this connection. It reads as follows:. . .

[Here follows Lincoln's letter of August 17, 1863, to James H. Hackett.]

If Mr. Lincoln had time to dilate upon the subject of his letter and to analyze the plays and passages to which he particularly refers, we would have an article on Shakespere which would doubtless have consigned to merited dust and oblivion the thousands of tomes that have been printed on that subject, and would have been accepted as the standard authority henceforth. New editions of Shakespere's plays, instead of having a long preface about what was thought and said of them by Bishop Warburton, Dr. Johnson, Stevens, Malone, Ben Jonson, Lord Shaftesbury, Goldsmith, Goethe, Voltaire and others, would simply contain Abraham Lincoln's commentary. Perhaps, after he retires to the shades of private life at Springfield, he may devote a few of his leisure moments to this pleasing task. Goethe was struck with the fact that in the literary circles of England the subject was Shakespere *und keine ende* — nothing but him, no end of Shakespere. Mr. Lincoln's criticism will preclude any such complaint in future. That will finish up the subject, and there will be nothing more to be said. Voltaire described the great dramatist as a savage who had some imagination; but that desperately profane Frenchman would not have hesitated, if he were still in the flesh, to have applied the same remark to our accomplished President.

Mr. Lincoln does not seem to be a passionate admirer of that soliloquy of Hamlet's: "To be or not to be," which schoolboys are so fond of declaiming, and which actors generally make such a bad mess of. There, again, he is right. It was Oliver Goldsmith, we believe, who took it to pieces and showed what arrant nonsense it was made up of. Mr. Lincoln has probably never read the criticism, and yet he has arrived at the same conclusion. Henceforth the *role* of Claudius, King of Denmark, will be sought after by accomplished actors, instead of being remitted to the greatest stick in the company; for Mr. Lincoln has discovered and made known the surpassing beauty of the King's soliloquy commencing

O, my offence is rank; it smells to heaven.

We suppose he has sometimes applied to his own case the lines
in it. —

> *Like a man to double business bound,*
> *I stand in pause where I shall first begin*
> *And both neglect.*

But, terse, forceful and elegant as is what Mr. Lincoln
modestly styles "this small attempt at criticism," the brightest
jewel in it is the sentence, "I should like to hear you
pronounce the opening speech of Richard the Third." How
delicately and dexterously the grave cares of his official position are combined with literary tastes. The sentiment is
apparent. It is not that he cares to hear Mr. Hackett, or any
other actor, declaim —

> Now is the winter of our discontent
> Made glorious summer —

but it is that the poet's dream should be realized by ourselves,
and that the time would soon arrive when we might truly and
happily say —

Grim visag'd war hath smoothed his wrinkled front.

We regard the short letter of Mr. Lincoln as by far the best
of his epistolary productions, and we expect it to enjoy that
immortality assured to the works of his favorite author.

In the meantime Hackett wrote again, on October 3, to let
Lincoln know of his next engagement at the National Theatre beginning on December 21, while other newspapers, taking their cue
from the New York *Herald,* joined in ridiculing Lincoln's
proficiency as a drama critic. On October 22 Hackett wrote a further letter, less in apology for making Lincoln's letter public, than
in certainty that the President was not likely to be so "thin
skinned" as to object:

Carlyle, Clinton Co., Illinois

Oct. 22, 1863

My dear Sir:

About a month since my son John K. Hackett of New York wrote to me how vexed he had been at the unwarrantable liberty taken by certain Newspaper Presses in publishing your kind, sensible & unpretending letter to me of "17 Aug't" last & more particularly at the editorial remarks upon & perversion of its subject-matter to antagonistic political purposes, accompanied by satirical abuse in general.

In order to calm my son's fears that it might give you cause to regret your having thus favored me with such original material, I replied that I felt assured that as a man of the world now and an experienced politician you were not likely to be so thin skinned, and that in my humble opinion such political squibs would probably affect your sensibilities about as much as would a charge of mustard seed shot at forty yards distance fired through a pop-gun barrel at the naturally armed alligator touch his nerves — Pray excuse the illustration! But, my son being a first rate shot with gun or pistol & thoroughly aware of their comparative effects, it was therefore an *argumentum ad hominen*.

I have just rec'd from my son the enclosed cut from the N.Y. Herald of 16th inst., transcribing an editorial from "The Liverpool (Eng.) Post of Oct. 1st," and as I perceive your letter was not quite correctly quoted therein & has been very improperly in Sept. last by the *Boston Courier,* and also because you may not have retained a copy, allow me to send you one of same which I caused to be printed for my friends' perusal without subjecting the original to consequent mutilation.

I wrote your excellency hence about "3d. Oct." inst. with a small package by mail which I hope came duly to your hand; and I intend to depart hence within a week for New York there to pass the winter.

I have the honor to be very respectfully Your obliged friend and obt servt even

Jas. H. Hackett.

The enclosed clipping reads as follows:

Perhaps no leader in a great contest ever stood so little chance of being a subject of hero worship as Abraham Lincoln, the President of the United States. That he was once a railsplitter would be pardoned if it could be proved that he were now a "swell." But there is nothing of the swell about "Old Abe." Every visitor that goes to Washington has something disrespectful to say of his very long legs and consequently very long pantaloons; of his shambling figure; of his awkward speech and double awkward silence; of his general unfitness in appearance and manners to mix in high society. Those who only know him from his exercitations in print conceive a but little better opinion of him. His grammar is decidedly self taught and perhaps not quite remembered; his style is no style at all; his arguments seem sometimes to have been written rather on the principle of Sampson making sport of the Philistines than as at all adapted to advance his cause; and some of his metaphors are voted decidedly below par *by the crowd of arrogant pretenders* to taste who never admired a saying that was tinged with vulgarity, *and never said one that could be suspected of vigor or originality.* When the enemies of the North have nothing else to say they deride the President; and when they feel the point of his homely jokes they bitterly denounce him as a sort of Nero fiddling away to a ribald tune while the empire he rules is in flames of civil war. Scarcely anyone has a good word to say for him; and even his own party in the States seem too ready to remain silent about his merits, and to base their defence of the administration on any grounds rather than confidence upon its head.

Yet a *worshipper of human heroes might possibly travel a great deal farther and fare much worse* for an idol than in selecting this same lanky American — the personification of free soil principles — the representative of the idea that slavery, without being forcibly interfered with, must not be allowed to spread itself over the North American continent — and the impersonation, also, of the victory of that idea — a victory, which, as it were, stands on the defensive against those who would turn it into defeat. Absolute truth, stern resolution, clear insight, solemn faithfulness, courage that cannot be daunted, hopefulness that cannot be dashed—these are qualities that go a long way to make up a hero, whatever side of the possessor of them may take in any lawful conflict. *And it would not be easy to dispute Mr. Lincoln's claim to all of these.* He has never given up a good servant or a sound principle. He has never shut his eyes to facts, or remained in ignorance of them. *He has never hesitated to do his work or faltered in doing it.* No resolution has remained *in nubilus* with him because it was a strong one. No measure has been adopted merely because "something must be done." The exigencies of a fanatical war have never betrayed him into fanaticism, and the sharp stings of satire have never drawn from him an exclamation of ill humor, or even an imprudent rejoinder.

Depend upon it, the whole history of the war proved that this quiet, unpretending, awkward man is on the whole a fitter subject for respect than ridicule even as a public man, leaving altogether aside the consideration, once a favorite in England, that he has raised himself literally from nothing. But it is not from the history of the war that we draw today an illustration of this conspicuous man's honest, generous and thoughtful character. We derive it from what little private life he has had while at the wheel — where he must have been a Ixion — of the great American ship. Last winter or spring — Mr. Lincoln does not well remember which — he went to the theatre and saw Hackett, *an excellent actor as few now in England need to be told.* Some time after Mr. Hackett sent the President a book with a complimentary note. But, having something more serious in hand, Mr. Lincoln omitted for sometime to use the player after his own honor, and did not acknowledge the present. At length, however, in August, the acknowledgment was sent. Now let us see in what terms Mr. Lincoln, the rough, uneducated, empty minded President, as some think him, addressed the actor whose Falstaff, after delighting tens of thousands had chanced to be played before him: —

[Lincoln's letter of August 17]

Now, to us this letter speaks for itself as favorably as any letter ever spoke. Its simplicity and candor are as fresh and delightful as new mown hay. *Only fancy a statesman, a President, confessing thus frankly he has never read Shakespeare through! How many British M.P.'s would have confessed it?* And yet how many of them there are who would have to own as much if they were put to it. We meet around intellectual or quasi intellectual dinner tables. We talk of Shelley as familiarly as of sherry. We affect to languish at the thought of Pascal, and chuckle hypocritically over a reference to Montaigne. We laugh consumedly at a quotation from Juvenal if the quoter looks humorous, *and pretend to be otherwise occupied if the expression of his countenance is not very readable.* We talk as familiarly of Rabelais as of last week's Punch; comment on the transcendentalism of "Sartor Resartus" without the faintest idea of the tenor of the book; and narrowly escape denouncing Thomas Carlyle downright, under the impression that he is Richard Carlisle, the infidel who outraged the orthodoxy of our fathers and mothers. There is no more abundant source of sham and pretension than the affectation in society of being well read in the "works which no gentleman's library should be without." Depend upon it, there is much good truth and honesty in any man, and especially in any public man who admires Shakespeare *and yet voluntarily says he has not read all his plays.*

But we are more pleased still with Mr. Lincoln for having read several of the plays many times over. *It is far better for a man to read one play twenty times, because he loves it, than to read twenty plays once, because they constitute the author's works and must be gone through.* "Lear," "Richard III.," "Henry VIII.," "Hamlet," and "Macbeth" would not be a bad library for any man who would make himself really master of them, and *for a ruler of men, who at the same time is a lover of human nature and a quaint humorist, they may well prove a continual feast.* The choice of "Macbeth" as principal favorite, and the preference of the less popular of Hamlet's soliloquies, also indicate the incisive use of his own wits which is one of the rarest indications of a man of power.

Long may Mr. Lincoln be able to find solace and enjoyment thus pleasantly and profitably, and may he never lack moral courage and graceful courtesy to do honor to those who, by illustrating the great dramatists, do almost all that is done effectually to keep them popularly alive. *In Mr. Hackett's case the honor is doubly due,* as many of our readers are aware. Not only is he a brilliant and unctious [sic] Falstaff, but a thoroughly estimable man. Once an opulent merchant, and afterwards unfortunate, he went on the stage and paid every creditor in full out of the new fortune he made in his new avocation. He is an honor to a noble profession, the credit of which is but too often inadequately sustained; and his distinguished correspondent is a man whose simple truth and cultivated intelligence will not forever be concealed by the unwieldiness of his frame or the uncouthness of his manners. *A contrast was wanted to the suave, deceitfulness and emptiness of James Buchanan, and one was found in Abraham Lincoln.*

Lincoln replied to both of Hackett's letters as follows:

Private

James H. Hackett   Executive Mansion
My dear Sir: Washington, Nov. 2, 1863.

Yours of Oct. 22nd. is received, as also was, in due course, that of Oct. 3rd. I look forward with pleasure to the fulfilment of the promise made in the former.

Give yourself no uneasiness on the subject mentioned in that of the 22nd.

My note to you I certainly did not expect to see in print; yet I have not been much shocked by the newspaper comments upon it. Those comments constitute a fair specimen of what has occurred to me through life. I have endured a great deal of ridicule without much malice; and have received a great deal of kindness, not quite free from ridicule. I am used to it. Yours truly

A. LINCOLN

There the correspondence rested so far as Lincoln was concerned, but Hacket continued to ply the President with letters and visits, discoursing on drama, offering political advice, and seeking appointment to the office of U.S. Consul at London, until the President dreaded the sight of the old man. Lincoln's secretary Noah Brooks related how Lincoln "almost groaned" upon learning late one night that Hackett was still waiting in the corridor outside the Executive Office door and said "that it seemed impossible for him to have any close relations with people in Washington without finding that the acquaintance thus formed generally ended with an application for office."

Lincoln's secretary John Hay recorded in his Diary Hackett's visit to the White House on December 13, 1863, as follows:

Dec. 13, 1863. . . Tonight Hackett arrived and spent the evening with the President. The conversation at first took a professional turn, the Tycoon showing a very intimate knowledge of those plays of Shakespeare where Falstaff figures. He was particularly anxious to know why one of the best scenes in the play, that where Falstaff & Prince Hal alternately assume the character of the King, is omitted in the representation. Hackett says it is admirable to read but ineffective on stage, that there is generally nothing distinctive about the actor who plays Henry to make an imitation striking. . . .

Hackett is a very amusing and garrulous talker. He had some good reminiscences of Houston, Crockett (the former he admires, the latter he thinks a dull man), McCarty and Prentiss.

On December 15, Hay recorded in his Diary a further visit to the theater to watch Hackett perform:

Tuesday, Dec. 15 1863. . . The President took Stoddard, Nicolay and me to Ford's with him to see Falstaff in *Henry IV*. . . . Hackett was most admirable. The President criticised his reading of a passage where Hackett said, "mainly *thrust* at me," the President thinking it should read "mainly thrust at *me*." I told the President I thought he was wrong; that "mainly" merely meant "strongly," "fiercely." The President thinks the dying speech of Hotspur an unnatural and unworthy thing — as who does not.

Aside from the Hackett episode, President Lincoln's reading and appreciation of Shakespeare is attested by several persons who had more or less intimate contacts with him: notably the artist F. B. Carpenter, who painted Lincoln and his Cabinet in the "Signing of the Emancipation Proclamation" which now hangs in the

Capitol in Washington, and who also wrote a book of reminiscences entitled *Six Months at the White House;* John W. Forney, editor of the *Philadelphia Press;* Senator Charles Sumner; and the Marquis de Chambrun, who accompanied Sumner and the Presidential party to visit the Army of the Potomac, April 5-10, 1865, following the fall of Richmond.

Carpenter related an occasion while he was painting Lincoln as follows:

> Presently the conversation turned upon Shakespeare, of whom it is well known Mr. Lincoln was very fond. He once remarked, "It matters not to me whether Shakespeare be well or ill acted; with him the thought suffices." Edwin Booth was playing an engagement at this time at Grover's Theatre. He had been announced for the coming evening in his famous part of *Hamlet.* The President had never witnessed his representation of this character, and he proposed being present. The mention of this play, which I afterward learned had at all times a peculiar charm for Mr. Lincoln's mind, waked up a train of thought I was not prepared for. Said he, — and his words have often returned to me with a sad interest since his own assassination, — "There is one passage of the play of 'Hamlet' which is very apt to be slurred over by the actor, or omitted altogether, which seems to be the choicest part of the play. It is the soliloquy of the king, after the murder. It always struck me as one of the finest touches of nature in he world."
>
> Then, throwing himself into the very spirit of this scene, he took up the words: —

> > *"O my offence is rank, it smells to heaven;*
> > *It hath the primal eldest curse upon 't,*
> > *A brother's murder! -- Pray can I not,*
> > *Though inclination be as sharp as will;*
> > *My stronger guilt defeats my strong intent;*
> > *And, like a man to double business bound,*
> > *I stand in pause where I shall first begin,*
> > *And both neglect. What if this cursed hand*
> > *Were thicker than itself with brother's blood?*
> > *Is there not rain enough in the sweet heavens*

To wash it white as snow? Whereto serves mercy
But to confront the visage of offence;
And what's in prayer but this twofold force --
To be forestalled ere we come to fall,
Or pardoned, being down? Then I'll look up;
My fault is past. But O what form of prayer
Can serve my turn? Forgive me my foul murder? --
That cannot be; since I am still possessed
of those effects for which I did the murder, --
My crown, my own ambition, and my queen.
May one be pardoned and retain the offence?
In the corrupted currents of this world,
Offence's gilded hand may shove by justice,
And oft 't is seen the wicked prize itself
Buys out the law; but 't is not so <u>above</u>.
There is no shuffling; there the action lies
In its true nature; and we ourselves compelled,
Even to the teeth and forehead of our faults,
To give in evidence. What then? what rests?
Try what repentance can; what can it not?
Yet what can it when one cannot repent?
         O wretched state! O bosom black as death!
O bruised soul that, struggling to be free,
Art more engaged! And heart with strings of steel,
Be soft as sinews of the new-born babe;
All may be well!"

He repeated this entire passage from memory, with a feeling and appreciation unsurpassed by anything I ever witnessed upon the stage. Remaining in thought for a few moments, he continued: "The opening of the play of 'King Richard the Third' seems to me often entirely misapprehended. It is quite common for an actor to come upon the stage, and, in a sophomoric style, to begin with a flourish: —

> *"'Now is the winter of our discontent*
> *Made glorious summer by this sun of York,*
> *And all the clouds that lowered upon our house,*
> *In the deep bosom of the ocean buried!'"*

"Now, " said he, "this is all wrong. Richard, you remember, had been, and was then, plotting the destruction of his brothers, to make room for himself. Outwardly, the most loyal to the newly crowned king, secretly he could scarcely contain his impatience at the obstacles still in the way of his own elevation. He appears upon the stage, just after the crowning of Edward, burning with repressed hate and jealousy. The prologue is the utterance of the most intense bitterness and satire."

Then, unconsciously assuming the character, Mr. Lincoln repeated, also from memory, Richard's soliloquy, rendering it with a degree of force and power that made it seem like a new creation to me. Though familiar with the passage from boyhood, I can truly say that never till that moment had I fully appreciated its spirit. I could not refrain from laying down my palette and brushes, and applauding heartily, upon his conclusion, saying, at the same time, half in earnest, that I was not sure but that he had made a mistake in the choice of a profession, considerably, as may be imagined, to his amusement.

Carpenter's implication is clear, that Lincoln's recitation was no mere declamation, but a profoundly subtle projection of Richard's psyche, as Lincoln understood it.

Similarly, Senator Charles Sumner in his *Memoirs* and the Marquis de Chambrun in his *Impressions of Lincoln and the Civil War* relate the following episode which took place following the fall of Richmond. This is from de Chambrun:

On Sunday, April 9th, we were proceeding up the Potomac. That whole day the conversation turned on literary subjects. Mr. Lincoln read aloud to us for several hours. Most of the passages he selected were from Shakespeare, especially *Macbeth*. The lines after the murder of Duncan, when the new king falls a prey to moral torment, were dramatically dwelt on. Now and then he paused to expatiate on how exact a picture Shakespeare here gives of a murderer's mind when, the dark deed achieved, its perpetrator already envies his victim's calm sleep. He read the scene over twice.

After several pages dealing with other matters the Marquis returned to the subject of Lincoln's love for Shakespeare:

> In discussing literature, his judgment showed a delicacy and
> sureness of taste which would do credit to a celebrated critic.
> Having formed his mind through the process of lonely
> meditation during his rough and humble life, he had been
> impressed by the two books which the Western pioneer always
> keeps in his log-cabin, the Bible and Shakespeare. From the
> Sacred Writings he absorbed the religious color in which he
> clothed his thoughts. From Shakespeare he learned to study
> the passions of humanity. I am inclined to think that this sort
> of intellectual culture, since it aids in preserving originality,
> is better suited to the development of a gifted mind than is
> regular education.

These are only a few of the better known episodes upon which
observations may be based, and from which inferences may be
drawn, as to what Shakespeare meant to and did for Lincoln. Primarily perhaps, it was Shakespeare's insight into human nature
which moved Lincoln most, with peculiar reference to his own experiences. It is easy to account for the terrific appeal of Shakespeare's
treatment of overpowering ambition in the characters of Macbeth,
Richard III, and Hamlet's uncle. Lincoln had known in many of
his overweening contemporaries, as well as in himself perhaps, the
power of personal ambition to drive men down paths of virtue as
well as vice. It is likewise easy to account for his repeated reading
of the historical plays *King John, Richard II, Henry IV, Henry
V, Henry VI,* and *Richard III,* not merely for their portrayal of
human character but also for their presentation of the horrors of
civil war and the struggle for sovereignty in its ambiguous disguises
as moral right and wrong. The one lesson that Shakespeare never
dismisses in the historical plays is the evil that good men and bad
alike do and suffer in the struggle for power, and the ambiguity
of human nature's strength and weakness, for good and evil, in
right and wrong, is ever present in his characters, both men and
women, from the highest to the lowest. As King Henry observed
in the Third Part of *King Henry VI* (Act II, Scene V),   after
listening to the lament of a son who has killed his father and the

lament of a father who has slain his son in battle, so Lincoln could
take to heart the lines:

> *Sad hearted men, much overgone with care,*
> *Here sits a king more woeful than you are.*

Like King Henry VI Lincoln had attained the ruler's seat in a
divided nation and almost daily was confronted with the special
horrors and tragedies of a civil war in which families were divided
in mutual slaughter. This was brought into his immediate family
by the death at Chickamauga of Confederate Brigadier General
Ben Hardin Helm, Mary Todd Lincoln's brother-in-law, for whose
grief-stricken but still rebellious widow, Emily Todd Helm, Lincoln
extended courtesies that almost breached military discipline as well
as political prudence, in bringing her through the lines and into
the White House in December 1863.

The shock to Lincoln of the tremendous casualties in the Battle
of the Wilderness was recounted by John W. Forney, who called
upon the President shortly after the casualty reports had come in
and found him reading *Macbeth*. "Let me read you this from
'Macbeth,' " he said to Forney. "I cannot read it like Forrest, who
is acting at the theater, but it comes to me tonight as a consolation:

> *"To-morrow, and tomorrow, and tomorrow,*
> *Creeps in this petty pace from day to day,*
> *To the last syllable of recorded time,*
> *And all our yesterdays have lighted fools*
> *The way to dusty death. Out, out, brief candle!*
> *Life's but a walking shadow, a poor player*
> *That struts and frets his hour upon the stage*
> *And then is heard no more: it is a tale*
> *Told by an idiot, full of sound and fury,*
> *Signifying nothing."*

One may wonder whether Lincoln really used the word
"consolation" in describing what this passage from *Macbeth* did
for him, but supposing he did, one suspects that his depth of
pessimism at this point must have been deep indeed, and that recognition of the fact Shakespeare had been there before him was in

effect more solace than any platitude of hope for the future.

Perhaps it was the range of Shakespeare's characters from the sublime to the ridiculous and from profound pessimism to infinite hope, a range which Lincoln shared, that accounted as much as anything for Lincoln's returning again and again to Shakespeare for "consolation" whenever he had opportunity to read for relaxation. Almost any play he happened to be reading could afford some application to his own condition at the particular moment; as for example, when he was reading *King John* while visiting Fortress Monroe during the Peninsular campaign in 1862. The President's son Willie, his father's special pride, had died in the White House on February 20, and Lincoln read to Colonel Le Grand B. Cannon the lines in Act III where Constance laments her lost son:

> *"And, father cardinal, I have heard you say*
> *That we shall see and know our friends in heaven.*
> *If that be true, I shall see my boy again..."*

"If that be true, I shall see my boy again. . ." he is reported to have said, "Colonel, did you ever dream of a lost friend and feel you were holding sweet communion with that friend, and yet have a sad consciousness that it was not a reality? — just so I dream of my boy Willie."

Returning to Lincoln's preference for the King's soliloquy rather than for Hamlet's famous "to be or not to be," we may ask a question: Why did Lincoln consider the King's soliloquy superior? It is the King's confession of guilt and of his inner struggle to pray and repent and to give himself up to justice. Dramatically, there may be sufficient reasons for omitting it from the acting version of the play, as is still customary. Nevertheless, it is the preeminent speech of the King which removes him from the category of mere villain and reveals him as a man, in whom the moral sense is not obliterated. Lincoln did not believe there was such a thing as a mere villain any more than Shakespeare did. How many times he said both publicly and privately concerning the popular villains of his own time, across the battle lines in the Confederacy, "Let us judge not that we be not judged." The Marquis de Chambrun records how he "twice repeated the same biblical sentence" to one who advocated that Jefferson Davis must be hanged because the "sight of Libby Prison rendered mercy impossible."

The King's soliloquy solicits sympathy and projects the common humanity, which the reader, be he ever so good, shares with the King. And at this particular moment of the play, the King's effort to pray should do more than Hamlet's own somewhat specious reasoning to justify to the audience Hamlet's avoidance of personal vengeance, a murder to repay a murder. Shakespearean tragedy is true to the ambiguity of human nature, in its scope for good and bad, right and wrong, which is never wholly resolved into an absolute.

Subtle psychology though it be, an actor's delight for projecting the introverted Prince's inner struggle and self-analysis, Hamlet's "to be or not to be" cannot match the moral profundity and does not excel the psychological subtlety of the extroverted King's grappling with his own conscience, which Carpenter described as having been read so impressively by Lincoln.

Surely it was this combination of subtlety and profundity which prompted Lincoln's remarks to Carpenter, "It matters not whether Shakespeare be well or ill acted; with him the thought suffices." On another occasion, on the way home from watching Edwin Booth's performance as Shylock in *The Merchant of Venice,* Lincoln is reported to have replied in answer to the question of how he liked the play: "It was a good performance but I had a thousand times rather read it at home, if it were not for Booth's acting. A farce, or a comedy is best played; a tragedy is best read at home." Both comments mark Lincoln as a thinking reader. This observation leads one to further speculation on Shakespeare's influence in the molding of Lincoln's thought and character, and perhaps to some extent, even on the pattern of action in Lincoln's life.

Edmund Wilson, in his essay on Lincoln, has not been the first to remark on what he so aptly phrases — "actually the poetry of Lincoln has not all been put into his writings. It was acted out in his life. . .he created himself as a poetic figure, and he thus imposed himself on the nation." How true this is cannot escape any literary student of Lincoln's life and works. As I have pointed out elsewhere, the essential effort of Lincoln's life was to identify himself, by words and in relationships to his contemporaries, as a representative, symbolic hero. He sought to play a role the action and words of which he would create for himself as circumstances and opportunity arose, but always with his mind's eye on the ultimate scene of the ultimate act, in which he would achieve his symbolic identity.

It was this role that gradually impressed itself upon his contemporaries, so vividly that even the mocking journalist who wrote *The New York Herald* article could not fail to note it, even though in ridicule; or so vividly that the sympathetic Frenchman de Chambrun could not escape the sense of dramatic fitness which seemed in retrospect to underlie Lincoln's reading aloud from *Macbeth* a few days before his assassination. It was as if Shakespeare had found the words before the fact, and Lincoln had appropriated them unto himself:

> *Besides, this Duncan*
> *Hath born his faculties so meek, hath been*
> *So clear in his great office, that his virtues*
> *Will plead like angels trumpet-tongued against*
> *The deep damnation of his taking off;*
>
> *Duncan is in his grave;*
> *After life's fitful fever he sleeps well;*
> *Treason has done his worst; nor steel, nor poison,*
> *Malice domestic, foreign levy, nothing*
> *Can touch him further.*

Early in life Lincoln subscribed to a philosophy that he himself defined as "the 'Doctrine of Necessity'— that is, that the human mind is impelled to action, or held in rest by some power, over which the mind itself has no control. . . . . " During his presidency he took many occasions to call this belief privately to the attention of his associates, or publicly to the attention of the whole nation, as in his Second Inaugural Address: "The Almighty has His own purposes. . . . If we shall suppose that American Slavery is one of those offences which, in the providence of God, must needs come, but which, having continued his appointed time, He now wills to remove, and that He gives to both North and South, this terrible war, as the woe due to those by whom the offence came, shall we discern therein any departure from those divine attributes which the believers in a Living God always ascribe to Him?" On one occasion during his Presidency Lincoln answered a question as to what his career might have been if he had received a political appointment in the Territory of Oregon in 1849, by saying: "I have always been a fatalist, what is to be will be, or rather, I have found all my life as Hamlet says:

> *"There is a divinity that shapes our ends,*
> *Rough-hew them how we will."*

That this attitude came solely from Shakespeare one cannot maintain, of course, but that the manifold applications of it in the plays with which Lincoln was so familiar were peculiarly pertinent in Lincoln's mind cannot, on the other hand, be escaped. To what extent then, one wonders, may Lincoln have adapted himself, consciously or subconsciously, to the spirit of Shakespearean tragedy in the role he sought to play in American history? With Shakespeare in mind, Lincoln's English biographer, Lord Charnwood, remarked that his great addresses are more like the speeches in tragic drama than like traditional oratory, and a truer observation was never made of the poetic quality of Lincoln's rhetoric. But one may pursue this thought even further, that among all the public figures in American history, Lincoln stands out as the character with a difference, part of this difference being that in dramatic actions as well as words, he seems to have been cast in a heroic role comparable to that of a Shakespearean hero. Although Lincoln took his bearings as timely politician from models closer to home — Jefferson and Clay, for example — it was Shakespeare who provided the steady vision of a timeless, tragic-comic image of man.

Lincoln and Shakespeare, Shakespeare and Lincoln! The joining of their names seems due as long as their common language lasts and their works are studied. The "psychographer" Gamaliel Bradford, who wrote such penetrating essays on many historical figures but never dared to trust his "psychography" on either Lincoln or Shakespeare, wrote a little known pamphlet called *The Haunted Biographer: Dialogues of the Dead* (1928), in which Lincoln and Shakespeare discourse as follows:

> *Shakespeare.* Curious, isn't it? We are both such great men and so different!
>
> *Lincoln.* Perhaps you exaggerate, so far as I am concerned. Circumstances just took me up and tossed me about, and planted me on the top. I have always felt that that was all.
>
> *Shakespeare.* No, Abe, between you and me, there should be none of those disguises. I might say, just as you do, that it was a matter of circumstance. But I really think that I was born great, and I think that you were.
>
> *Lincoln.* It may be so, it may be so. But are others born little? And I so often feel myself so immensely like the others?
>
> *Shakespeare.* You can't feel more like them than I did. But somewhere, somehow, there must have been just a little something. — Still melancholy, Abe? Like my own Jaques, you seem to suck melancholy from everything — melancholy or fun, even from songs.
>
> *Lincoln.* Most of all from songs, especially from the serene, pervading, magnificent splendor of yours. But I am sure you knew the melancholy, too, Will, every bit as much as Jaques and I.
>
> *Shakespeare.* Perhaps, perhaps. Those who are born different always know it, I think, and for that matter, most of those who are born the same. As you say, songs can breed it and nurse it; but, oh, Abe, there is nothing like the magic of songs to whiff it away.
>
> *Lincoln.* Do you know, I sometimes believe I should have done better to make songs. Could you have dealt with men, Will?
>
> *Shakespeare.* I don't know. I sometimes thought I could; but not as you did, not as you did, not with your superb gift. And that is chiefly what makes us melancholy, the thought of what we should like to do and could not.

THE ESSENTIALS OF LINCOLN'S STATESMANSHIP

"If we could first know *where* we are, and *whither* we are tending, we could better judge *what* to do, and how to do it." This was the theme with which Lincoln opened his House Divided speech in 1858, at the beginning of his campaign against Stephen A. Douglas for the U.S. Senate. It was more than this, however, the axiom upon which, when elected President two years later, he consistently attempted to conduct his course of action in the effort to reunite the divided house and to preserve the constitutional framework of its government. Such a truism may seem a simple platitude to the human intellect, but to the practical reason which must decide upon a course of action, it is most difficult to apply. There are too many imponderables of relationship and minutiae of fact in defining where we are, and there are too many possibilities of error in predicting just where we are going, when society is made up of human beings motivated by not one but many drives and banded together in groups for the purpose of going places which lie in divergent and sometimes opposite directions, the same individual often being a member of more than one of these groups and at best only dimly aware that they are not heading in the same direction, or at worst totally unaware that if he succeeds with one group in attaining its goal he may defeat his purpose of attaining the goal of another group in which he is also a determined campaigner.

George Bernard Shaw once observed, "The practical men know where they are, but not always whither we are going, whereas the thinkers who know whither we are going do not always know where we are." The great panjandrum stated even this truism too simply in his *Everybody's Political What's What* (p. 49) for he showed that even among practical men few accurately know where they are, and among thinkers few actually know whither we are going. It is sometimes a notion among historians a century after an event that they can weigh the evidence and decide who did actually know at the time, but there is always at least one historian who weighs the same evidence and concludes contrariwise.

In his day Jefferson Davis felt that Lincoln's position on slavery was a threat to regiment sovereign states and the liberties of citizens into a Union dominated from Washington by Northern capitalists. Most Democrats then believed that Lincoln's statement of the alternatives "*all* one thing or *all* the other" was not a true statement of alternatives, because they denied Lincoln's charge that extension of slavery into the territories would "push it forward till it shall become alike lawful in *all* the states, *old* as well as *new—North* as well as *South.*" Many believed that Lincoln's statement was merely the lever a crafty demagogue used to elevate himself into a position of prominence and, by creating fear of the legitimate and orderly development of honest and high-minded government by statesmen like Davis, Franklin Pierce, and James Buchanan, to acquire through election to office the power to *make* the country "*all* one thing," and that thing a federally dominated government run for the benefit of Northern industry and commerce, whose interest in exploiting so-called "free labor" was concealed by a hypocritical abhorrence of the alleged immorality of slavery.

We cannot dismiss this view entirely, for the reason that there is a mixture of truth in it. Jefferson Davis and his contemporaries who agreed with him did know to some extent whither we were tending, and did not like the whither, and therefore tried to put a stop to the tendency. During the decade which preceded the Civil War, they were able, not to stop it but to hold it back. They recognized that extension of slavery into the territories, enabling the admission of new slave states, was the sine qua non for the continuation in power of an agrarian oligarchy founded chiefly on wealth consisting of land and slave labor to work the land. Although a few of them were troubled by the questionable morality of owning black men, they had inherited the system of slavery and did not intend to give up or permit the destruction by inimical political forces of this half of the wealth upon which their power and their way of life was founded. Not one of them had been able to transcend the primitive morality of the slavocracy as Lincoln had done in the most memorable single statement he had ever made about the morality of slavery: "As I would not be a *slave,* so I would not be a *master.*" The political bulwark of the slavocracy was state government rather than federal, simply because slavery was incapable of limitless expansion, unlike the wealth of factories and commerce, machinery and technology, exploiting free labor, which was becoming the preponderant wealth of the nation, outweighing even land in the national balance and spreading into new territories without regard to boundaries, subsidized and encouraged by favorable federal as well as state legislation. Slavery was incapable of expansion first because tied to the land, and second because slave owners were only dimly aware, in isolated places in the South, that slaves as well as free laborers could be made into fairly competent factory hands by a modicum of training. Thirdly, it was incapable because slave owners in general were unwilling to risk the only kind of capital improvement which would increase the value of their slave property—namely, education.

State sovereignty became the sacred dogma of the slave interest because it seemed to afford the only means of preserving and extending in any degree at all the kind of wealth which, together with land, furnished the foundation of its political power.

It was not that Jefferson Davis did not see whither we were tending, but that he did not see that political power and control alone could not either permanently hold back the tendency or turn it to the purposes of the slave interest. And he, like his peers among the leaders in the slave states, would accept no alternative to maintaining the national status quo except to secede from the nation and set up separate governments dedicated to maintaining the local status quo. This was the limit of his vision as a statesman, and it appealed to his peers so well that they chose him as President

of the new Confederacy in 1861. It was also the most certain guarantee of the failure of that Confederacy as a government that its
basic principle was to hold the line, oppose change, and combat
all efforts, internal as well as external, to modify socially,
economically, or politically the agrarian slavocracy which ruled it.

To return to the year 1858, when Lincoln said "If we could first
know *where* we are, and *whither* we are tending, we could better
judge what to do, and how to do it. . . . I believe this government
cannot endure, permanently half *slave* and half *free* . . . . It will
become *all* one thing or *all* the other . . . ." As Davis and his
peers could not, or would not, understand, this was not a threat,
but a prediction. Lincoln meant no threat to abolish the states, but
only to recognize their secondary and gradually diminishing
sovereignty as a result of the inevitable expansion of federal authority under the Constitution, as the Constitution would continue to
be interpreted by the courts and amended by the people, and as
legislation would be enacted by the Congress to embody the will
of the electorate. He meant no immediate threat even to   slave
property as such, although he did believe that ultimately the competition between slave and free labor would reduce the effectiveness
of slave property to the point at which it would become a luxury
too expensive even for a wealthy society to maintain in a
competitive world economy. What he did mean, as he explained
later (February 14, 1860), was that "this government cannot *last
always,* half slave and half free." The first duty of public men,
in Lincoln's view, was to recognize that the status quo can never
be maintained permanently, and that the object of every public
man, of whatever persuasion, should be to work with the possible
(where we are) toward the inevitable (whither we are tending). As
a practical man, he knew where we were with considerable accuracy, as anyone who has studied his writings must admit. As a
thinker, he did not know precisely where we were going; certainly
in the matter of the struggle between capital and labor he pretended
to no historical prophecy such as his contemporary Karl Marx
would venture, but his study of history convinced him that although
basic human nature could change but slowly, if at all, the forms
of society and government must change to adapt themselves to the

discoveries and inventions which the human mind makes in   its quest for knowledge.

During the years 1858-1859 Lincoln worked up a lecture on the subject "Discoveries and Inventions," which may seem today   a somewhat   minor effort when compared with his great political speeches of   the   same   period,   but   which   is   tremendously significant   in helping us understand his statesmanship. Its theme was that the mind of man discovers and the life of man is changed by what is discovered. Although he rather liked the word "prog-ress" as applied to this process in general, he gave a humorous cast to his discussion of some of the results. Like Emerson, he was aware that progress may be devious and at times   in   "Young America" ambiguous, if not deceptive. The most incontrovertible aspect of the human condition as Lincoln saw it, however, was the creative power of the human mind, "impelled to action or held in rest by some power over which the mind itself has no control" (*The Collected Works of Abraham Lincoln* I, 382).

Here are a few selected sentences from the   two   manuscript remnants of the lecture on "Discoveries and Inventions," which will give an idea of the general drift of Lincoln's thesis and perhaps suggest its importance to an understanding of his statesmanship. One of the fragments begins thus:

> All creation is a mine, and every man a miner.

> The whole earth, and all *within* it, *upon* it, and *round about* it, including *himself,* in his physical, moral, and intellectual nature, and his susceptibilities, are   the   infinitely   various "leads" from which, man, from the first, was to dig out his destiny.

> Man is not the only animal who labors; but he is the only one who *improves* his workmanship. This improvement, he ef-fects by *Discoveries,* and *Inventions* (*C.W.,* II, 437).

> The great difference between Young America and Old Fogy, is the result of *Discoveries, Inventions,* and *Improvements.* These, in turn, are the result of *observation, reflection,* and *experiment.*

The inclination to exchange thoughts with one another is probably an original impulse of our nature . . . . What one observes, and would himself infer nothing from, he tells to another, and that other at once sees a valuable hint in it. A result is thus reached which neither *alone* would have arrived at. . . . *Writing* -- the art of communicating thoughts to the mind, through the eye--is the great invention of the world. . . .by means of writing, the seeds of invention were more permanently preserved, and more widely sown. . . . At length printing came. . . . It is very probable--almost certain--that the great mass of men, at that time, were utterly unconscious, that their *conditions,* or their *minds* were capable of improvements. . . . To emancipate the mind from this false and under estimate of itself, is the great task which printing came into the world to perform (*C.W.,* III, 358, 359, 360, 363).

But enough. Such history, or philosophy of history, is so much a part of our elementary understanding today that we may dismiss it as too obvious to merit an accolade. And yet, how many of the public men of Lincoln's day, or of our own, truly perceive the import of this point-of-view and try to frame their policies in accord with it?

On this basic concept Lincoln formulated his central philosophy of government--as the mind of man discovers and invents, society changes, and as society changes, *"Legislation* and *adjudication* must follow, and conform to, the progress of society"* (C.W.,* II, 459). Whether we like it or not, or whether we understand whither we are going, we are going nevertheless, and the statesman at the best is he who in his time works with the current of events which he does not control, but which he may use to gain limited objectives on the way to an ultimate destiny which he perceives only in very general outline, if at all. This was Lincoln's success as a statesman, to have been more right than wrong in his judgments of where we were and to have perceived whither we were tending well enough to guide himself, and for a short period of four years his nation, toward its destiny.

As to where we were in March 1861, it then seemed to many that the Union was in the process of inevitable disintegration, and that the wave of the future moved toward at least two, and possibly more, individual regional governments, and that to resist this trend by force of arms was foolhardy. It was widely believed that local and regional interests in the North and the Middle West as well as the South would welcome and rally to the cause of state governments or regional confederacies, and that the governments of European nations would welcome and promptly recognize this divisive move-ment for reasons of self-interest. There were likewise many who believed that such divisiveness simply would not, could not, work in the era of the steam engine and the telegraph, which had increased the interdependency even of nations which had long histories of sep-arated and theoretically sovereign existence.

Lincoln tried to make clear to the South the obsolescence of the political philosophy of its leaders.

> Physically speaking, we cannot separate. We cannot remove our respective sections from each other, nor build an impassable wall between them. . . . They cannot but remain face to face; and intercourse, either amicable or hostile, must continue between them. . . . Suppose you go to war, you can-not fight always; and when, after much loss on both sides, and no gain on either, you cease fighting, the identical old questions, as to terms of intercourse, are again upon you. (*C.W.*, IV, 269).

Of course, Lincoln had more than this general philosophy as jus-tification for his action. He had in the Constitution the legal basis for his view that "the Union of these states is perpetual" (*C.W.*, IV, 264), and that even if the Constitution was a mere contract it could not be "peaceably unmade, by less than all the parties who made it" *(C.W.,* IV, 265). It was therefore his first and principal duty as President to maintain the Union, peaceably if possible, but if necessary, by force. But whatever of abstract right and wrong there may have been in the divergent views of Lincoln and Davis concerning the legal meaning of the Constitution, there can be little question today that Lincoln's view rather than that of Davis was consonant with the tendency throughout western civilization toward broader and tighter political bonds between all men, to keep pace with the discoveries and inventions which were changing the lives of men everywhere. And, although this is no place to elaborate the details, there can be little question today that the North's superior adaptability to, and use of, discoveries and inventions — the tools of industrial and technological civilization — finally enabled the Union to defeat the Confederacy, once Lincoln had motivated and organized the Union for the war that neither North nor South wanted.

At almost any given date during the Civil War, Lincoln's understanding of where we were at that moment is demonstrably so superior to that of his critics as to make them seem absurd in the long view of history. In the beginning most people thought that the war would be short. General Winfield Scott, in command of the United States Army, even thought that peace could be restored without much bloodshed. Lincoln, however, began preparing for a long war, without knowing, of course, how long it would last. Four days after issuing his call for troops, Lincoln proclaimed a blockade of the Southern ports, which he knew could not immediately affect the South, but which proved in the long run a most decisive factor. There was much debate among his Cabinet as to the wisdom of proclaiming a blockade rather than merely issuing an order closing the Southern ports. The latter, it was argued, would enable seizure of goods and arrest of smugglers, without forfeiture of ships, and would avoid the danger of antagonizing other nations. Blockade, it was pointed out, was an act of war and implied recognition of the South as a nation. Whether blockade was, in spite of the risk, a more effective deterrent than merely closing the ports, or whether it was an unnecessary diplomatic mistake, the main point to keep in mind is that it strangled the South.

Likewise, it was the long view that motivated Lincoln's non-military policies and decisions from the beginning, with a view toward keeping the border states in the Union and strengthening their allegiance, while he utilized the North's superior resources to build the largest army the world had yet seen, in order to mount simultaneous attacks on several fronts, thus minimizing the South's advantage of having shorter lines of supply and communication. There are plenty of military mistakes in the Union's execution of Lincoln's war policy, some of them perhaps directly attributable to Lincoln himself, but of his overall policy, no responsible critic has ever concluded that it was anything but the best.

In regard to the abolishment of slavery, also, it was the long view that determined Lincoln's policy. Even after two years of bloody fighting, he was reluctant to take the action which seemed so obviously and immediately necessary to so many, not because he doubted that slavery should or would be abolished, but because he knew that enduring results required that legislative action be taken. Even when he finally issued the Emancipation Proclamation on grounds of military necessity, he knew that until Congress amended the constitution and the states ratified, his proclamation was of dubious long-range effect. His statesmanship was at its best in the splendid rhetoric with which he exhorted and persuaded and in the personal political maneuvers which he employed to get the Negro's freedom ratified by the representatives of the people, who alone could make the action stick. His intentions in regard to citizenship for the Negro likewise demonstrated how well he knew where we were. His instructions to General Nathaniel P. Banks (August 5, 1863) and his suggestion to Governor Michael Hahn (March 13, 1864) regarding education and suffrage for the Negro citizens in the occupied portion of Louisiana showed his understanding of the need to move gradually but forcefully, following the same philosophy that he followed regarding emancipation. The laws must be changed, the Negro educated, and the white citizen brought to understand that the abolition of slavery was the beginning of something that must go on for years, as well as the end of something that had gone on for years. It is ridiculous to try to maintain today, as some men do, that because Lincoln admitted that the Negro was not in fact the white man's equal in his day, therefore he did not conceive that the Negro could be the white man's equal in fact in the time to come. He did conceive the Negro's possible equality and began working toward that end. We cannot know for sure what Lincoln would have done had he not been assassinated, but to assume that he would have done less than to advocate and work for achievement of equality for the Negro is not compatible with his course up to the end of his life.

In regard to foreign relations, Lincoln's understanding of where we were proved considerably superior to that held by the man he appointed Secretary of State. On April 1, 1861, William H. Seward seriously proposed to "demand explanations from Spain and France, categorically, at once," and "to seek explanations from Great Britain and Russia, and send agents into Canada, Mexico, and Central America, to rouse a vigorous continental spirit of independence against European intervention. And if satisfactory explanations are not received from Spain and France [I] would convene Congress and declare war against them" (*C.W.*,IV, 317). Why? The sole object would be to consolidate patriotic feeling against foreign powers and thus arouse lagging Union sentiment. Lincoln ignored this proposal. Although he did not completely restrain Seward from sending belligerent instructions to U.S. ministers abroad, he did see to it in the *Trent* incident that British sovereignty would not be challenged. The imprisoned Confederate emissaries Mason and Slidell were released, and when British soldiers were embarked for Canada, Lincoln offered them the choice of disembarking at Portland, Maine, and taking U.S. trains to their destination. The offer was refused, but Lincoln had doubly made the point that he sought no conflict with a foreign power.

Although official Britain and France were overtly neither friendly nor unfriendly, the people of both countries were predominantly in sympathy with the Union because of the Confederacy's avowed intention to perpetuate slavery. Lincoln augmented this sympathy by appointing anti-slavery men to posts abroad and by sending over, or encouraging to go on their own, as many prominent abolitionists as possible to preach and lecture. They served the Union cause better abroad than at home, where they constantly badgered Lincoln to take the step he was not ready to take in emancipating the slaves. Lincoln was glad to have Henry Ward Beecher preach to the British that the war was a war to end slavery, but at home Lincoln preferred to emphasize that it was a war to preserve the Union.

Certainly Lincoln needed to motivate the Union cause at home, but Seward's way was incredibly impractical, even if psychologically understandable, holding a certain "tried and true" promise of demagogic effectiveness with a considerable chauvinistic element of the population. It is hard today to understand how an intelligent adviser could have made Seward's proposal, with any serious belief that the seceded states would return to the Union in order to preserve the very government they had refused to acknowledge. Lincoln and Seward were agreed on the need for motivation, but fortunately it was Lincoln and not Seward whose responsibility it was to provide the motivation.

Although the problem of motivation was paramount, organization and administration were required to give effect to the motivation.

Organization could not of itself persuade or coerce free men to fight, simply for organization's sake, but it could enable them to fight effectively. Lincoln's statesmanship in organizing and administering the government of the Union to fight the Civil War was largely an achievement in delegating responsibility to his Cabinet. Secretary of the Treasury Chase maintained that there was in fact no administration by the President but that each Department ran itself. So long as each Department produced the needed results, as Chase's department certainly did, this was just what Lincoln wanted, and he interfered and overruled only when political exigencies seemed to demand it. Policies rather than administrative details are the statesman's primary responsibility, and only when administration fails to carry policies forward can the statesman afford to spend his time interfering with administration. Chase's criticism of Lincoln's failure to administer is a fair indication that Chase would have been far less of a statesman as President than Lincoln; the fact that Lincoln utilized Chase's valuable service as an administrator in spite of his political maneuvering for the presidency, so long as that maneuvering did not seriously jeopardize the main object of winning the war, is in itself something for students of statesmanship to ponder.

Although the need for motivation was paramount, on February 11, 1861, when Lincoln began his journey to Washington, there was uncertainty as to what would provide it. Some abolitionists were perhaps sufficiently motivated to fight in order to abolish slavery, but they were a relatively small portion of the populace. Others among the antislavery segment were glad to see the South secede, carrying with it the moral cancer of slavery. The by no means negligible segment in the North which favored the perpetuation of slavery was also divided, some willing to see the slave states secede, some desirous of persuading them to remain in the Union with guarantees, some clinging to Douglas' doctrine of popular sovereignty as sufficient unto the future. Perhaps the largest segment of the people, however, without regard to party politics, actually agreed with Lincoln that although slavery was at bottom of the disintegration of the Union, and must be dealt with in due course, it was not the paramount issue. The paramount issue was the preservation of the Union, and Lincoln's first object was to consolidate support on this alone. He said in his first Inaugural, "This country, with its institutions, belongs to the people who inhabit it. Whenever they grow weary of the existing government, they can exercise their *constitutional* right of amending it, or their *revolutionary* right to dismember or overthrow it" (*C.W.*, IV, 269). The question was, did the majority of the people actually wish to dismember or overthrow the government? If they did not, would they fight to prevent a minority from dismembering it?

The motivation which Lincoln undertook to develop, both rationally and emotionally, and which provided the North with a will to win, was as Alexander Stephens later observed with truth, a kind of religious mysticism which raised the idea of the Union to sacred proportions, as a symbol of what Lincoln called in his address to the Senate of New Jersey, February 21, 1861, "that something more than National Independence; that something that held out a great promise to all the people of the world to all time to come"; or again, the next day in his address in Independence Hall, "that which gave promise that in due time the weight would be lifted from the shoulders of all men"; and again in his Message to Congress in Special Session, July 4, 1861, "that form and substance of government whose leading object is to elevate the condition of men; to lift artificial weights from all shoulders; to clear the paths of laudable pursuit for all; to afford all an unfettered start and a fair chance in the race of life"; and most memorably in his Gettysburg Address, November 19, 1863, "that government of the people, by the people, for the people, shall not perish from the earth."

These are only a few of the memorable passages in which Lincoln undertook to identify in the minds of the people, the Union as the bulwark of their individual and collective hope for future freedom and opportunity. If today these words seem too obvious to represent statesmanship at the highest pitch of creative thought, if a cynic should be inclined to say "so what—could not even a simpleton have arrived at this?"—perhaps we should reflect that the best proof of statesmanship is the ability to say and do in one generation what will seem obvious to the next. Lincoln was certainly not unaware of posterity, but he knew that a statesman cannot address posterity successfully except through his contemporaries. The politician or statesman who appeals to posterity to judge his cause has already lost it. Apparently Robert E. Lee knew this, if Jefferson Davis did not, and it is a great misfortune of our nation today that some of our contemporaries choose to emulate Davis, who spent his remaining years after the Civil War trying to prove how right he had been, just as his letters and speeches during the war had always carried the burden of asserting his rightness. Lincoln on the contrary seldom claimed to *be right,* but in all his letters and speeches maintained that he sought to *find* the *right,* and avowed his belief that in the long run "right makes might," even though he recognized that in the short run what appears to be the triumph of right may not satisfy even the winner. One may suppose, on the basis of a knowledge of Lincoln's writings, that he would deprecate today, if he were alive, any effort to argue how right or even how successful his statesmanship had been. He might even quote from his own Second Inaugural, "The prayers of both could not be answered; that of neither has been answered fully. The Almighty has his own purposes. . . with firmness in the right, as God gives us to see the right, let us strive on to finish the work we are in" *(C.W.,* VIII, 333).

This is an old-fashioned view which may not satisfy some of us, but it is the sum of that other side of Lincoln's statesmanship. On the one hand he believed in the creativity of the mind of man which discovers and through discovery inevitably modifies and changes the patterns of human society; on the other hand, he believed that God wills the ultimate change. Whether the statesman prefers to use the terms "will of God" or "necessity" (Lincoln used both, Karl Marx only the one) to name the inevitable, the success of his statesmanship depends on the degree to which he is able to anticipate "whither we are tending."

Lincoln's statesmanship helped bring on a war he did not want, helped abolish slavery that perhaps could not have continued forever anyway, helped preserve a Union that could not be preserved as it was, helped create new economic and social problems that could not have been completely avoided in any event—and withal took its place in history as a remarkable and unique achievement which can furnish a neat, specific pattern for no would-be statesmen in our day or in any day to come. Lincoln's statesmanship was the mirror of the man, and so personal that it cannot be reduced in terms of either success or failure to a rule of thumb. Yet Lincoln's practical-mystical philosophy may be worth more than any specific pattern for success. We must try to know where we are and whither we are tending in order to decide what to do and how to do it. What we want may influence what we do and how we do it. What other people want will likewise influence what they do and how they do it. But the imponderable factor in the modern world as in Lincoln's day, is the creative mind of man which forces change upon us whether we want it or not, and we must try to provide for the necessity of change in a compatible manner or the necessity of change may provide for us in an incompatible manner.

There is a passage in Lincoln's instructions to General Banks, referred to earlier, which seems to me to say very simply what was the sum of his philosophy of life and government in a changing world, and which describes in a very succinct way just what his practice of statesmanship added up to.

> While I very well know what I would be glad for Louisiana to do, it is quite a different thing for me to assume direction of the matter. I would be glad for her to make a new Constitution recognizing the emancipation proclamation, and adopting emancipation in those parts of the state to which

the proclamation does not apply. And while she is at it, I think it would not be objectionable for her to adopt some practical system by which the two races could gradually live themselves out of their old relation to each other, and both come out better prepared for the new *(C.W., VI, 365)*.

This is merely the general application to the problem then confronting people in Louisiana of the principle which Lincoln saw as the only long-range solution to all human relations in a changing world—to adopt a practical system by which men can live themselves out of their old relation to each other and into the new relation required by man's discovery and creation of new things and new ways of thinking about old things. He had phrased the same view in his magnificent exhortation to the Congress on December 1, 1862. "The dogmas of the quiet past are inadequate to the stormy present. . . . As our case is new, so we must think anew, and act anew. We must disenthrall ourselves, and then we shall save our country" *(C.W., V, 537)*.

Although Lincoln had accepted violence, when it was forced on him, as one means of living out of an old relation into a new, he had consistently advocated that the frame of government under which we live could provide adequately the practical system of living out of old and into new relations, by legislation and adjudication which follow and conform to the progress of society. But suppose legislation and adjudication do not follow and conform to the progress of society. Lincoln's answer to that in the instance of the Dred Scott decision was to "offer no resistance" but "do what we can to have it [the Supreme Court] overrule" *(C.W., II, 401)* this decision as it had overruled others. And he saw no reason not to have "a patient confidence in the ultimate justice of the people" *(C.W., IV, 270)* who make up society.

In our day, when statesmen are contending on the international scene with problems fundamentally the same as, though particularly variant from, those obtaining at home, Lincoln's statesmanship commends itself to those who will study it.

This brings us to the question of whether Lincoln's philosophy, based upon the evolutionary view of human history which grew out of the industrial revolution, is valid in the present day when confronted by the deterministic philosophy of his contemporary, Karl Marx, which also grew out of the industrial revolution. Some people are shocked if one points out that there is any area of agreement between Lincoln and Marx, but unless we recognize the area of agreement we cannot understand how much wider is their area of disagreement. They agreed on the basic relationship between capital and labor—that (to use Lincoln's words rather than Marx's) "labor is prior to, and independent of capital" *(C.W.,* III, 478). They agreed on the fact of class struggle and that the then forthcoming century was the era of the rising proletariat (though Lincoln did not use the word, preferring "laboring classes"). They agreed that the industrial revolution had made universal education the sine qua non of society and government. They agreed that equality of opportunity for all men and amelioration of the condition of mankind were legitimate objects of government, and that government was the means by which men could do collectively what they could not do at all, or so well, for themselves individually.

They agreed that an understanding of the relationship of natural freedom and natural necessity is the only solid foundation for human institutions, but they did not agree on what is natural freedom or natural necessity. Creative mind and continuously transforming matter were the elements as Lincoln conceived them; continuously transforming matter and conforming mind were the elements as Marx conceived them. Whereas Lincoln believed that men should try to better understand natural freedom in order to create out of their better understanding the human institutions necessary to enjoy it, Marx believed that men should try better to understand natural necessity in order to conform to it.

In the Marxian view the future is determined. Thus Mr. Khrushchev as a Marxist could state categorically, "We will bury you," because he believed the answer is already in his possession. Likewise, Russian propaganda can assume that communism is the final truth and that repeating its shibboleths and exterminating those who do not accept them will enlighten human society into the pattern dictated by natural necessity as defined by Marx—namely, a classless society regimented by communist dogma.

In the Lincolnian view the future is not determined, but problematical, because no humanly conceived dogma or definition is adequate to the infinite, and to the as yet uncreated future. Thus Lincoln could and did state: "In great contests each party claims to act in accordance with the will of God. Both may be, and one must be, wrong. In the present civil war it is quite possible that God's purpose is something different from the purpose of either party; and yet the human instrumentalities, working just as they do, are of the best adaptation to effect his purpose."

The points of fundamental difference between Lincoln's philosophy and Marx's continue with Marx's assumption that societies of the future, like all societies he knew of, would operate against a background of scarcity. Lincoln assumed that discovery and invention knew no bounds comprehensible to the human imagination. It would be silly to maintain that Lincoln had any specific inklings of the scientific revolution taking place in our day, but it is a fact that his general philosophy of human creativity and exploitation of nature posited a boundless possibility. A further difference lies in Lincoln's full recognition of the fact that ideas come into being as a result of individual men pursuing each his particular aim in his own particular situation. Lincoln would have scoffed at an economic determinism which recognizes authoritarian collectivization as the primary means of ameliorating mankind, simply because of its inflexibility, but he recognized that collectivization by consent was a very good way for many individuals to attain common objectives, economic or otherwise. Where Marx and Engels promulgated the doctrine, derived from Spinoza via Hegel, that man's freedom lies in the recognition of necessity, Lincoln believed and reiterated time and again that man's necessity lies in the recognition of freedom, and that whatever chains are forged by authoritarians will assuredly be broken, though few, if any, may know the precise time in advance. He knew no less than Marx and Engels the wisdom of recognizing true necessity, but their understanding of necessity was at the opposite pole from his. Whereas theirs was fixed to a theory of dialectical materialism projecting a classless society, his was fixed to a theory of what might be called dialectical idealism, projecting a society in which classes and masses as he and his contemporaries knew them would perhaps have no place or meaning, but in which individuals would still be individual, and would band together of choice and of need to achieve their common aims, to seek truth as well as to dispense it, and to become that which remains to become.

It is one of the curiosities of the history of Marxism in the twentieth century that it should attract a leading philosopher of man's freedom, Jean Paul Sartre (outside the iron curtain be it noted), to join the communist cause in promulgating a blend of Marxism and what is called existentialism, which in many respects is closer to Lincoln's philosophy than it is to Marx.

We are living today in an even more explosive era than Lincoln's, although so far the violence is still chiefly outside our national borders. The emerging civilization is even more unpredictable in our day. Ideas, discoveries, and inventions are accelerating the democratization and socialization of this civilization at a rate no contemporary of Lincoln's, practical or theoretical, could have forecast. The chain reaction of ideas, which began long before Lincoln or Marx, still provides the revolutionary energy that is going off in what appear falsely to be isolated explosions in the most remote as well as the nearest areas of the world, and which appear, equally falsely, to some of our contemporaries, to be nothing but the Marxist subversion of peace, when the reality beneath this appearance is merely being dressed by communism in Marxist clothes, which have been all too readily available, in default of a supply of other revolutionary clothing suitable to the rapid change which underdeveloped countries all seek and hope for. Thinkers somewhat to left of center like Sartre, in opposition to the status quo, embrace communism as the only effective means by which the status quo can be overthrown, but are worried about the inflexibility of the authoritarian communist state on the far left, which recognizes no necessity of freedom. As one who considers himself to be perhaps at center, I admit to some concern on occasion about the flexibility of our constitutional state which must contain, adopt, and adapt these forces of change to an orderly transition, in which men will find practical means of living out of their old relation into a new one, without an authoritarian state either to right or left.

Lincoln's contemporary, the Danish philosopher Sören Kierkegaard, to whom Sartre and so many intellectuals are today acknowledging indebtedness for their ideas on human freedom, really offers in this connection nothing that Lincoln did not know, namely, that man creates his future but cannot entirely control it, and hence that future is brought about, to use Lincoln's words, "by some power over which the mind itself has no control." It might be well if the practical men of our day could spend as much time studying Lincoln as the intellectuals are spending on Kierkegaard, for Lincoln was perhaps the most practical man in our history, and his practicality, sui generis, makes more sense in the world of deeds than does the existentialism about which we hear so much. Perhaps such study would increase our respect for seeking practical ways of living out of old relations into new ones, and decrease our devotion to dogma, whether patterned after Karl Marx, Adam Smith, Saint Thomas, John Calvin, Sören Kierkegaard, or whomever the dogmatist prefers.

In closing, I must confess that I had no intention, when I began writing this paper, of showing Lincoln's statesmanship to be avant-garde in the twentieth century, but only to try to summarize what seem to me to have been the essential principles which guided his actions a hundred years ago. I trust there will be people around a century from now, with a perspective double our own, to study him and assess his statesmanship in that day. I venture to predict that his philosophy and his deeds will look even more realistic and statesmanlike then than they do now.

A TOUCHSTONE FOR GREATNESS: THOUGHTS ON LINCOLN'S BIRTHDAY

As regularly as February 12 rolls around, I get invited to speak to some audience about Abraham Lincoln, and I am troubled about what to say.

Perhaps what most of Lincoln's admirers want in a Lincoln's birthday speech or sermon is to be indulged in patriotic sentimentality — an anecdotal sketch of the personality of Lincoln or a eulogy of his character. It is not the hard truths that Lincoln lived by or the harsh deeds by which he enforced his authority that is wanted so much as a "tribute" to our greatest man. Idolatry is perhaps the word for this, or a very near thing to it. One notes that Lincoln's birthday, although not a national holiday, has been more widely observed by such memorial services than any other.

I can certainly understand this enduring interest, having become preoccupied with Lincoln myself many years ago — as a student more skeptical than otherwise — but with the result that after becoming immersed in study of Lincoln I forever after found the study of most other great men somehow lacking. It is hard not to be a Lincoln idolater, even after you really come to know him. The more he is studied, the larger he looms.

But let me ask, what is the use of this idolatry? What good is it aside from providing a sort of pious secular adjunct to, or substitute for, going to church and worshipping the person of Jesus? Maybe it is for some people a sort of substitute religion. I

247

occasionally needle myself with this question. My father was a Methodist preacher, and I very easily decided *that* was one thing I *couldn't be*. Every year when February rolls around and I am asked to speak, I ask the questions, Why am I preaching? and What am I preaching?

There are some trite answers to these questions — such as Longfellow's famous lines:

> *Lives of great men all remind us*
> *We can make our lives sublime,*
> *And departing, leave behind us*
> *Footprints on the sands of time.*

I do not mean to scoff at this, for it is a truth most amply illustrated by Lincoln's own example. He greatly admired Jefferson and Washington, and his study of their lives and works did in large measure mold the character and inspire the achievement of Lincoln himself.

He gave very explicit testimony on this point in a speech he made in Trenton, New Jersey, on his way to Washington, February 21, 1861:

> May I be pardoned if, upon this occasion, I mention that away back in my childhood, the earliest days of my being able to read, I got hold of a small book, such a one as few of the younger members have ever seen, 'Weem's Life of Washington.' I remember all the accounts there given of the battle fields and struggles for the liberties of the country, and none fixed themselves upon my imagination so deeply as the struggle here at Trenton, New Jersey. The crossing of the river; the contest with the Hessians; the great hardships endured at that time, all fixed themselves on my memory more than any single revolutionary event; and you all know, for you have all been boys, how these early impressions last longer than any others. I recollect thinking then, boy even though I was, that there must have been something more than common that those men struggled for. I am exceedingly anxious that that thing which they struggled for; that something even more than National Independence; that something that held out a great promise to all the people of the world to all time to come;

I am exceedingly anxious that this Union, the Constitution, and the liberties of the people shall be perpetuated in accordance with the original idea for which that struggle was made, and I shall be most happy indeed if I shall be an humble instrument in the hands of the Almighty, and of this, his almost chosen people, for perpetuating the object of that great struggle.

It is difficult, if not impossible, for me to read that passage, for the hundredth time, without feeling something of Lincoln's patriotic piety. But . . .

This quoting of Lincoln can be dangerous business. The White Citizens' Councils throughout the South have distributed a leaflet on which my name as editor of Lincoln's *Collected Works* appears rather larger than I like to see it for the purpose involved — as if I as well as Lincoln were responsible for the idea it seeks to spread. The leaflet quotation from Lincoln begins "I am not, nor ever have been in favor of bringing about in any way the social and political equality of the white and black races — I am not nor ever have been in favor of making voters or jurors of negroes. . ." etc.

This cannot be dismissed by referring to the old adage about the devil quoting scripture for his own purpose, for Lincoln meant every word of it, when he said it — that is, when he was trying to get elected to the Senate against Douglas in 1858. And it is absolutely useless to point out to the White Citizens' Council that Lincoln changed his mind and recommended to Governor Michael Hahn, the first free-state governor of Louisiana, in 1864, that the new Louisiana constitution should define the elective franchise to include Negroes. Lincoln was a nineteenth-century, not a twentieth-century man. But he was not stuck completely in his era. He did not remain bound by his 1858 ideas, even six years later in 1864. And it is pitiable to see twentieth-century men in our day wishing to remain stuck in the year 1858 and citing Lincoln as their authority. But such is *one* of the uses of scripture, and of history — to mislead others, and to mislead oneself.

In reading what Lincoln is reliably reported to have said on several occasions when speaking directly to Negroes, rather than about

Negroes or slavery or the black race in general, I am impressed with what seems to me to have been not at all his belief or feeling that the Negro race was inferior, but rather that the white race, as he had known its individual representatives very profoundly and personally, was capable of but a very limited scope for anything but self-interest. It was for this reason that he advised a group of free Negroes to consider colonizing in Central America. I suspect that if Lincoln had been born a century later he might have sympathized with, if not agreed with, the black nationalists of our day. But I think his basic political philosophy would probably be no different today than it was then, on a man-to-man basis, that black and white alike will continue to seek what seems to them to be in their own best interest, but that conflict of interest can be resolved best by seeking for a common interest, through a government dedicated to a certain proposition. And I believe he would have encouraged blacks and whites alike to use every device of government possible to achieve their own best interest by that medium rather than by violence.

For reasons best known to himself, I suppose, the Negro senior editor of *Ebony,* Lerone Bennett, Jr., wrote in the February 1968 issue of his magazine that Lincoln was a "conservative white supremacist." Mr. Bennett is more complete in his facts and quotations than is the White Citizens' Council, and yet by emphasis he succeeds in distorting the historical Lincoln almost as radically. Such statements as that Lincoln "shared the racial prejudices of most of his white contemporaries" and "was a firm believer in white supremacy" vastly misrepresent the historical Lincoln, who was deeply anxious that the words *all men are created equal* should be recognized as applying to Negro no less than white, and that "the great promise to all the people of the world to all time to come. . . shall be perpetuated. . . . " Mr. Bennett succeeds in creating a mythical Lincoln almost as far removed from history as the myth of the Emancipator which he resolved to demolish.

Were I a Negro American in search of the historical Lincoln, I should certainly question the validity of conclusions such as Lerone Bennett's when the testimony of Lincoln's contemporary, ex-slave Frederick Douglass, is available and does not   support

Bennett's statement. Frederick Douglass was certainly no "Uncle Tom," and what he said about Lincoln rings clear.

> In all my interviews with Mr. Lincoln I was impressed with his entire freedom from popular prejudice against the colored race. He was the first great man that I talked with in the United States freely, who in no single instance reminded me of the difference between himself and myself, of the difference of color, and I thought that all the more remarkable because he came from a State where there were black laws. I account partially for his kindness to me because of the similarity with which I had fought my way up, we both starting at the lowest round of the ladder. . . .

Can any American today, of whatever biological or cultural heritage, be more honored or respected than to be treated by his fellowman as Lincoln treated Douglass? There is no honor greater than to be treated as an equal by a truly great man.

Lincoln had something to say about such misuses of history as that of Lerone Bennett, when confronted by his antagonist Stephen A. Douglas's contention that the powers of the Constitution of the United States intended that the Constitution should prohibit the control of slavery by the federal government in the territories. Lincoln devoted his Cooper Union speech to refuting the idea and summarized his argument with this observation:

> If any man at this day sincerely believes that a proper division of local from federal authority, or any part of the Constitution, forbids the Federal Government to control as to slavery in the federal territories, he is right to say so, and to enforce his position by all truthful evidence and fair argument which he can. But he has no right to mislead others, who have less access to history, and less leisure to study it, into the false belief that "our fathers who framed the Government under which we live" were of the same opinion — thus substituting falsehood and deception for truthful evidence and fair argument.

But there are worse things than Lerone Bennett's carefully argued case for Lincoln's racism, which can be understood, even if not forgiven, in terms of the Black Power push to obliterate all evidence that white men ever treated black men other than badly. Worse by far is the frequent indifference of modern "liberal" journalism to historical fact, as for example, when *The New York Review of Books* (June 15, 1967), out to get President Johnson for alleged lying, cites President Lincoln's alleged use of dishonesty for political purposes, by stating categorically that "Lincoln lied to Greeley for purposes of seduction." Twice challenged to produce a credible source or retract, the *Review* simply ignored my letters.

Trying to project Lincoln into our own day is a very tricky business in any event, and sometimes has its amusing aspect. Several years ago I received a letter from a professional magazine writer who wanted to know what I thought Lincoln would have been like on TV. It appeared that Arthur M. Schlesinger, Jr., had written an article for the *Saturday Evening Post,* in which he said he "shuddered" to think what TV would have done to Lincoln, Jefferson, and other public men in our past history. Hence, my opinion was being sought on what TV would have done to Lincoln. I would have put the question the other way around: What would Lincoln have done to TV or with TV? After all, TV is but one of the media. It is merely the most recent extension of the rostrum or stage, as it was formerly an extension of the forum or public square. The newspaper is still one of the media, even though radio and TV have short-circuited it to some extent. The printed word was merely an extension of the written word, which was itself merely an extension of the spoken word, enabling it to be carried beyond the immediate audience to people everywhere who could read. Any man who could talk as effectively to his fellowmen as Lincoln did, would most certainly have learned to adapt the medium of TV to his purpose, very effectively.

If Marshall McLuhan's most sensible thesis in a sometimes nonsensical argument *(The Medium is the Massage)* is correct — namely, that electronic communication is turning the world into a global village — then it would be my guess that Abraham Lincoln reincarnate might operate as effectively in the global village as he did in the frontier village. In 1832 the villagers of New Salem, Illinois, voted in Lincoln's first race for the state legislature 277 for Lincoln and only 7 for his opponent.

The point is that any extension or improvement in communication can be used by man to increase the common understanding and to convey reason, sympathy, and good will — at least as well as their opposites.

This brings me to the Lincoln quotation which President Lyndon Johnson echoed so effectively in his State of the Union Message, in January 1967. " 'If we could first know *where* we are, and whither we are tending, we could better judge *what* to do and *how* to do it.' " This was the axiom upon which Lincoln consistently attempted to conduct his thinking and his actions both as a private citizen and as a public man, and in this any man might well try to emulate him.

But alas, there lies a true tragedy of our time, and it was LBJ himself who sought to point the parallel. I say this as an admirer of President Johnson for what he could and did accomplish, not as a scoffer at what he did not and could not.

I must confess that for me Lincoln has become a kind of touchstone to test greatness in other men. His usefulness in this respect is not limited to testing those who have succeeded him, or those who preceded him, in the White House, or those who have been leaders of other peoples or other nations, past or present. Although the greatness of other public men is perhaps more readily assayed by comparison with Lincoln, even the greatness of poets, scientists, or whatever geniuses of a more private cast, is not unsusceptible to the test. For even in pursuit of science or art the ultimate of greatness lies less in talent or genius than in character. The degrees of greatness between Shakespeare and Shelley are thus not primarily degrees of difference in mastery of words, or poetic forms, or even in height of imagination, but rather degrees in comprehensive humanity. It is scope that sets Lincoln, as well as Shakespeare, in the relationship to his fellowmen which scarcely permits them to match him overall in human *being*.

Hence I have been led to ask myself on occasion, just what is the quality of *being* in Lincoln which seems to loom so large the more I have studied him? His human kindness, his political acuity, his paradoxical heroism of humility with power, his creative imagination, his sense of destiny — these yes, and so much more, all fused together by his utter but only gradually developed belief in his own and every other man's absolute identity. This seems to me to be the discovery or invention (Lincoln saw these terms as somewhat interchangeable names) which he conceived that Jefferson had patented in the name of every citizen of the new republic in perpetuity, but which every man, including himself, would have to reinvent and rediscover anew.

A man passes through time, place, and action in his life. Time, place, and action also pass through him — his mind, emotion, and physical being. Do time, place, action account for him any more than he accounts for them? Throughout his life Lincoln seemed to answer this question equivocally yes and no.

In the first case, a man is merely one of many, moving and being moved in the flux of time and matter. The destiny of this *one* is only part of the overall destiny determined by necessity, fate, God — or whatever name is given the creative force.

In the second case, the entity time-place-action — an entity because in this case *they* are aspects of only *one* thing, the subjective *experience* of one man — is merely what is moving or being moved by a man in the flux of his will to be. Thus, time-place-action are his destiny created by him, imagined into being consciously and subconsciously.

In the first case we have what is generally understood as the "real" framework of the objectively studied universe. In the second case we have what is generally understood as the "unreal" framework of the subjectively imagined universe of one man's mind. The first is customarily conceived of as "discovered," the second is customarily conceived of as "invented," but from time immemorial men have believed, and acted on the belief, that the "unreal" can be "realized" to some degree, depending on the will of men individually and collectively to create correspondence between unreal imagination and real fact. Thus discovery and invention are names for the same achievement — seeing what was foreseen — and human life is an interaction between the real world and the imagined world, at what the scientifically sophisticated might call the "interface" of the real and the imagined.

Thus the "proposition" that "all men are created equal"

bothered Lincoln all his life as an unreality to be realized, and from his equivocal yes and no, he thought and acted out his creative determinism in regard to the proposition. In the more practical everyday problems of running the war, likewise he conceived of himself, as well as others, as in a real sense, creating destiny. In a moment of solitude sometime in September 1862 he summarized his thought on this problem of man creating his destiny vis-à-vis God, and put it down on a scrap of paper:

> The will of God prevails. In great contests each party claims to act in accordance with the will of God. Both *may* be, and one *must* be wrong. God cannot be *for,* and *against* the same thing at the same time. In the present civil war it is quite possible that God's purpose is something different from the purpose of either party — and yet the human instrumentalities, working just as they do, are of the best adaptation to effect His purpose. I am almost ready to say this is probably true — that God wills this contest, and wills that it shall not end yet. By his mere quiet power, on the minds of the now contestants, He could have either *saved* or *destroyed* the Union without a human contest. Yet the contest began. And having begun He could give the final victory to either side any day. Yet the contest proceeds.

I confess that I never read this passage without a feeling of exaltation that I otherwise get only from reading certain passages in Shakespeare and the Bible. It is a soliloquy of the greatest tragic hero in our history, uttered ot his "real" agony, an agony "realized" in the destiny created by the poet Lincoln was, out of the time-place-action into which he was born. For Lincoln's life seems to me to have been created out of his imagination as certainly as any poem was ever created out of a great poet's imagination. And from first to last his story seems, the more it is studied, the best evidence for each man's unique incarnation, in which all men are created equal because the ultimate of equality is each man's uniqueness.

Perhaps the outstanding trend in Western literature and science during the last century has been the reduction of human beings, along with the rest of nature, to abstractions. Whether it be Joyce

or Beckett, Freud or Marx, Einstein or Muller, the trend is to reduce every phenomenon, including human identities, to abstract
symbols. There is rarely or never such a thing as "a character"
in a modern novel. The nineteenth century may have had its David
Copperfield or Huckleberry Finn or Becky Sharp or Daisy Miller,
but we have only Leopold Blooms and Lady Chatterleys or their
even more abstracted imitations, largely faceless and gutless, albeit
the most excellent representation of human biological and
psychological entities, abstractly conceived and depicted with
perception and skill. In drama today there is not a single character
with so much identity as Falstaff or Hamlet, although it is clear
that Shakespeare was also symbolizing. The difference is that
Shakespeare's characters, as Elizabethans, can have identity and
at the same time represent profound abstract truths of human nature, whereas we seem to have conceived that since identity does
not exist in reality, it cannot in fiction. Modern man is perhaps
a meaning of some sort in a context of some sort, but without
substance or individual lineaments. He may have feelings of guilt
but no guilt, feelings of joy but no joy. All is abstraction. Even the
courts seem to have come to recognize the nonexistence of personal
crime. Whatever the culprit performed was not his so much as his
parents' or society's fault. Crime cannot be personal because evil
is a mere abstraction. Nor can one pat himself on the back for
a good deed — abstractly it is at best only an act of self-interest.

Thus where writers in earlier times wrote about fictional people
as if they were real, modern authors write about their neighbors
as if they were fiction, and we have the fairy tales of Samuel
Beckett, Edward Albee, Philip Roth, Gore Vidal, and others. In
our fairy tales, more grim than the brothers Grimm, physiology
and psychology are named Alexander Portnoy and Myra
Breckenridge.

In such an age it is sometimes refreshing to study biography and
history, particularly when the record is of a man whose identity
is so palpably real and recognizable. It is not the myth or legend
— though that has its kind of poetic meaning also — but the
factual, actual, unique, and memorable individual Lincoln who
illuminates mankind.

Robert Frost wrote many memorable lines during his long life as a poet. One of them comes to mind here as particularly appropriate!

The fact is the sweetest dream that labor knows.

How particularly true of the fact that proves out the dream! That is what Frost was talking about in the poem "Mowing," where the accomplished fact is the relatively simple one of cutting a wide swath, not metaphorically but really, for love. When the fact accomplished is a total human life, with the lineaments of Abraham Lincoln, or Frederick Douglass, no less, one becomes aware of what the abstract truths and symbols of literature, as well as the theories and symbols of science, are all about. And one learns to appreciate not only what mankind is, but also what a man can be.